McDOUGAL LITTELL

BLEU 1

Discovering FRENCH
Nouveau!

Unit 6 Resource Book

Components authored by Jean-Paul Valette and Rebecca M. Valette:

- Workbook
- Communipak
- Assessment Program
- Video Program
- Audio Program

Components authored by Sloane Publications:

- Family Letter, *Patricia Smith*
- Absent Student Copymasters, *E. Kristina Baer*
- Family Involvement, *Patricia Smith*
- Multiple Choice Test Items, *Nicole Dicop-Hineline*

Other Components

- Video Activities, *T. Jeffrey Richards, Philip D. Korfe, Consultant*
- Comprehensive (Semester) Tests, *T. Jeffrey Richards*
- Activités pour tous, *Patricia L. Ménard*

ISBN-13: 978-0-618-29831-0   ISBN-10: 0-618-29831-2

7 8 9 10 11 — MDO — 10 09 08 07

Table of Contents
Unité 6. Le shopping

To the Teacher

The Unit Resource Books that accompany each unit of *Discovering French, Nouveau!–Bleu* provide a wide variety of materials to practice, expand on, and assess the material in the *Discovering French, Nouveau!–Bleu* student text.

Components

Following is a list of components included in each Unit Resource Book, correlated to each **Leçon:**
- Workbook, Teacher's Edition
- *Activités pour tous*, Teacher's Edition
- Lesson Plans
- Block Scheduling Lesson Plans
- Family Letter
- Absent Student Copymasters
- Family Involvement
- Video Activities
- Videoscripts
- Audioscripts
- Lesson Quizzes

Unit Resources include the following materials:
- Communipak
- *Activités pour tous* Reading, Teacher's Edition
- Workbook Reading and Culture Activities, Teacher's Edition
- Lesson Plans for *Images*
- Block Scheduling Lesson Plans for *Images*
- Assessment
  Unit Test
  Listening Comprehension Performance Test
  Speaking Performance Test
  Reading Comprehension Performance Test
  Writing Performance Test
  Multiple Choice Test Items
  Comprehensive Test
  Test Scoring Tools

- Audioscripts
- Videoscripts for *Images*
- Answer Key

Component Description

Workbook, Teacher's Edition

The *Discovering French, Nouveau!–Bleu* Workbook directly references the student text. It provides additional practice to allow students to build their control of French and develop French proficiency. The activities provide guided communicative practice in meaningful contexts and frequent opportunity for self-expression.

Listening Activities give students the opportunity to demonstrate comprehension of spoken French in a variety of realistic contexts. Students listen to excerpts from the CD that accompanies the *Discovering French, Nouveau!–Bleu* program while working through listening activities to improve both general and discrete comprehension skills.

Writing Activities give students the chance to develop their writing skills and put into practice what they have learned in class. The last activity is called *Communication* and encourages students to express themselves in various additional communicative situations.

The Reading and Culture Activities contain realia (illustrations and objects from real life) from French-speaking countries and various kinds of cultural activities. Each unit includes one set of Reading and Culture Activities.

Activités pour tous, Teacher's Edition

The activities in *Activités pour tous* include vocabulary, grammar, and reading practice at varying levels of difficulty. Each practice section is three pages long, with each page corresponding to a level of difficulty (A, B, and C). A is the easiest and C is the most challenging.

Lesson Plans

These lesson plans follow the general sequence of a *Discovering French, Nouveau!–Bleu* lesson. Teachers using these plans should become familiar with both the overall structure of a *Discovering French, Nouveau!–Bleu* lesson and with the format of the lesson plans and available ancillaries before translating these plans to a daily sequence.

Block Scheduling Lesson Plans

These plans are structured to help teachers maximize the advantages of block scheduling, while minimizing the challenges of longer periods.

Family Letter and Family Involvement

This section offers strategies and activities to increase family support for students' study of French language and culture.

Absent Student Copymasters

The Absent Student Copymasters enable students who miss part of a **Leçon** to go over the material on their own. The Absent Student Copymasters also offer strategies and techniques to help students understand new or challenging information. If possible, make a copy of the CD, video, or DVD available, either as a loan to an absent student or for use in the school library or language lab.

Video Activities and Videoscript

The Video Activities that accompany the Video or DVD for each module focus students' attention on each video section and reinforce the material presented in the module. A transcript of the Videoscript is included for each **Leçon**.

Audioscripts

This section provides scripts for the Audio Program and includes vocabulary presentations, dialogues, readings and reading summaries, audio for Workbook and Student Text activities, and audio for Lesson Quizzes.

Communipak

The Communication section contains five types of oral communication activities introduced sequentially by level of challenge or difficulty. Designed to encourage students to use French for communication in conversational exchanges, they include *Interviews*, *Tu as la parole*, *Conversations*, *Échanges*, and *Tête à tête* activities.

Assessment

Lesson Quizzes

The Lesson Quizzes provide short accuracy-based vocabulary and structured assessments. They measure how well students have mastered the new conversational phrases, structures, and vocabulary in the lesson. Also designed to encourage students to review material in a given lesson before continuing further in the unit, the quizzes provide an opportunity for focused cyclical re-entry and review.

Unit Tests

The Unit Tests are intended to be administered upon completion of each unit. They may be given in the language laboratory or in the classroom. The total possible score for each test is 100 points. Scoring suggestions for each section appear on the test sheets. The Answer Key for the Unit Tests appears at the end of the Unit Resource Book.

There is one Unit Test for each of the eight units in *Discovering French, Nouveau!–Bleu*. Each test is available in two versions: Form A and Form B. A complete Audioscript is given for the listening portion of the tests; the recordings of these sections appear on CDs 13–16.

Speaking Performance Test

These tests enable teachers to evaluate students' comprehension, ability to respond in French, and overall fluency. Designed to be administered to students individually, each test consists of two sections, *Conversations* and *Tu as la parole*.

Reading Comprehension Performance Test

These tests allow for evaluation of students' ability to understand material written in French. The Reading Comprehension Performance Test is designed for group administration. Each test contains several reading selections, in a variety of styles. Each selection is accompanied by one to four related multiple-choice questions in English.

Listening Comprehension Performance Test

The Listening Comprehension Test is designed for group administration. Each test contains ten short listening items, each accompanied by a multiple-choice question. The test is divided into two parts, *Conversations* and *Questions et réponses*. The listening selections are recorded on CD, and the full script is also provided so that the teacher can administer the test either by playing the CD or by reading the selections aloud.

Writing Performance Test

The Writing Performance Test gives students the opportunity to demonstrate how well they can use the material in the unit for self-expression. The emphasis is not on the production of specific grammar forms, but rather on the communication of meaning. Each test contains several guided writing activities, which vary in format from unit to unit.

Multiple Choice Test Items

These are the print version of the multiple choice questions from the Test Generator. They are contextualized and focus on vocabulary, grammar, reading, writing, and cultural knowledge.

Answer Key

The Answer Key includes answers that correspond to the following material:

- Video Activities
- Lesson Quizzes
- Communipak Activities
- Unit Tests
- Comprehensive Tests
- Performance Tests
- Multiple Choice Test Items

Nom _____

Classe _____ Date _____

Discovering
FRENCH
Nouveau!

B L E U

Unité 6
Leçon 17

Workbook TE

Unité 6. Le shopping

LEÇON 17   Le français pratique: L'achat des vêtements

LISTENING ACTIVITIES

Section 1. Les vêtements et les accessoires

A. Écoutez et répétez.

B. Compréhension orale

 a. _6_

 **b.** _11_

 c. _3_

 d. _8_

 e. _12_

 f. _2_

 g. _5_

 h. _1_

 i. _16_

 j. _14_

 k. _9_

 l. _4_

 m. _7_

 n. ____

 o. _10_

p. _13_

Discovering French, Nouveau! Bleu

Unité 6, Leçon 17
Workbook

149

URB
p. 1

Nom _____

Classe _____ Date _____

C. Questions et réponses

▶ Vous désirez?
Je cherche un tee-shirt.

▶

...des chaussures.

...une chemise.

...un pantalon.

...des lunettes de soleil.

...des chaussettes.

D. Compréhension orale

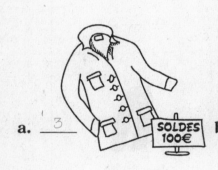
a. ___3___ SOLDES 100€

b. ___2___

c. ___1___ 210€

Section 2. Les nombres de 100 à 1000

E. Écoutez et répétez.

100	200	500	800
101	300	600	900
102	400	700	1000

Nom _____

Classe _____ Date _____ _____

Discovering
FRENCH
Nouveau!

B L E U

Unité 6
Leçon 17

Workbook TE

F. Questions et réponses

▶ —Combien coûte la veste?
—Elle coûte 100 euros.

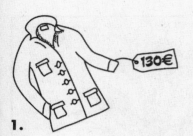

1.

—... le manteau?
— Il coûte 130 euros.

2.

—... l'imperméable?
—Il coûte 200 euros.

3.

—... la robe?
—Elle coûte 390 euros.

Section 3. Conversations

G. La réponse logique

1. a. J'ai une veste bleue.
   b. Je porte des bottes.
   c. Je cherche un imperméable.

2. a. Un blouson.
   b. Une boutique.
   c. Un grand magasin.

3. a. Un imper.
   b. Des bottes.
   c. Mon maillot de bain.

4. a. Il est trop grand.
   b. Il est démodé.
   c. 160 euros.

5. a. Oui, il est marron.
   b. Oui, il est très joli.
   c. Non, il est grand.

6. a. Non, elle est bon marché.
   b. Non, il est démodé.
   c. Non, il est trop petit.

Section 4. Dictée

H. Écoutez et écrivez.

—Qu'est-ce que tu penses du ___manteau___ rouge ?

—Il est ___génial___.

—Combien est-ce qu'il ___coûte___ ?

— ___210___ euros.

—Oh là là ! Il n'est pas ___bon marché___ !

URB
p. 3

Discovering French, Nouveau! Bleu

Unité 6, Leçon 17
Workbook

151

Nom _____

Classe _____ Date _____

Discovering
FRENCH
Nouveau!

B L E U

WRITING ACTIVITIES

A/B **1. Une affiche de mode** *(A fashion poster)*

You are working in the ad department of a fashion designer. Complete the poster below with the names of the articles of clothing.

URB
p. 4

152

Unité 6, Leçon 17
Workbook

Discovering French, Nouveau! Bleu

Nom _____

Classe _____ Date _____

Discovering
FRENCH
Nouveau!

B L E U

Unité 6
Leçon 17   Workbook TE

2. Qu'est-ce que vous portez? (sample answers)

Describe in detail what you are wearing. Give the colors of each item of clothing. Then select two other people (one male and one female) and describe their clothes in the same manner.

▶ Aujourd'hui, je porte une chemise verte et jaune, un pantalon noir, . . .

1. Aujourd'hui, je porte un jean bleu, un pull noir, un manteau rouge et des tennis blancs.

   _____

2. M. Denis _____ porte un pantalon marron, une chemise blanche, une cravate bleue
   et rouge et une veste bleue.

3. Kristen _____ porte un pull vert et jaune, une jupe jaune, un blouson orange et
   des chaussures marron.

Nom _____

Classe _____ Date _____

3. Les valises *(Suitcases)* (sample answers)

Imagine you are planning for four trips. Make a list of at least four items of clothing that you will pack in each of the following suitcases.

1. un week-end à la plage

un short · des polos · des sandales · des tee-shirts · un maillot de bain · des lunettes de soleil · un sweat · une casquette

2. un week-end de ski

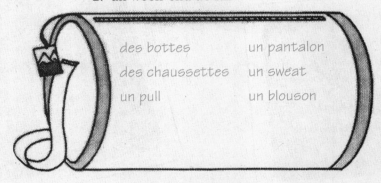

des bottes · un pantalon · des chaussettes · un sweat · un pull · un blouson

3. un mariage élégant

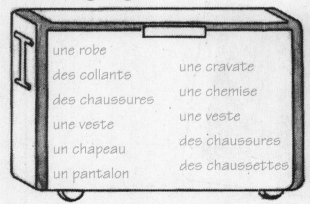

une robe · des collants · une cravate · des chaussures · une chemise · une veste · une veste · un chapeau · des chaussures · un pantalon · des chaussettes

4. une semaine à Québec

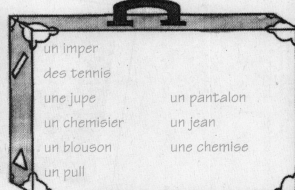

un imper · des tennis · une jupe · un pantalon · un chemisier · un jean · un blouson · une chemise · un pull

Nom

Classe _____ Date _____

Discovering
FRENCH
Nouveau!

BLEU

Unité 6
Leçon 17

Workbook TE

4. Conversations : Dans un magasin

Complete the dialogues on the basis of the illustrations. Use expressions from page 262 of your student text.

1.

—Vous désirez, _____ monsieur ?

—Je cherche une cravate _____.

2.

—Pardon, mademoiselle.

Combien coûtent les bottes _____ ?

—Elles coûtent cent vingt _____ euros.

3.

—S'il vous plaît, madame, quel est le prix de la robe

_____ ?

—Elle coûte mille euros _____.

4.

—Est-ce que le manteau est bon marché _____ ?

Oh là là, non. Il est très cher _____.

Il coûte cinq cents _____ euros.

5.

—Qu'est-ce que tu penses de ma veste _____ ?

—Elle est trop longue _____.

6.

—Comment trouves-tu mon pantalon _____

_____ ?

—Il est trop court _____.

Discovering French, Nouveau! Bleu

URB
p. 7

Unité 6, Leçon 17
Workbook

155

Nom _____

Classe _____ Date _____

Discovering FRENCH Nouveau!

B L E U

Unité 6
Leçon 17

Activités pour tous TE

Unité 6. Le shopping

LEÇON 17 Le français pratique: L'achat des vêtements

A

Activité 1 La mode

Classify the following articles of clothing as primarily for men and women or just for women.

	HOMMES & FEMMES	FEMMES
une chemise	×	
un pantalon	×	
une robe		×
une ceinture	×	
un chemisier		×
des collants		×

Activité 2 L'intrus

Select the word that doesn't fit with the others.

1. une boutique   un magasin   des collants
2. des baskets   des sandales   des tennis
3. des sandales   un pantalon   un maillot de bain
4. une ceinture   une casquette   un chapeau
5. une jupe   une robe   une veste
6. un polo   un manteau   un imper

Activité 3 Au grand magasin

You are out shopping with a French-speaking friend. Get your friend's opinion on the various articles of clothing below. Fill in the blanks, using **penses** or **trouves,** circling the correct articles, and naming the articles of clothing.

1. Qu'est-ce que tu _penses_ _du_/ des / les _short_ ?

2. Comment est-ce que tu _trouves_ _le_/ les / des _jean_ ?

3. Qu'est-ce que tu _penses_ du /_des_/ les _chaussettes_ ?

4. Comment est-ce que tu _trouves_ le /_les_/ des _chaussures_ ?

Nom _____

Classe _____ Date _____

Discovering
FRENCH
Nouveau!

BLEU

B

Activité 1   Qu'est-ce que je porte?

Circle the two clothing items that would be appropriate for the situation described.

1. En hiver quand il neige, je porte: (des bottes)   (un pull)   une cravate

2. À la plage, je porte: un chemisier   (un maillot de bain)   (des sandales)

3. Pour regarder un match au stade, je porte: (une casquette)   une robe   (un jean)

4. Pour faire du jogging, je porte: des collants   (des baskets)   (un survêtement)

5. Pour aller au restaurant, je porte: (un pantalon)   un short   (une chemise)

Activité 2   Où va Olivia?

First, fill in the blanks with the names of the articles of clothing.
Then, decide where Olivia is going.

Olivia porte . . .   Elle va . . .

_c_ 1.   et

un pantalon   un polo   a. à la plage.

_d_ 2. et

des baskets   un tee-shirt   b. en ville et il pleut.

_b_ 3. et

des bottes   un imper   c. à l'école.

_a_ 4. et

un short   des lunettes de soleil   d. au gymnase.

Activité 3   Au grand magasin

Match each question with the best answer.

_d_ 1. —Vous désirez, mademoiselle?   a. —Il coûte 145 euros.

_a_ 2. —Combien est-ce qu'il coûte?   b. —Je pense qu'il est moche.

_e_ 3. —Qu'est-ce que tu vas acheter?   c. —Je ne pense pas.

_b_ 4. —Comment trouves-tu le blouson?   d. —Je cherche un maillot de bain.

_c_ 5. —Tu penses que c'est bon marché?   e. —Je vais acheter des baskets.

Nom

Classe _____ Date _____

**Discovering
FRENCH**
Nouveau!

BLEU

Unité 6
Leçon 17 Activités pour tous TE

C

Activité 1 Mes habitudes (Sample Answers)

Write answers in French to the following questions.

1. Est-ce que tu aimes faire du shopping?

   Oui, j'aime beaucoup faire du shopping!

2. Quelle sorte de magasin est-ce que tu préfères?

   Je préfère les grands magasins.

3. Est-ce que tu préfères acheter des vêtements élégants ou des vêtements de sport?

   Je préfère acheter des vêtements de sport.

4. Quelle est ta couleur favorite pour les vêtements?

   J'aime le beige.

5. Combien est-ce que tu dépenses *(spend)* pour un pantalon élégant? Pour un jean?

   Pour un pantalon élégant, je dépense $65. Pour un jean, je dépense $40.

Activité 2 Contraire ou synonyme? (Sample Answers)

In the left column, write adjectives with the *opposite* meaning. In the right column, list items of clothing that are rough *synonyms* of the items provided.

Contraires	Synonymes
1. joli *moche*	1. un jean *un pantalon*
2. démodé *à la mode*	2. une casquette *un chapeau*
3. grand *petit*	3. un manteau *un imper*
4. long *court*	4. une chemise *un chemisier*
5. cher *bon marché*	5. des tennis *des baskets*

Activité 3 Mes vêtements (Sample Answers)

Write sentences listing at least three items of clothing that you wear in these situations.

1. Pour aller à la plage, *je mets des sandales et des lunettes de soleil, un maillot de bain et des sandales*.

2. Quand je vais au centre commercial, *je porte un pantalon, un pull sympa et des chaussures*.

3. En hiver quand il fait froid, *je mets un manteau, un chapeau et des bottes*.

4. Pour aller à une soirée, *je mets mon pull préféré, une jupe et des chaussures*.

5. Quand je dîne dans un restaurant élégant, *je porte une belle veste, des collants et une robe élégante*.

LEÇON 17 Le français pratique: L'achat des vêtements, page 256

Objectives

Communicative Functions and Topics

To talk about clothing, accessories, and stores that sell clothes
To talk about what people are wearing and where to go shopping
To say whether clothes fit and what they look like
To ask for help from a salesperson and find out prices
To use expressions of opinion
To use numbers to 1000 to discuss prices

Linguistic Goals To use regular *-er* verbs in the present tense

Cultural Goals To be aware of the French concept of style

Motivation and Focus

❑ Students can identify the type of store and clothing in the photo on pages 254–255. Ask about their favorite places to buy clothes and the types of clothes they like. Discuss the importance of clothes and style. Read *Thème et Objectifs* on page 254 to preview content of the unit.

Presentation and Explanation

❑ *Lesson Opener:* Ask students to identify the types of stores in the photos on pages 256–257. Use SETTING THE STAGE, page 256 of the TE, to find out students' favorite shopping places. Have them read the captions, encouraging comments on similarities and differences between their favorite stores and those in the photos. Read *Accent sur . . .*, page 256. Use CRITICAL THINKING SKILLS, page 257 of the TE, to point out French words used in fashion.

❑ *Vocabulary A:* Use **Overhead Transparency** 35 to introduce clothes, page 258. Model the clothing items and have students repeat. Explain the LANGUAGE NOTES, page 258 of the TE. Students can identify clothing they are wearing.

❑ *Vocabulary B:* Introduce accessories, page 260, with **Overhead Transparency** 36.

❑ *Vocabulary C:* Present vocabulary and expressions for getting help from a salesperson and discussing clothes with a friend, page 262. Use **Overhead Transparency** 37 to clarify meaning. Students can repeat the words and expressions. Use **Audio** CD 3, Track 20 to practice numbers from 100 to 1000.

Guided Practice and Checking Understanding

❑ Use the activities suggested on pages A94–A98 of **Overhead Transparencies** with Transparencies 35–37 to practice clothing vocabulary.

❑ Check students' listening comprehension with **Audio** CD 10, Tracks 1–8 or **Audioscript** pages 32–34, and **Workbook** Listening Activities A–H (pages 149–151).

❑ Have students do **Video Activities** pages 23–27 as they watch **Video** Module 17 or listen as you read the **Videoscript,** pages 29–30.

❑ Do the COMPREHENSION Activity with clothing on page 258 of the TE.

Discovering
FRENCH *Nouveau!*

BLEU

Unité 6
Leçon 17

Lesson Plans

Independent Practice

❑ Do the oral practice activities on pages 259–263 for homework. Then arrange students in pairs for PAIR PRACTICE with Activities 1, 4, and 7–8.
❑ Use any of **Communipak** *Interviews* 1–4, pages 140–141, *Conversations* 1–2, pages 144–145, *Échange* 1, page 148, or *Tête à tête* 1, pages 151–152, for additional practice with clothing vocabulary. **Video Activities** page 28 is suitable for small-group work.
❑ Have students do the activities in **Activités pour tous**, pages 91–93.

Monitoring and Adjusting

❑ Assign Writing Activities 1–4 in the **Workbook** (pages 152–155).
❑ Monitor listening skills with SUPPLEMENTARY LISTENING PRACTICE, page 259 of the TE. Use the suggestions for EXPANSION and VARIATION activities on pages 259 and 261 of the TE to challenge more advanced students.

Assessment

❑ Use Quiz 17 on pages 35–36 after students have completed the lesson's activities. You can adapt the questions to the class's specific needs with the **Test Generator.**

Reteaching

❑ Redo any appropriate activities in the **Workbook.**
❑ Use **Teacher to Teacher** pages 18–19 to reteach clothing items.
❑ Have students watch the **Video** to reteach parts of the lesson or for make-up work.

Extension and Enrichment

❑ Play the GAME, page 262 of the TE, with **Overhead Transparency** 12. Do the CHALLENGE ACTIVITY: UNE IDOLE on page 263 of the TE. See the SUPPLEMENTARY VOCABULARY lists, pages 258 and 261 of the TE, for additional clothing and store items.

Summary and Closure

❑ Use Transparency S15 and the suggestions at the bottom of page A25 of **Overhead Transparencies** to summarize vocabulary and expressions used in shopping for clothes.
❑ Use the suggestions for PORTFOLIO assessment on page 265 of the TE.

End-of-Lesson Activities

❑ *À votre tour!:* Students can prepare and practice Activities 1–4, pages 264–265. Use **Audio CD** 3, Tracks 21–23 with Activities 1–3. Assign written self-expression Activities 5 or 6 for homework.

LEÇON 17   Le français pratique: L'achat des vêtements, page 256

Block Schedule (3 Days to Complete)

Objectives

Communicative Functions and Topics	To talk about clothing, accessories, and stores that sell clothes
	To talk about what people are wearing and where to go shopping
	To say whether clothes fit and what they look like
	To ask for help from a salesperson and find out prices
	To use expressions of opinion
	To use numbers to 1000 to discuss prices
Linguistic Goals	To use regular *-er* verbs in the present tense
Cultural Goals	To be aware of the French concept of style

Day 1

Motivation and Focus

❑ Students can identify the type of store and clothing in the photo on pages 254–255. Ask about their favorite places to buy clothes and the types of clothes they like. Discuss the importance of clothes and style. Read *Thème et Objectifs* on page 254 to preview content of the unit.

Presentation and Explanation

❑ *Lesson Opener:* Ask students to identify the types of stores in the photos on pages 256–257. Use SETTING THE STAGE, page 256 of the TE, to find out students' favorite shopping places. Have them read the captions, encouraging comments on similarities and differences between their favorite stores and those in the photos. Read *Accent sur . . .*, page 256. Use CRITICAL THINKING SKILLS, page 257 of the TE, to point out French words used in fashion.

❑ *Vocabulary A:* Use **Overhead Transparency** 35 to introduce clothes, page 258. Model the clothing items and have students repeat. Explain the LANGUAGE NOTES, page 258 of the TE. Students can identify clothing they are wearing.

❑ *Vocabulary B:* Introduce accessories, page 260, with **Overhead Transparency** 36.

❑ *Vocabulary C:* Present vocabulary and expressions for getting help from a salesperson and discussing clothes with a friend, page 262. Use **Overhead Transparency** 37 to clarify meaning. Students can repeat the words and expressions. Use **Audio** CD 3, Track 20 to practice numbers from 100 to 1000.

Guided Practice and Checking Understanding

❑ Use the activities suggested on pages A94–A98 of **Overhead Transparencies** with Transparencies 35–37 to practice clothing vocabulary.

❑ Check students' listening comprehension with **Audio** CD 10, Tracks 1–8 or **Audioscript** pages 32–34, and **Workbook** Listening Activities A–H (pages 149–151).

Discovering FRENCH *Nouveau!*

BLEU

Unité 6
Leçon 17

Block Scheduling
Lesson Plans

Day 2

Motivation and Focus

❑ Have students do **Video Activities** pages 23–27 as they watch **Video** Module 17 or listen as you read the **Videoscript,** pages 29–30.

❑ Do the COMPREHENSION Activity with clothing on page 258 of the TE.

Independent Practice

❑ Do the oral practice activities on pages 259–263 for homework. Then arrange students in pairs for PAIR PRACTICE with Activities 1, 4, and 7–8.

❑ Use any of **Communipak** *Interviews* 1–4, pages 140–141, *Conversations* 1–2, pages 144–145, *Échange* 1, page 148, or *Tête à tête* 1, pages 151–152, for additional practice with clothing vocabulary. **Video Activities** page 28 is suitable for small-group work.

❑ Have students do the activities in **Activités pour tous**, pages 91–93.

Monitoring and Adjusting

❑ Assign Writing Activities 1–4 in the **Workbook** (pages 152–155).

❑ Monitor listening skills with SUPPLEMENTARY LISTENING PRACTICE, page 259 of the TE. Use the EXPANSION and VARIATION activities on pages 259 and 261 of the TE.

Day 3

End-of-Lesson Activities

❑ *À votre tour!:* Students can prepare and practice Activities 1–4, pages 264–265. Assign written self-expression Activities 5 or 6 for homework.

Reteaching (as needed)

❑ Redo any appropriate activities in the **Workbook.**

❑ Use **Teacher to Teacher** pages 18–19 to reteach clothing items.

Extension and Enrichment

❑ Play the GAME, page 262 of the TE, with **Overhead Transparency** 12. Do the CHALLENGE ACTIVITY: UNE IDOLE on page 263 of the TE.

❑ Use **Block Scheduling Copymasters**, pages 129–136.

❑ For expansion activities, direct students to www.classzone.com

Summary and Closure

❑ Use Transparency S15 and the suggestions at the bottom of page A25 of **Overhead Transparencies** to summarize vocabulary and expressions used in shopping for clothes.

❑ Use the suggestions for PORTFOLIO ASSESSMENT on page 265 of the TE.

Assessment

❑ Use Quiz 17 on pages 35–36 after students have completed the lesson. You can adapt the questions to your class's specific needs with the **Test Generator**.

Date:

Dear Family:

We are currently working on Unit 6 in the *Discovering French, Nouveau!–Bleu* program. In this unit, students are learning to name and describe clothing, to discuss style, to make comparisons, and to distinguish between certain people or objects. Students are also learning grammar—they are learning to use demonstrative adjectives and interrogative pronouns; to conjugate verbs with spelling changes such as **acheter** (to buy) and **préférer** (to prefer) as well as other verbs like them; to conjugate the irregular verb **mettre** (to put or place); to conjugate regular **–ir** verbs; to form certain irregular adjectives; and to use the imperative.

Through completing the activities, students employ critical thinking skills as they compare the French language and the culture of France with their own community. They also connect to other academic subjects, using their knowledge of French to access new information.

Please feel free to call me with any questions or concerns you might have as your student practices reading, writing, listening, and speaking in French.

Sincerely,

Nom _____

Classe _____ Date _____ _____

Discovering
FRENCH
Nouveau!

B L E U

Unité 6
Leçon 17

Absent Student
Copymasters

LEÇON 17 Le français pratique: L'achat des vêtements, pages 254–257

Materials Checklist

- **Student Text**
- **Video 3** or **DVD 2**; Counter 40:29–42:04

Steps to Follow

- Unit Opener: Look at the photograph on pp. 254–255. What types of stores do you see? Are they specialty shops or department stores? How can you tell? What items can you buy in Derby? Can you guess what items you might find in Salamander? How is this shopping area the same as or different from shopping areas in your town?
- Read *Accent sur…l'élégance française* (pp. 256–257). Look at the photographs and read the captions.
- Watch **Video 3** or **DVD 2**; Counter 40:29–42:04. Repeat everything you hear.

If You Don't Understand . . .

- Watch the **Video** or **DVD** in a quiet place. Try to stay focused. If you get lost, stop the **Video** or **DVD**. Replay it and find your place.
- Say aloud anything you write. Make sure you understand everything you say.
- Write down any questions so that you can ask your partner or your teacher later.

Self-Check

Answer the following questions. You may review the reading to find the answer.

1. En France, où est-ce que vous achetez les vêtements élégants et chers?
2. En France, où est-ce que vous achetez les vêtements de bonne qualité et pas trop chers?
3. En France, où est-ce que vous achetez les chaussures de sport?

Answers

1. En France, vous achetez les vêtements élégants et chers dans une boutique. 2. En France, vous achetez les vêtements de bonne qualité et pas trop chers dans une grande surface. 3. En France, vous achetez les chaussures de sport dans un magasin de chaussures.

Nom _____

Classe _____ Date _____

A. Vocabulaire: Les vêtements, pages 258–259

Materials Checklist

- **Student Text**
- **Audio** CD 10, Track 1
- **Video 3** or **DVD 2**; Counter 37:12–38:08
- **Workbook**

Steps to Follow

- Study *Vocabulaire: Les vêtements* (pp. 258–259). Copy the model sentences and the new words on a separate sheet of paper. Circle the nouns that end in –*eaux* in the plural.
- Watch **Video 3** or **DVD 2**; Counter 37:12–38:08. Repeat everything you hear.
- Do Activity 1 in the text (p. 259). Write the parts for both speakers on a separate sheet of paper. Read both parts aloud.
- Do Activity 2 in the text (p. 259). Write the answers in complete sentences. For items 2, 3, and 4, base your answers on what you imagine these people are wearing today.
- Do Writing Activities A/B, 1–2 in the **Workbook** (pages 152–153).
- Do Listening Activity A in the **Workbook** (p. 149). Use **Audio CD** 10, Track 1.

If You Don't Understand . . .

- Watch the **Video** or **DVD** in a quiet place. Try to stay focused. If you get lost, stop the **Video** or **DVD**. Replay it and find your place.
- Listen to the **CD** in a quiet place. Try to stay focused. If you get lost, stop the **CD**. Replay it and find your place.
- On a separate sheet of paper, write down the words that are underlined in the text. Check for meaning.
- Say aloud anything you write. Make sure you understand everything you say.
- Write down any questions so that you can ask your partner or your teacher later.

Self-Check

Use the vocabulary in parentheses to answer the following questions. Use **un** or **une** as appropriate.

1. Qu'est-ce que tu portes aujourd'hui? (casquette, polo, jean)
2. Qu'est-ce que Jean porte aujourd'hui? (chemise, pantalon, chaussures)
3. Il pleut. Qu'est-ce que je vais mettre? (imperméable)
4. Qu'est-ce que Marie-Louise va acheter? (veste)
5. Qu'est-ce que nous allons porter demain? (pull, jean)
6. Qu'est-ce qu'il va mettre ce soir? (manteau, pantalon)

Answers

1. Je porte une casquette, un polo et un jean. 2. Aujourd'hui, Jean porte une chemise, un pantalon et des chaussures. 3. Tu vas (vous allez) mettre un imperméable. 4. Marie-Louise va acheter une veste. 5. Demain, nous allons porter un pull et un jean. 6. Ce soir, il va mettre un manteau et un pantalon.

Nom _____

Classe _____ Date _____

Discovering
FRENCH
Nouveau!

B L E U

Unité 6
Leçon 17
Absent Student
Copymasters

B. Vocabulaire: D'autres vêtements et accessoires,
pages 260–261

Materials Checklist

- **Student Text**
- **Audio** CD 10, Track 2

- **Video 3** or **DVD 2**; Counter 38:08–39:08
- **Workbook**

Steps to Follow

- Study *Vocabulaire: D'autres vêtements et accessoires* (p. 260). Copy the words on a separate sheet of paper. Check meanings.
- Watch **Video 3** or **DVD 2**; Counter 38:08–39:08. Repeat everything you hear.
- Do Activity 3 in the text (p. 260). Write your answers on a separate sheet of paper.
- Do Activity 4 in the text (p. 261). Write the parts for both speakers in complete sentences. Read both parts aloud.
- Do Activity 5 in the text (p. 261). Set a timer for five minutes and time yourself. Write complete sentences on a separate sheet of paper.
- Do Activity 6 in the text (p. 261). Write your answers in complete sentences on a separate sheet of paper.
- Do Writing Activity A/B, 3 in the **Workbook** (page 154).
- Do Listening Activity B in the **Workbook** (p. 149). Use **Audio CD** 10, Track 2.

If You Don't Understand . . .

- Watch the **Video** or **DVD** in a quiet place. Try to stay focused. If you get lost, stop the **Video** or **DVD**. Replay it and find your place.
- Listen to the **CD** in a quiet place. Try to stay focused. If you get lost, stop the **CD**. Replay it and find your place.
- Reread the activity directions. Put the directions in your own words.
- Read the model several times. Be sure you understand it.
- Say aloud everything that you write. Be sure you understand what you are saying.
- When writing a sentence, ask yourself, "What do I mean? What am I trying to say?"
- Write down any questions so that you can ask your partner or your teacher later.

Self-Check

Write complete sentences using the following expressions. Use the appropriate form of the indefinite article.

Anne / bottes / aller à la campagne

Anne porte des bottes. Elle va aller à la campagne.

1. Jean / maillot de bain / nager
2. Hélène et Louise / lunettes de soleil / aller à la plage
3. Sophie / short / jouer au tennis

Answers

1. Jean porte un maillot de bain. Il va nager. 2. Hélène et Louise portent des lunettes de soleil. Elles vont à la plage. 3. Sophie porte un short. Elle va jouer au tennis.

Nom _____

Classe _____ Date _____

C. Vocabulaire: Dans un magasin, pages 262–263

Materials Checklist

- **Student Text**
- **Audio** CD 3, Track 20-23; CD 10, Tracks 3–8
- **Video 3** or **DVD 2;** Counter 34:40–37:11; 39:09–40:28
- **Workbook**

Steps to Follow

- Study *Vocabulaire: Dans un magasin* (p. 262). Copy the new words and expressions on a separate sheet of paper. Underline the feminine adjective endings, for example, *chère*, *petite*, *géniale*.
- Study *Les nombres de 100 à 1000* (p. 263). Copy the chart on a separate sheet of paper.
- Watch **Video 3** or **DVD 2;** Counter 34:40–37:11; 39:09–40:28, or listen to **Audio** CD 3, Track 20. Repeat everything you hear.
- Do Activities 7 and 8 in the text (p. 263). Write the parts for both speakers in complete sentences on a separate sheet of paper. Read both parts aloud.
- Do Writing Activity A/B, 4 in the **Workbook** (page 155).
- Do Listening Activities C–H in the **Workbook** (pp. 150–151). Use **Audio CD** 10, Tracks 3–8.
- Do Activities 1-6 of *À votre tour!* in the text (pp. 264-265). Use *Audio CD 3*, Tracks 21-23 with Activities 1-3.

If You Don't Understand . . .

- Reread the activity directions. Put the directions in your own words.
- Read the model several times before beginning so you are certain what to do. Copy the model. Say aloud everything that you write. Listen and be sure you understand what you are saying.
- Watch the **Video** or **DVD** in a quiet place. Try to stay focused. If you get lost, stop the **Video** or **DVD**. Replay it and find your place.
- Listen to the **CDs** in a quiet place. Try to stay focused. If you get lost, stop the **CDs**. Replay them and find your place.
- Write down any questions so that you can ask your partner or your teacher later.

Self-Check

Write questions and answers using the following expressions. Write out the numbers. Underline the definite article and the adjective in each sentence.

maillot de bain / rose / 125 euros

Combien coûte le maillot de bain rose? Il coûte cent vingt-cinq euros.

1. blouson / joli / 150 euros
2. pantalon / vert / 180 euros
3. chemise / joli / 275 euros
4. veste / gris / 220 euros
5. jean / noir / 100 euros

Answers

1. Combien coûte le joli blouson? Il coûte cent cinquante euros. 2. Combien coûte le pantalon vert? Il coûte cent quatre-vingts euros. 3. Combien coûte la jolie chemise? Elle coûte deux cent soixante-quinze euros. 4. Combien coûte la veste grise? Elle coûte deux cent vingt euros. 5. Combien coûte le jean noir? Il coûte cent euros.

Nom _____

Classe _____ Date _____

Discovering
FRENCH
Nouveau!

BLEU

Unité 6
Leçon 17
Family Involvement

LEÇON 17 Le français pratique: L'achat des vêtements

Pour aller en ville

Interview a family member. Ask him or her to identify what he or she would wear to go into the city. Choose among the examples given.

- First, explain your assignment.
- Then, model the pronunciation of the words below the pictures. Point to the picture as you model each answer.
- Ask the question, **Qu'est-ce que tu portes pour aller en ville?**
- When you have the answer, complete the sentence at the bottom of the page.

 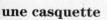

une casquette   **un tee-shirt**   **un chapeau**   **un jean**   **un pantalon**

une robe   **une chemise**   **un chemisier**   **un jogging**   **une veste**

Pour aller en ville, _____ porte _____

_____.

Nom _____

Classe _____ Date _____

Un mariage

Tell a family member to imagine that he or she is going to an elegant wedding. Find out what he or she would wear.

- First, explain your assignment.
- Then, model the pronunciation of the words below the pictures. Point to the picture as you model each answer. Give any necessary English equivalents.
- Ask the question, **Qu'est-ce que tu portes pour aller à un mariage élégant?**
- When you have an answer, complete the sentence at the bottom of the page.

une robe courte et élégante

un jean bon marché

un pantalon à la mode

une jolie robe longue

des collants

un chapeau

une veste

des chaussures élégantes

_____ porte _____

Nom _____

Classe _____ Date _____

Discovering FRENCH *Nouveau!*

BLEU

Unité 6
Leçon 17
Video Activities

MODULE 17 Le français pratique: L'achat des vêtements

Video 3, DVD 2

17.1 Activité 1. Dominique et Stéphanie

Counter 34:40–35:55

Where are Stéphanie and Dominique today and what are they doing? Watch the video and circle the letter of the correct completion to each sentence below.

1. Nous sommes samedi . . .
   a. après-midi   b. matin   c. soir

2. Stéphanie et Dominique sont . . .
   a. au gymnase   b. à la maison   c. en ville

3. Elles font . . .
   a. du shopping   b. une promenade   c. un match

4. Le pull jaune est . . .
   a. joli   b. super   c. moche

5. Stéphanie et Dominique entrent dans . . .
   a. un supermarché   b. une boutique   c. un magasin

6. Stéphanie regarde une robe . . .
   a. rouge   b. verte   c. bleue

7. Les robes sont très . . .
   a. belles   b. chères   c. bon marché

8. Les Galeries Lafayette sont un grand . . .
   a. musée   b. centre commercial   c. magasin

17.2 Activité 2. Dialogue:
Aux Galeries Lafayette
Counter 35:56–37:11

What does Dominique buy at the Galeries Lafayette? Watch the video and circle the letter of the missing word or words in each exchange.

Scène 1

DOMINIQUE: Regarde la robe!

STÉPHANIE: Eh bien, dis donc, elle

n'est pas _____.

a. moche   b. jolie

c. bon marché   d. chère

Scène 2

STÉPHANIE: Qu'est-ce que tu penses

de ce _____?

DOMINIQUE: Il est chouette . . . mais il

est trop _____ pour toi.

a. blouson   b. polo

c. grand   d. petit

Scène 3

LA VENDEUSE: Que désirez-vous mademoiselle?

DOMINIQUE: Je cherche un _____.

LA VENDEUSE: De quelle couleur?

DOMINIQUE: Je voudrais un polo _____.

a. blouson   ⓑ polo

c. jaune   d. bleu

Scène 4

LA VENDEUSE: Comment trouvez-vous ce polo?

DOMINIQUE: Il est _____.

Combien est-ce qu'il coûte?

LA VENDEUSE: Il est _____.

DOMINIQUE: D'accord, je le prends.

a. mal   b. bien

c. bon marché   d. en solde

Nom _____

Classe _____ Date _____ _____

Discovering
FRENCH
Nouveau!

B L E U

Unité 6
Leçon 17
Video Activities

17.3 Activité 3. Je cherche . . .

People are shopping for clothes. As you watch the video, number the items (1–16) in the order you hear them.

a. _____ un pantalon

b. _____ un imperméable

c. _____ une cravate

d. _____ une robe

e. _____ un polo

f. _____ des chaussettes

g. _____ des lunettes de soleil

h. _____ des tennis

i. _____ une chemise

j. _____ un manteau

k. _____ un jean

l. _____ une veste

m. _____ un pull

n. _____ des chaussures

o. _____ un maillot de bain

p. _____ un survêtement

17.4 Activité 4. Vous désirez?

What are people in the video looking for? After you watch the video segment, fill in the blanks below with the names of the clothing items pictured.

1._____ 2._____ 3._____

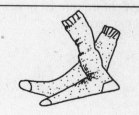

4._____ 5._____ 6._____

17.5 Activité 5. Combien coûte la veste?

Counter 39:09–39:52

How much do things cost? As you watch the video, draw a line from each item of clothing to the corresponding price.

1. la veste   a. 125 euros

2. le blouson   b. 230 euros

3. l'imperméable   c. 75 euros

4. les chaussures   d. 150 euros

17.6 Activité 6. Qu'est-ce que tu en penses?

Counter 39:53–40:28

What do the people in the video say about their friends' choices in clothing? For each exchange, circle the letter of the correct completion as you hear it.

1. —Comment trouves-tu ma robe?
   —Elle est très . . .   a. chouette
                               b. moche

2. —Comment trouves-tu mon pantalon?
   —Il est trop . . .   a. grand
                               b. long

3. —Qu'est-ce que tu penses de ma chemise?
   —Elle est . . .   a. à la mode
                               b. un peu démodée

4. —Qu'est-ce que tu penses de mon manteau?
   —Il est trop . . .   a. court
                               b. petit

Nom _____

Discovering FRENCH *Nouveau!*

Nom _____

Classe _____ Date _____ _____

BLEU

🗣 **17.7 Activité 7.** Où acheter les vêtements?

Counter 40:29–42:04

A. Before you watch the **Vignette culturelle,** answer the following question.

Question personnelle: Where do you usually buy your clothes—at department stores, specialty shops, or discount places?

Réponse: _____

B. After you watch the **Vignette culturelle,** read the descriptions below of different places where you can buy clothes in France. Fill in the blank in each item below with the correct place name from the box.

une boutique de mode	un marché aux puces
un grand magasin	une boutique de soldes

1. Ici les vêtements sont élégants, mais ils sont chers. C'est _____.

2. Ici il y a toujours un grand choix de vêtements. La qualité est bonne et les prix sont raisonnables. C'est _____.

3. Là, on peut acheter des vêtements à des prix intéressants. C'est _____

   _____.

4. Quand on n'a pas beaucoup d'argent on peut aller où l'atmosphère est pittoresque et les vêtements sont drôles. C'est _____.

C. Question personnelle: If you were in France, at which of the four stores above would you go shopping for clothes? Why?

Réponse: _____

Discovering French, Nouveau! Bleu

Nom _____

Classe _____ Date _____

 Activité 8. Dans un magasin

With a classmate, imagine you are on a shopping trip in France. Take turns pretending to try on the different items listed below, and have a conversation about how the item looks—use your imagination! Decide whether to buy the item or not. Continue until all the items have been tried on.

un pantalon	**un pull**	**une chemise**	**un manteau**	**une veste**
	un imperméable	**des chaussures**	**des lunettes de soleil**	

▶ ÉLÈVE 1: **Comment trouves-tu ce pull?**

ÉLÈVE 2: **Euh . . . il est trop grand pour toi.**

ÉLÈVE 1: **D'accord. Je ne le prends pas.**

 | *Phrases utiles*
Comment trouves-tu . . .?
Il/Elle est . . .
Ils/Elles sont . . .

MODULE 17 Le français pratique: L'achat des vêtements

Video 3, DVD 2

17.1 Introduction: Listening— Le shopping
Counter 34:40–35:55

Nous sommes samedi après-midi. Stéphanie et Dominique sont en ville. Qu'est-ce qu'elles font? Elles font du shopping.

DOMINIQUE: Regarde, il est chouette, ce polo rayé.

STÉPHANIE: Ah oui, c'est vrai. Regarde ce pull jaune.

DOMINIQUE: Ah, oui, il est super.

STÉPHANIE: On entre?

DOMINIQUE: D'accord.

Stéphanie et Dominique entrent dans une boutique. Il y a beaucoup de jolis vêtements ici. Dominique regarde une robe bleue. Stéphanie regarde une robe rouge. Malheureusement, les robes sont très chères.

Finalement, Stéphanie et Dominique vont aux Galeries Lafayette. Les Galeries Lafayette sont un grand magasin. Ici on peut acheter beaucoup de vêtements différents.

17.2 Dialogue: Aux Galeries Lafayette
Counter 35:56–37:11

DOMINIQUE: Regarde la robe.

STÉPHANIE: Eh bien, dis donc, elle n'est pas bon marché!

STÉPHANIE: Qu'est-ce que tu penses de ce blouson?

DOMINIQUE: Il est chouette . . . mais il est trop grand pour toi!

VENDEUSE: Que désirez-vous, mademoiselle?

DOMINIQUE: Je cherche un polo.

VENDEUSE: De quelle couleur?

DOMINIQUE: Je voudrais un polo jaune.

DOMINIQUE: Comment tu me trouves comme ça?

VENDEUSE: Comment trouvez-vous ce polo?

DOMINIQUE: Il est bien. Combien est-ce qu'il coûte?

VENDEUSE: Il est en solde . . .

DOMINIQUE: D'accord, je le prends.

17.3 Mini-scenes: Listening— Qu'est-ce que vous cherchez?
Counter 37:12–38:08

In France, you'll certainly want to go clothes shopping. You may need to let the salesperson know what you're looking for. Let's learn the names of clothing by asking these shoppers what they're looking for.

Qu'est-ce que vous cherchez?

—Je cherche un pantalon.
—Je cherche une chemise.
—Je cherche un imperméable.
—Je cherche un manteau.
—Je cherche une cravate.
—Je cherche un jean.
—Je cherche une veste.
—Je cherche une robe.
—Je cherche un pull.
—Je cherche un polo.
—Je cherche des chaussettes.
—Je cherche des chaussures.
—Je cherche un maillot de bain.
—Je cherche des lunettes de soleil.
—Je cherche des tennis.
—Je cherche un survêtement.

17.4 Mini-scenes: Speaking— Vous désirez?
Counter 38:09–39:08

Now it's your turn to go shopping. A salesperson will ask you what you want. Answer according to the picture.

—Vous désirez? [screen card]
—Je cherche un tee-shirt.

—Vous désirez? [screen card]
—Je cherche des chaussures.

—Vous désirez? [screen card]
—Je cherche une chemise.

—Vous désirez? [screen card]
—Je cherche un pantalon.

—Vous désirez? [screen card]
—Je cherche des lunettes de soleil.

—Vous désirez? [screen card]
—Je cherche des chaussettes.

17.5 Mini-scenes: Speaking— Combien coûte la veste?

Counter 39:09–39:52

When we go shopping, we also want to know what things cost. Imagine you're shopping with a friend. When she asks you the price of an item, tell her what it says on the price tag.

—Combien coûte la veste? [screen card]
—Elle coûte 150 euros.

— Combien coûte le blouson? [screen card]
—Il coûte 125 euros.

— Combien coûte l'imperméable? [screen card]
—Il coûte 230 euros.

— Combien coûtent les chaussures? [screen card]
—Elles coûtent 75 euros.

17.6 Mini-scenes: Listening— Comment trouves-tu ma robe?

Counter 39:53–40:28

When we buy clothes, we want to know how we look in them. Watch.

VÉRONIQUE: Comment trouves-tu ma robe?
DELPHINE: Elle est très chouette.

LE MARI: Comment trouves-tu mon pantalon?
LA FEMME: Euh . . . il est trop long.
DOMINIQUE: Qu'est-ce que tu penses de ma chemise?
JEAN-MARC: Euh . . . elle est un peu démodée.

—Qu'est-ce que tu penses de mon manteau? Il est très bon marché.
—Oui, mais il est trop petit.

17.7 Vignette culturelle: Où acheter les vêtements?

Counter 40:29–42:04

Où est-ce que vous achetez vos vêtements? Les jeunes Français ont beaucoup de possibilités. Ils peuvent aller dans une boutique de mode. Ici les vêtements sont élégants, mais ils sont chers.

Ils peuvent aller dans un grand magasin. Ici il y a toujours un grand choix de vêtements. La qualité est bonne et les prix sont raisonnables.

Ils peuvent aussi aller dans une boutique de soldes. Là, ils peuvent acheter des vêtements à des prix intéressants! Quand on n'a pas beaucoup d'argent, on peut aller au marché aux puces. Là, l'atmosphère est pittoresque. Les vêtements sont drôles, et les prix sont imbattables.

LEÇON 17 Le français pratique: L'achat des vêtements

PE AUDIO

CD 3, Track 20
Les nombres de 100 à 1000, p. 263

Repeat the numbers after the speaker.
Écoutez et répétez.

100 # 101 # 102

200 # 300 # 400

500 # 600 # 700

800 # 900 # 1000

À votre tour!

CD 3, Track 21
1. Écoutez bien!, p. 264

Thomas and Frédéric are both getting ready to leave on vacation. Listen to the following sentences which mention items that they are packing. If the item belongs to Thomas, mark A. If the item belongs to Frédéric, mark B. You will hear each sentence twice.

Let's begin. Commençons.

1. Il a une casquette. #
2. Où est sa ceinture? #
3. Quand il pleut, il porte un imperméable. #
4. Il a un blouson noir. #
5. Ses chaussures sont marron. #
6. Le pull est sur le lit. #
7. Il porte souvent des sandales. #
8. Oui, c'est sa cravate. #
9. Ce survêtement est très cher. #
10. J'aime bien la veste. #
11. Il a des chaussettes blanches. #
12. Tiens, voilà ses lunettes de soleil. #
13. Quand il fait chaud, il porte un tee-shirt. #
14. Le pantalon est dans la valise. #

CD 3, Track 22
2. Créa-Dialogue, p. 264

Listen to some sample *Créa-dialogues.*
Écoutez les conversations.

Modèle: —Vous désirez, mademoiselle?
—Je cherche un pantalon.
—Comment trouvez-vous le pantalon gris?
—Il est joli. Combien est-ce qu'il coûte?
—Soixante dollars.
—Oh là là, il est cher!

Maintenant, écoutez le dialogue numéro 1.

—Vous désirez, monsieur?
—Je cherche un pull.
—Comment trouvez-vous le pull rouge?
—Il est élégant. Combien est-ce qu'il coûte?
—Trente dollars.
—Il est bon marché.

CD 3, Track 23
3. Conversation dirigée, p. 265

Listen to the conversation. *Écoutez la conversation entre Sophie et Christophe.*

SOPHIE: Qu'est-ce que tu cherches Christophe?
CHRISTOPHE: Je cherche une casquette.
SOPHIE: Comment trouves-tu la casquette jaune?
CHRISTOPHE: Elle est géniale, mais je vais acheter la casquette bleue.
SOPHIE: Combien est-ce qu'elle coûte?
CHRISTOPHE: Elle coûte 5 euros.
SOPHIE: Elle est bon marché, mais elle est trop petite.

Unité 6 Leçon 17

Audioscripts

Discovering
FRENCH
Nouveau!

BLEU

WORKBOOK AUDIO

Section 1. Les vêtements et les accessoires

CD 10, Track 1

A. Écoutez et répétez. p. 149

Listen to the names of various items of clothing. Repeat each item after the speaker.

Commençons.

un blouson #

un manteau #

un pantalon #

un chapeau #

un pull #

un imper #

un jean #

un polo #

une chemise #

une veste #

une casquette #

une cravate #

un chemisier #

une jupe #

une robe #

des collants #

CD 10, Track 2

B. Compréhension orale, p. 149

You will hear different shoppers answer the question: *Qu'est-ce que vous cherchez?* Look at the pictures in your Workbook and match each shopper with the corresponding item of clothing.

Modèle: 1. —Qu'est-ce que vous cherchez?
—Je cherche un pantalon.

You would write "1" under the picture "h": the pair of pants.

2. —Qu'est-ce que vous cherchez?
—Je cherche une chemise. #

3. —Qu'est-ce que vous cherchez?
—Je cherche un imperméable. #

4. —Qu'est-ce que vous cherchez?
—Je cherche un manteau. #

5. Je cherche une cravate. #

6. Je cherche un jean. #

7. Je cherche une veste. #

8. Je cherche une robe. #

9. Je cherche un pull. #

10. Je cherche un polo. #

11. Je cherche des chaussettes. #

12. Je cherche des chaussures. #

13. Je cherche un maillot de bain. #

14. Je cherche des lunettes de soleil. #

15. Je cherche des tennis. #

16. Je cherche un survêtement.

Now check your answers. You should have matched the clothing with the pictures as follows: a-6, b-11, c-3, d-8, e-12, f-2, g-5, h-1, i-16, j-14, k-9, l-4, m-7, n-15, o-10, and p-13.

CD 10, Track 3

C. Questions et réponses, p. 150

Now it's your turn to go shopping. A salesperson will ask you what you want. Answer according to the picture in your Workbook. If you are not sure of the response, listen for the confirmation.

Modèle: Vous désirez?
Je cherche un tee-shirt.

1. Vous désirez? #Je cherche des chaussures.
2. Vous désirez? #Je cherche une chemise.
3. Vous désirez? #Je cherche un pantalon.
4. Vous désirez? #Je cherche des lunettes de soleil.

5. Vous désirez? #Je cherche des chaussettes.

CD 10, Track 4

D. Compréhension orale, p. 150

Today Dominique and Stéphanie are shopping at the Galeries Lafayette. You will hear them talking about three different items. Look at your Workbook, and match each conversation with the corresponding picture.

Scène 1.

DOMINIQUE: Regarde la robe.
STÉPHANIE: Elle est jolie. Combien coûte-t-elle?
DOMINIQUE: 210 euros.
STÉPHANIE: Eh bien, dis donc, elle n'est pas bon marché! #

Scène 2.

STÉPHANIE: Qu'est-ce que tu penses de ce blouson?
DOMINIQUE: Il est chouette . . . mais il est trop grand pour toi! #

Scène 3.

VENDEUSE: Que désirez-vous mademoiselle?
DOMINIQUE: Je cherche un manteau.
VENDEUSE: Comment trouvez-vous ce manteau blanc?
DOMINIQUE: Il est bien. Combien est-ce qu'il coûte?
VENDEUSE: Il est en solde . . . à cent euros.
DOMINIQUE: D'accord, je le prends. #

Now check your answers. You should have matched the conversations with the pictures as follows: a-3, b-2, and c-1.

Section 2. Les nombres de 100 à 1000

CD 10, Track 5

E. Écoutez et répétez. p. 150

Listen and repeat the numbers in your Workbook after the speaker.

Commençons.

100 #	101 #	102 #	200 #	300 #
400 #	500 #	600 #	700 #	800 #
900 #	1000 #			

CD 10, Track 6

F. Questions et réponses, p. 151

Now imagine you are shopping with your French friend Sophie who wants to know how much certain items cost. Consult the price tags in your Workbook and answer her accordingly.

Modèle:

— Combien coûte la veste? #
— Elle coûte 100 euros.

Commençons.

1. — Combien coûte le manteau? #
   — Il coûte 130 euros.
2. — Combien coûte l'imperméable? #
   — Il coûte 200 euros.
3. — Combien coûte la robe? #
   — Elle coûte 390 euros.

Section 3. Conversations

CD 10, Track 7

G. La réponse logique, p. 151

You will hear a series of short questions, each one read twice. In your Workbook, circle the letter (a, b, or c) corresponding to the most logical answer.

Commençons.

1. Vous désirez, monsieur? #
2. Qu'est-ce que tu vas acheter? #
3. Qu'est-ce que tu vas mettre pour aller à la plage? #
4. Combien coûte l'imper? #
5. Tu trouves le blouson marron génial? #
6. Est-ce que ta veste est chère? #

Now check your answers. You should have circled 1-c, 2-a, 3-c, 4-c, 5-b, and 6-a.

Section 4. Dictée

CD 10, Track 8

H. Écoutez et écrivez. p. 151

You will hear a short dialogue spoken twice. First listen carefully to what the people are saying. The second time you hear the dialogue, fill in the missing words.

Écoutez.

—Qu'est-ce que tu penses du manteau rouge?
—Il est génial.
—Combien est-ce qu'il coûte?
—Deux cent dix euros.
—Oh là là! Il n'est pas bon marché!

Listen again and fill in the missing words.

LESSON 17 QUIZ

Part I: Listening

CD 15, Track 9

A. Conversations

You will hear a series of short conversations between Cécile and Christophe. Listen to each conversation carefully. Then answer the corresponding questions on your answer sheet by circling the appropriate letter (a, b, or c). You will hear each conversation twice.

Let's begin.

1. CÉCILE: Qu'est-ce que tu cherches?
   CHRISTOPHE: Je cherche ma casquette.

2. CHRISTOPHE: Tu vas mettre ton imper?
   CÉCILE: Bien sûr! Il pleut.

3. CHRISTOPHE: Qu'est-ce que tu vas acheter à ton frère pour son anniversaire?
   CÉCILE: Une ceinture.

4. CÉCILE: Qu'est-ce que tu penses de ma veste verte?
   CHRISTOPHE: Elle est chouette!

5. CHRISTOPHE: Combien coûte ton manteau?
   CÉCILE: Il coûte 200 euros.
   CHRISTOPHE: Oh là là! Il est cher!

6. CÉCILE: Où vas-tu, Christophe?
   CHRISTOPHE: Je vais au centre commercial.
   CÉCILE: Ah bon? Qu'est-ce que tu vas acheter?
   CHRISTOPHE: Des lunettes de soleil.

7. CHRISTOPHE: Tu vas en ville?
   CÉCILE: Oui, je vais acheter une chemise.
   CHRISTOPHE: Où est-ce que tu achètes tes vêtements?
   CÉCILE: Dans les grands magasins.

8. CÉCILE: Qu'est-ce que tu cherches?
   CHRISTOPHE: Des bottes.
   CÉCILE: Qu'est-ce que tu penses des bottes marron?
   CHRISTOPHE: Elles sont bon marché, mais elles sont démodées.

Nom _____

Classe _____ Date _____ _____

QUIZ 17

Part I: Listening

A. Conversations (40 points)

You will hear a series of short conversations between Cécile and Christophe. Listen to each conversation carefully. Then answer the corresponding questions on your answer sheet by circling the appropriate letter (a, b, or c). You will hear each conversation twice.

1. What is Christophe looking for?
   a. His cap.
   b. His overcoat.
   c. His wallet.

2. What is Cécile going to put on?
   a. Her new dress.
   b. A sweatshirt.
   c. A raincoat.

3. What is Cécile going to buy her brother for his birthday?
   a. A belt.
   b. A jogging suit.
   c. A shirt.

4. What does Christophe think of Cécile's new jacket?
   a. He likes it.
   b. He doesn't like it.
   c. He thinks it's too long.

5. How much does Cécile's coat cost?
   a. 100 euros.
   b. 200 euros.
   c. 1000 euros.

6. What is Christophe going to buy?
   a. Swimming trunks.
   b. Hightops.
   c. Sunglasses.

7. Where does Cécile buy her clothes?
   a. In department stores.
   b. In expensive shops.
   c. At the flea market.

8. Where are Cécile and Christophe?
   a. At home.
   b. In a shoe store.
   c. At the supermarket.

Part II: Writing

B. Au grand magasin (30 points)

Cécile and Laure are going shopping. Indicate what they are going to buy by writing out the names of the following items. Use **un**, **une**, or **des**, as appropriate.

Cécile et Laure vont acheter . . .

1. _____   2. _____   3. _____

Nom _____

Classe _____ Date _____

Discovering
FRENCH
Nouveau!

B L E U

4. _____   5. _____   6. _____

7. _____   8. _____

9. _____   10. _____

C. Les nombres (10 points)

Write the following numbers in digits.

1. _____ huit cents   4. _____ mille cinq cents

2. _____ trois mille   5. _____ douze mille

3. _____ deux mille six cent cinquante

D. Expression personnelle (20 points)

Describe FOUR items that you are wearing now and give the COLOR of each. Be sure to use **un**, **une**, and **des**, as appropriate.

Aujourd'hui, je porte . . .

- _____

- _____

- _____

- _____

Nom _____

Classe _____ Date _____

Discovering FRENCH *Nouveau!*

B L E U

Unité 6
Leçon 18
Workbook TE

LEÇON 18 Rien n'est parfait!

LISTENING ACTIVITIES

Section 1. Acheter et préférer

A. Écoutez et répétez.

J'achète une veste. #
Tu achètes une cravate. #
Il achète un imper. #
Nous achetons un jean. #
Vous achetez un chemisier. #
Elles achètent un pull. #

Je préfère la veste bleue. #
Tu préfères la cravate jaune. #
Il préfère l'imper gris. #
Nous préférons le jean noir. #
Vous préférez le chemisier blanc. #
Elles préfèrent le pull rouge. #

Section 2. Ce et quel

B. Écoutez et répétez.

  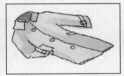  

le blouson   la veste   l'imper   les chaussures   les affiches

C. Écoutez et parlez.

Modèle: une casquette
         Regarde cette casquette.

1. un pull *Regarde ce pull.*
2. une guitare *Regarde cette guitare.*
3. des vestes *Regarde ces vestes.*
4. un vélo *Regarde ce vélo.*
5. des tee-shirts *Regarde ces tee-shirts.*
6. des lunettes *Regarde ces lunettes.*
7. un ordinateur *Regarde cet ordinateur.*
8. des appareils-photo *Regarde ces appareils-photo.*

Nom _____

Classe _____ Date _____ _____

D. Écoutez et parlez.

Modèle: Je vais acheter une veste.
Quelle veste?

1. Quel blouson?   2. Quelles photos?   3. Quel CD?   4. Quelle affiche?   5. Quelles affiches?

Section 3. Conversations

E. La réponse logique

1. a.) Oui, il est génial.
   b. Oui, j'ai un tee-shirt.
   c. Oui, je porte une chemise.

2. a. Oui, c'est vrai.
   b.) Un jean et un polo.
   c. J'ai une classe de français.

3. a. Ma guitare.
   b. Des CD.
   c.) Mon copain Nicolas.

4. a.) Des sandwichs.
   b. Ma cousine.
   c. Un survêtement.

5. a. Je n'étudie pas.
   b.) Je voudrais aller à la piscine.
   c. Oui, je fais une promenade.

Section 4. Dictée

F. Écoutez et écrivez.

— ___Quels___ vêtements est-ce que tu vas ___mettre___ pour le pique-nique?

— ___Ce___ jean et ___cette___ chemise bleue.

— Et ___quelles___ chaussures est-ce que tu vas porter?

— ___Ces___ tennis.

Nom _____

Classe _____ Date _____

Discovering FRENCH Nouveau!

BLEU

Unité 6
Leçon 18
Workbook TE

WRITING ACTIVITIES

A 1. Au centre commercial

Friends are shopping. Say what everyone is buying by completing the sentences with the appropriate forms of **acheter**.

1. Nous _achetons_ des vêtements.

2. Claire _achète_ une ceinture.

3. Vous _achetez_ une casquette.

4. Virginie et Christine _achètent_ des CD.

5. Tu _achètes_ une veste.

6. Marc _achète_ un survêtement.

7. J'_achète_ un sweat.

8. Mes copains _achètent_ des chaussures.

2. Une boum

Christine has invited her friends to a party. Some of them are bringing other friends. Others are bringing things for the party. Complete the sentences below with the appropriate forms of **amener** or **apporter**.

1. François _apporte_ des sandwichs.

2. Stéphanie _amène_ un copain.

3. Nous _apportons_ des CD.

4. Vous _amenez_ vos cousins.

5. Tu _apportes_ ta guitare.

6. Nous _amenons_ des copines.

7. Vous _apportez_ un DVD.

8. Marc et Roger _amènent_ leur soeur.

URB
p. 39

Discovering French, Nouveau! Bleu

Unité 6, Leçon 18
Workbook

159

Nom _____

Classe _____ Date _____

B L E U

B 3. Dans la rue

Olivier and Béatrice are walking in town. Olivier is pointing out various people and commenting on various things he sees. Complete his questions, as in the model.

▶ Tu connais _ces filles_____?

  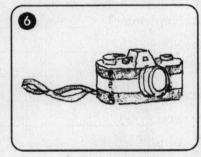

1. Qui sont _ces garçons?_____?

2. Regarde _cette voiture_____!

3. Veux-tu aller dans _ce café?_____?

4. Regarde _cette veste_____!

5. Comment trouves-tu _ces chaussures?_____?

6. Combien coûte _cet appareil-photo?_____?

Nom _____

Classe _____ Date _____

Discovering FRENCH Nouveau!

B L E U

Unité 6
Leçon 18
Workbook TE

B/C 4. Conversations

Complete the following mini-dialogues.

▶ —__Quelle__ cravate préfères-tu?
—Je préfère __cette cravate__ jaune.

1. —__Quel__ imperméable vas-tu acheter?
—Je vais acheter __cet imperméable__ beige.

2. —__Quelles__ bottes vas-tu mettre?
—Je vais mettre __ces bottes__ noires.

3. —__Quels__ blousons préfères-tu?
—Je préfère __ces blousons__ bleus.

4. —__Quelle__ veste vas-tu porter pour la boum?
—__Cette veste__ verte.

D 5. Qu'est-ce qu'ils mettent?

Read what the following people are doing or are going to do. Then complete the second sentence with the verb **mettre** and one of the items in the box. Be logical!

la table	la télé	un maillot de bain
la radio	un survêtement	des vêtements élégants

1. Julien va nager. Il _met un maillot de bain_.
2. Vous allez dîner. Vous _mettez la table_.
3. Nous allons écouter le concert. Nous _mettons la radio_.
4. Tu vas regarder le match de foot. Tu _mets la télé_.
5. Je vais faire du jogging. Je _mets un survêtement_.
6. Mes cousins vont à un mariage. Ils _mettent des vêtements élégants_.

Nom _____

Classe _____ Date _____

6.  Communication (sample answers)

Some French friends have invited you to a picnic.

Write a short paragraph saying . . .

- *what clothes you are going to wear to the picnic*

- *what items you are going to bring to the picnic*

- *whom you are going to bring along*

> Je vais mettre un jean, un pull et un blouson.
>
> _____
>
> Je vais apporter ma guitare,
>
> une radiocassette et des CD.
>
> Je vais amener mon copain Pierre et ma
>
> cousine Louise.

Nom _____

Classe _____ Date _____

Discovering FRENCH Nouveau!

B L E U

Unité 6
Leçon 18
Activités pour tous TE

LEÇON 18 Rien n'est parfait!

A

Activité 1 Dialogues

Circle the correct verbs for the following dialogues.

1. —Alors, qu'est-ce que *tu préfères* / *tu mets?*
   —Je vais *acheter* / *apporter* le rouge.

2. —Tu vas au pique-nique cet après-midi?
   —Oui, et *j'espère* / *j'achète* *apporter* / *amener* ma cousine.

3. —Ce soir, est-ce que *tu mets* / *tu apportes* une robe ou un pantalon?
   —*Je mets* / *J'apporte* un pantalon.

4. —Est-ce que *vous amenez* / *vous apportez* les boissons à la fête?
   —Oui, *nous achetons* / *nous espérons* les boissons cet après-midi. Qu'est-ce qu'ils
   préfèrent / *espèrent?*

Activité 2 Qu'est-ce que tu préfères?

Making your selections from the box, fill in the blanks with the correct forms of **quel.** Each
form will be used once.

quel   quelle   quels   quelles

1. __Quelle__ musique est-ce que tu préfères—la musique rap ou la musique country?

2. Je ne sais pas __quelles__ chaussures vont mieux avec cette robe. Les noires ou les bleues?

3. __Quel__ pantalon est-ce que tu préfères—le beige ou le gris?

4. __Quels__ copains est-ce qu'elle invite ce soir?

Activité 3 De nouveaux vêtements

You are shopping for clothes with your best friend. Fill in the blanks with the correct form of
the demonstrative adjective **ce.**

1. Tu aimes __ce__ pull?

2. J'aime __cet__ imper!

3. __Cette__ ceinture est parfaite pour mon pantalon.

4. Qu'est-ce que tu penses de __ce__ short?

5. Je vais acheter __ces__ baskets.

Nom _____

Classe _____ Date _____

Discovering
FRENCH
Nouveau!

B L E U

B

Activité 1 Voyage en France

Vanessa is trying to decide what to bring on a trip to France and she is explaining everything over the phone to her friend Christine who lives there. Choose the correct verb forms to complete the paragraph.

Bon, alors, *j'apporte* / *j'amène* ma robe bleue pour dîner au restaurant. Mais *je dois acheter* / *j'achète* des chaussures élégantes. Pour nos promenades en montagne, *j'apporte* / *je mets* mon jean et mes baskets. Et *j'espère* / *j'espères*   *apporter* / *trouver* de nouveaux vêtements dans une grande surface ou dans un grand magasin en France. Je n'ai pas de maillot de bain ou d'imper et *je cherche* / *je trouve* une belle veste sympa.

Activité 2 Questions avec quel

Making your selections from the box, fill in the blanks with the correct forms of **quel**. Each form will be used once or more.

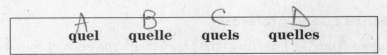

A	B	C	D
quel	**quelle**	**quels**	**quelles**

1. __Quel__ programme est-ce que tu regardes?

2. Je ne sais pas __quels__ chapitres je dois étudier pour l'examen.

3. __Quelle__ veste est-ce que tu vas mettre aujourd'hui?

4. Alors, __quelles__ chaussures est-ce que je dois acheter pour mettre avec ce sac?

5. __Quel__ temps fait-il aujourd'hui?

Activité 3 De nouveaux vêtements

You are shopping for clothes with your best friend. Fill in the blanks with the correct forms of the demonstrative adjective **ce** and **ci / là** when necessary.

—Regarde __ce__ pull! Comment le trouves-tu?

—Il est vraiment beau.

—C'est décidé: j'achète le pull bleu. Et toi?

—Tu préfères __ce__ pantalon-__ci__ ou __cette__ jupe-__là__?

—Je préfère la jupe.

—Moi aussi. Et puis, __cet__ imper est parfait. J'achète la jupe et l'imper.

Nom _____

Classe _____ Date _____ _____

Discovering
FRENCH
Nouveau!

B L E U

Unité 6
Leçon 18
Activités pour tous TE

C

Activité 1   Achats de vêtements

Complete each sentence with a form of **acheter, préférer,** or **mettre.**

1. Aujourd'hui, je vais _acheter_ (*acheter*) un pull. Je vais
   mettre (*mettre*) ce pull pour aller au restaurant ce soir.

2. Qu'est-ce que tu _préfères_ (*préférer*)? Le bleu ou le vert? Yvonne et moi,
   nous _préférons_ (*préférer*) le bleu.

3. Tu _mets_ (*mettre*) ce chemisier avec cette jupe?
   J' _espère_ (*espérer*) que non!

4. Pour l'anniversaire de Mimi aujourd'hui, Serge et moi, nous _achetons_
   (*acheter*) des CD. Et toi, tu _achètes_ (*acheter*) le gâteau?

5. Nous _espérons_ (*espérer*) arriver à 7 heures et nous allons
   amener (*amener*) notre cousine. D'accord?

Activité 2   Questions avec quel

Write the question that would produce each response. Use a form of **quel.**

1. _À quelle heure rentres-tu_ ?   Je rentre à dix heures.

2. _Quelle est la date, aujourd'hui_ ?   C'est le deux mars.

3. _Quelles sont tes chaussures préférées_ ?   Mes chaussures préférées sont des tennis.

4. _Quel est ton livre préféré_ ?   Mon livre préféré est «Le Petit Prince.»

5. _Quelle veste est-ce que tu cherches_ ?   Je cherche ma veste noire.

Activité 3   Ces photos de vacances

Your friend Aline is commenting on photos she brought back from her annual vacation in
Juan-les-Pins, in the South of France. Complete the paragraph with the correct forms of the
demonstrative adjective **ce.**

_Ce_ quartier est vraiment sympa. Il y a beaucoup de boutiques et de cafés.

Dans _cette_ boutique, j'achète toujours des cadeaux. _Cet_ hôtel est

cher, il est près de la plage. _Ce_ parc est amusant: l'été, il y a des concerts.

Sur _cette_ photo, c'est un copain de mon frère. Il est mignon, non?

LEÇON 18 Rien n'est parfait!, page 266

Objectives

Communicative Functions and Topics	To talk about clothing and accessories and describe what clothes look like. To talk about where to buy clothes. To emphasize a remark
Linguistic Goals	To use the verbs *mettre*, *acheter*, and *préférer*, the demonstrative *ce*, and the interrogative *quel?* To pronounce the letters *"e"* and *"è"*
Cultural Goals	To learn about French department stores

Motivation and Focus

❑ Use the WARM-UP AND REVIEW activity, page 266 of the TE, with **Overhead Transparency** 38 to review clothing items and prices.

❑ Have students brainstorm a list of questions to consider before buying clothes. Students can look at the photos on pages 266–267 for some ideas: size, color, price.

Presentation and Explanation

❑ *Lesson Opener:* Play **Video** 18.1 or **Audio** CD 3, Tracks 24–25, or act out the scenes on pages 266–267. Replay with students repeating. Have them read the conversations silently; then discuss the clothing Frédéric is thinking about buying and why he doesn't buy it.

❑ *Note culturelle:* Read and discuss *Le grand magasin*, page 266. Share the NOTE CULTURELLE on page 267 of the TE.

❑ *Grammar A:* Present the verbs on page 268, pointing out accent changes. Play **Audio** CD 3, Track 26. Introduce other verbs with the same patterns in the *Vocabulaire* box, page 269.

❑ *Grammar B:* Explain use and forms of the demonstrative adjective *ce*, page 270.

❑ *Grammar C:* Introduce the forms of the interrogative adjective *quel*, page 271. Show how they are used with various nouns to ask questions.

❑ *Grammar D:* Present the forms of the irregular verb *mettre*, page 272. Ask students to repeat the forms, pointing out the silent "t" in singular forms.

❑ *Prononciation:* Explain and model the pronunciation of the letters *"e"* and *"è,"* page 273. Play **Audio** CD 3, Track 27 and have students practice the sounds of the vowels.

Guided Practice and Checking Understanding

❑ Practice verb forms with **Overhead Transparency** 16 and the suggestions on page A63. Use Transparency 38 and the activities on pages A99–A100 to practice numbers 100–1000, *ce* and *quel*, and *préférer* and *acheter*.

❑ Use **Audio** CD 10, Tracks 9–14, or **Audioscript** pages 63–65 to check listening skills as students do **Workbook** Listening Activities A–F (pages 157–158).

❑ Check understanding of the opening text with *Compréhension* on page 267. Replay **Video** Module 18, or read **Videoscript** pages 60–61, and have students complete the activities on pages 56–58 of the **Video Activities.**

Independent Practice

❑ Practice new vocabulary and grammatical constructions with the Activities on pages 268–273. Students can work alone or do Activities 1–3 and 7–9 for homework. Ask students to work in pairs to do Activities 4–6 as PAIR PRACTICE.

Discovering
FRENCH
Nouveau!

BLEU

Unité 6
Leçon 18
Lesson Plans

❏ In pairs, have students prepare *Échange* 2, page 149, of **Communipak.** Invite pairs to present their conversations to the class. Students can play the game on page 59 of the **Video Activities** to practice forms of *ce* and *quel.*

❏ Have students do the activities in **Activités pour tous**, pages 95–97.

Monitoring and Adjusting

❏ Assign the Writing Activities in the **Workbook** (pages 159–162).

❏ Monitor student's use of the lesson's structures as they work on the practice activities. Refer them to the grammar explanations on pages 268–272 as needed. Refer to TEACHING STRATEGIES and LANGUAGE NOTES in the TE margins for further explanations. Use LISTENING ACTIVITY: PRÉFÉRENCES, page 271 of the TE, to monitor understanding of interrogative adjective forms.

Assessment

❏ After students have completed all of the lesson's activities, administer Quiz 18 on pages 66–67. Use the **Test Generator** to adjust the questions to your class's needs.

Reteaching

❏ Have students redo activities in the **Workbook** that correspond to structures or functions that students find difficult.

Extension and Enrichment

❏ Play the game described in the TEACHING NOTE on page 272 of the TE.

Summary and Closure

❏ Use Transparency S15 and the suggestions on the bottom of page A25 of **Overhead Transparencies** to summarize the lesson's vocabulary and structures.

❏ Do PORTFOLIO ASSESSMENT on page 275 of the TE.

End-of-Lesson Activities

❏ *À votre tour!:* Have students practice Activities 1–3, pages 274–275, in pairs. Use **Audio** CD 3, Tracks 28–29 with Activities 1–2. Invite pairs to present their exchanges to the class. Assign the composition, Activity 4 on page 275, for homework.

Discovering
FRENCH
Nouveau!

B L E U

LEÇON 18   Rien n'est parfait!, page 266

Block Schedule (3 Days to Complete)

Objectives

Communicative Functions and Topics	To talk about clothing and accessories and describe what clothes look like. To talk about where to buy clothes To emphasize a remark
Linguistic Goals	To use the verbs *mettre, acheter,* and *préférer,* the demonstrative *ce,* and the interrogative *quel?* To pronounce the letters *"e"* and *"è"*
Cultural Goals	To learn about French department stores

Day 1

Motivation and Focus

❏ Use the WARM-UP AND REVIEW activity, page 266 of the TE, with **Overhead Transparency** 38 to review clothing items and prices.

❏ Have students brainstorm a list of questions to consider before buying clothes. Students can look at the photos on pages 266–267 for some ideas: size, color, price.

Presentation and Explanation

❏ *Lesson Opener:* Play **Video** 18.1 or **Audio** CD 3, Tracks 24–25, or act out the scenes on pages 266–267. Replay with students repeating. Have them read the conversations silently; then discuss the clothing Frédéric is thinking about buying and why he doesn't buy it.

❏ *Note culturelle:* Read and discuss *Le grand magasin,* page 266. Share the NOTE CULTURELLE on page 267 of the TE.

❏ *Grammar A:* Present the verbs on page 268, pointing out accent changes. Play **Audio** CD 3, Track 26. Introduce other verbs with the same patterns in the *Vocabulaire* box, page 269.

❏ *Grammar B:* Explain use and forms of the demonstrative adjective *ce,* page 270.

❏ *Grammar C:* Introduce the forms of the interrogative adjective *quel,* page 271. Show how they are used with various nouns to ask questions.

❏ *Grammar D:* Present the forms of the irregular verb *mettre,* page 272. Ask students to repeat the forms, pointing out the silent "t" in singular forms.

❏ *Prononciation:* Explain and model the pronunciation of the letters *"e"* and *"è,"* page 273. Play **Audio** CD 3, Track 27 and have students practice the sounds of the vowels.

Guided Practice and Checking Understanding

❏ Practice verb forms with **Overhead Transparency** 16 and the suggestions on page A63. Use Transparency 38 and the activities on pages A99–A100 to practice numbers 100–1000, *ce* and *quel,* and *préférer* and *acheter.*

❏ Use **Audio** CD 10, Tracks 9–14, or **Audioscript** pages 63–65 to check listening skills as students do **Workbook** Listening Activities A–F (pages 157–158).

Discovering
FRENCH
Nouveau!

BLEU

Unité 6
Leçon 18
Block Scheduling
Lesson Plans

Day 2

Motivation and Focus

❏ Check understanding of the opening text with *Compréhension* on page 267. Replay **Video** Module 18, or read **Videoscript** pages 60–61, and have students complete the activities on pages 56–58 of the **Video Activities.**

Independent Practice

❏ Practice new vocabulary and grammatical constructions with the activities on pages 268–273. Students can work alone or do Activities 1–3 and 7–9 for homework. Ask students to work in pairs to do Activities 4–6 as PAIR PRACTICE.

❏ In pairs, have students prepare *Échange* 2, page 149, of **Communipak.** Invite pairs to present their conversations to the class. Students can play the game on page 59 of the **Video Activities** to practice forms of *ce* and *quel.*

❏ Have students do the activities in **Activités pour tous**, pages 95–97.

Monitoring and Adjusting

❏ Assign the Writing Activities in the **Workbook** (pages 159–162).

❏ Monitor student's use of the lesson's structures as they work on the practice activities. Refer them to the grammar explanations on pages 268–272 as needed. Refer to TEACHING STRATEGIES and LANGUAGE NOTES in the TE margins for further explanations. Use LISTENING ACTIVITY: PRÉFÉRENCES, page 271 of the TE, to monitor understanding of interrogative adjective forms.

Day 3

End-of-Lesson Activities

❏ *À votre tour!:* Have students practice Activities 1–3, pages 274–275, in pairs. Use **Audio** CD 3, Tracks 28–29 with Activities 1–2. Invite pairs to present their exchanges to the class. Assign the composition, Activity 4 on page 275, for homework.

Reteaching (as needed)

❏ Have students redo activities in the **Workbook** that correspond to structures or functions that students find difficult.

Extension and Enrichment

❏ Use **Block Scheduling Copymasters**, pages 137–144.

❏ Play the game described in the TEACHING NOTE on page 272 of the TE.

❏ For expansion activities, direct students to www.classzone.com.

Summary and Closure

❏ Use Transparency S15 and the suggestions on the bottom of page A25 of **Overhead Transparencies** to summarize the lesson's vocabulary and structures.

❏ Do PORTFOLIO ASSESSMENT on page 275 of the TE.

Assessment

❏ After students have completed the lesson, administer Quiz 18 on pages 66–67. Use the **Test Generator** to adjust the questions to your class's needs.

Nom _____

Classe _____ Date _____

Discovering
FRENCH
Nouveau

BLEU

LEÇON 18   Rien n'est parfait!, pages 266–267

Materials Checklist

- **Student Text**
- **Audio** CD 3, Tracks 24–25
- **Video 3** or **DVD 2;** Counter 42:45–43:44

Steps to Follow

- Read *Rien n'est parfait!: Scènes 1–3* (pp. 266–267). Look at the photographs for each scene.
- Read the questions in *Compréhension* (p. 267) before you watch the video or listen to the audio.
- Watch **Video 3** or **DVD 2;** Counter 42:45–43:44, or listen to **Audio** CD 3, Tracks 24–25. Repeat everything you hear.
- Read *Note culturelle* (p. 266).
- Answer the questions in *Compréhension* (p. 267). Write your answers in complete sentences on a separate sheet of paper.

If You Don't Understand . . .

- Watch the **Video** or **DVD** in a quiet place. Try to stay focused. If you get lost, stop the **Video** or **DVD**. Replay it and find your place.
- Listen to the **CD** in a quiet place. Try to stay focused. If you get lost, stop the **CD**. Replay it and find your place.
- Repeat aloud with the audio. Try to sound like the people on the recording.
- Say aloud anything you write. Make sure you understand everything you say.
- Write down any questions so that you can ask your teacher or your partner later.

Self-Check

Answer the following questions in complete sentences on a separate sheet of paper.

1. Qu'est-ce que c'est qu'un grand magasin?
2. Est-ce que l'idée du grand magasin est une idée américaine?
3. Qu'est-ce qu'on peut acheter dans un grand magasin?
4. Comment s'appelle le premier grand magasin français?

Answers

1. Un grand magasin est un magasin de 4 ou 5 étages où on peut acheter des produits différents.   2. L'idée du grand magasin est une idée française.   3. Dans un grand magasin, on peut acheter toutes sortes de produits: des vêtements, des parfums, des meubles, etc.   4. Le premier grand magasin français s'appelle le Bon Marché.

Nom _____

Classe _____ Date _____

Discovering
FRENCH
Nouveau!

B L E U

Unité 6
Leçon 18
Absent Student
Copymasters

A. Les verbes *acheter* et *préférer,* page 268
Vocabulaire: Verbes comme *(like)* *acheter* et *préférer,*
page 269

Materials Checklist

- **Student Text**
- **Audio** CD 3, Track 26; CD 10, Track 9
- **Workbook**

Steps to Follow

- Study *Les verbes acheter et préférer* (p. 268). Copy the present conjugation of these verbs on a separate sheet of paper. Circle the letter *é,* the letter *è,* and the letter *e* in the stem.
- Listen to **Audio** CD 3, Track 26. Repeat everything you hear.
- Do Activity 1 in the text (p. 268). Write the answers in complete sentences on a separate sheet of paper. Be sure to write out the numbers, for example, *15 = quinze.*
- Study *Vocabulaire: Verbes comme (like) **acheter** et **préférer*** (p. 269). Write the present conjugation of ***acheter, amener, préférer,*** and ***espérer*** on a separate sheet of paper. Circle the letter *é,* the letter *è,* and the letter *e* in the stem.
- Do Activity 2 in the text (p. 269). Write your answers in complete sentences.
- Do Writing Activities A, 1–2 in the **Workbook** (page 159).
- Do Listening Activity A in the **Workbook** (page 157). Use **Audio** CD 10, Track 9.

If You Don't Understand . . .

- Listen to the **CDs** in a quiet place. Try to stay focused. If you get lost, stop the **CDs**. Replay them and find your place.
- Repeat aloud with the audio. Try to sound like the people on the recording.
- Reread the activity directions. Put the directions in your own words.
- Read the model several times. Be sure you understand it. Underline the new expressions, for example, *Tu amènes ton copain.*
- Say aloud everything you write. Make sure you understand everything you say.
- When writing a sentence, ask yourself, "What do I mean? What am I trying to say?"
- Write down any questions so that you can ask your teacher or your partner later.

Self-Check

Complete the following sentences with the appropriate form of **acheter, préférer, amener, apporter,** or **espérer.** Write the complete sentences on a separate sheet of paper.

1. Qu'est-ce que tu . . . au pique-nique? Le pain ou le jambon?
2. Qu'est-ce que vous . . . au grand magasin?
3. Qu'est-ce qu'il . . . ? Jouer au tennis ou nager?
4. Est-ce qu'elles . . . voyager cet été?
5. Est-ce que nous . . . Jean-Marc à la boum?

Answers

1. Qu'est-ce que tu apportes au pique-nique?   2. Qu'est-ce que vous achetez au grand magasin?   3. Qu'est-ce qu'il préfère?   4. Est-ce qu'elles espèrent voyager cet été?   5. Est-ce que nous amenons Jean-Marc à la boum?

Nom _____

Classe _____ Date _____

B. L'adjectif démonstratif *ce,* page 270

Materials Checklist

- **Student Text**
- **Audio** CD 10, Tracks 11, 13
- **Video 3** or **DVD 2**; Counter 43:45–44:58
- **Workbook**

Steps to Follow

- Watch **Video 3** or **DVD 2**; Counter 43:45–44:58. Repeat everything you hear.
- Study *L'adjectif demonstratif ce* (p. 270). Copy the chart on a separate sheet of paper. Underline the liaisons, for example, ***cet homme***.
- Do Activity 4 in the text (p. 270). Write complete sentences. Underline the liaisons, for example, ***cet imper.***
- Do Activity 5 in the text (p. 270). Write the parts for both speakers on a separate sheet of paper. Read both parts aloud.
- Do Writing Activity B, 3 in the **Workbook** (page 160).
- Do Listening Activities C, E in the **Workbook** (pages 157–158). Use **Audio** CD 10, Tracks 11, 13.

If You Don't Understand . . .

- Watch the **Video** or **DVD** in a quiet place. Try to stay focused. If you get lost, stop the **Video** or **DVD**. Replay it and find your place.
- Listen to the **CD** in a quiet place. Try to stay focused. If you get lost, stop the **CD**. Replay it and find your place.
- Reread the activity directions. Put the directions in your own words.
- Read the model several times. Be sure you understand it.
- Say aloud everything that you write. Make sure you understand what you are saying.
- When writing a sentence, ask yourself, "What do I mean? What am I trying to say?"
- Write down questions so that you can ask your partner or your teacher later.

Self-Check

Complete these sentences with the correct form of the demonstrative adjective. Check agreement. Write the complete sentences on a separate sheet of paper.

1. . . . jolie voiture est à moi.
2. . . . chaussures sont élégantes, n'est-ce pas?
3. J'achète . . . stylo-ci.
4. Tu apportes . . . pain-là au pique-nique?
5. Comment s'appelle . . . petit garcon?

Answers

Nom _____

Classe _____ Date _____

C. L'adjectif interrogatif *quel?* page 271
D. Le verb *mettre,* pages 272–273

Materials Checklist

- **Student Text**
- **Audio** CD 3, Tracks 27–29; CD 10, Tracks 10, 12, 14
- **Video 3** or **DVD 2**; Counter 44:59–46:09
- **Workbook**

Steps to Follow

- Study *L'adjectif interrogatif quel?* (p. 271). Copy the chart on a separate sheet of paper. Underline the liaison in the plural forms, for example, *quelles affiches*.
- Watch **Video 3** or **DVD 2**; Counter 44:59–46:09. Repeat everything you hear.
- Do Activity 6 in the text (p. 271). Write the parts for both speakers on a separate sheet of paper. Underline the expressions *quel, quelle, quels,* and *quelles.*
- Do Activity 7 in the text (p. 271). Write the answers on a separate sheet of paper.
- Study *Le verbe mettre* (p. 272). Copy the conjugation.
- Do Activities 8–9 in the text (pp. 272–273). Write sentences on a separate sheet of paper.
- Read the list of words in *Prononciation: Les lettres «e» et «è»* in the text (p. 273). Listen to **Audio** CD 3, Track 27. Repeat what you hear.
- Do Writing Activities B/C, 4 and D, 5 in the **Workbook** (page 161).
- Do Listening Activities B, D, F in the **Workbook** (pages 157–158). Use **Audio** CD 10, Tracks 10, 12, 14.
- Do Activities 1–4 of *À votre tour!* in the text (pp. 274–275). Use **Audio** CD 3, Tracks 28–29 with Activities 1–2.

If You Don't Understand . . .

- Watch the **Video** or **DVD** in a quiet place. Try to stay focused. If you get lost, stop the **Video** or **DVD**. Replay it and find your place.
- Listen to the **CDs** in a quiet place. Try to stay focused. If you get lost, stop the **CDs**. Replay them and find your place.
- Listen once without repeating. Then replay and repeat aloud with the audio. Try to sound like the people on the recording. Imitate their sounds. Pause the **CDs** if you can't keep up.
- Reread the activity directions. Put the directions in your own words.
- Read the model several times so you are certain what to do. Copy the model. Say aloud everything that you write. Listen and be sure you understand what you are saying.
- Write down any questions so that you can ask your teacher or your partner later.

Self-Check

Answer the following questions, using the correct forms of the demonstrative adjective **ce**. Write in complete sentences on a separate sheet of paper.

1. Qu'est-ce que tu mets ce soir? (pantalon noir / chemise blanche)
2. Il va pleuvoir demain. Qu'est-ce vous allez mettre? (grand imper jaune)
3. Qu'est-ce que Jean met pour aller à la boum? (jean / veste)
4. Qu'est-ce que nous mettons pour aller au match de foot? (pull / jean)

Answers

1. Je mets ce pantalon noir et cette chemise blanche. 2. Je vais mettre ce grand imper jaune. 3. Il met ce jean et cette veste. 4. Nous mettons ces pulls et ces jeans.

Nom _____

Classe _____ Date _____

LEÇON 18   Rien n'est parfait!

Les préférences

Interview a family member. Ask a family member to choose which of the following items he or she likes best.

- First, explain your assignment.
- Next, model the pronunciation of the words above the pictures. Point to the picture as you model each answer.
- Then ask each question, pointing again to the picture as you ask **-ci** or **-là**.
- After you have asked each question, complete the sentences that follow.

Tu préfères ces chaussures-ci   **ou ces chaussures-là?**

_____ **préfère** _____.

Tu préfères cette maison-ci   **ou cette maison-là?**

_____ **préfère** _____.

Tu préfères ce chien-ci   **ou ce chien-là?**

_____ **préfère** _____.

Nom _____

Classe _____ Date _____ _____

Discovering
FRENCH *Nouveau!*

BLEU

Unité 6
Leçon 18

Family Involvement

Quelle voiture . . . ?

Interview a family member. Ask a family member which car he or she prefers.

- First, explain your assignment.
- Model the pronunciation of the word **voiture**. Ask the family member to point to his or her choice and answer using **cette**.
- Ask the question, **Quelle voiture préfères-tu?**
- When you have an answer, complete the sentence at the bottom of the page.

 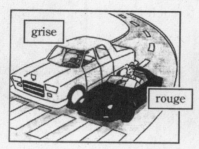 

Quelle voiture préfères-tu?

_____ **préfère** _____

_____ .

Discovering
FRENCH
Nouveau!

B L E U

MODULE 18   Rien n'est parfait!

Video 3, DVD 2

18 Activité 1. Frédéric et
Jean-Claude   Counter 42:15–42:44

Where are Frédéric and Jean-Claude going?
Watch the video to find out. Then circle the
letter of the correct completion to each
statement below.

1. Frédéric et Jean-Claude vont
   acheter des . . .
   a. livres   b. CD   c. vêtements

2. Ils vont dans . . .
   a. un centre commercial   b. un grand magasin c. une boutique

3. Ce magasin s'appelle . . .
   a. Le Bon Marché   b. Le Printemps   c. La Samaritaine

18.1 Activité 2. Au Bon Marché   Counter 42:45–43:44

What clothes are Frédéric and Jean-Claude shopping for at the Bon Marché? Watch the video
and circle **vrai** if a statement below is true and **faux** if it is false.

1. Le pull est bleu.   **vrai**   **faux**

2. Il est très chouette.   **vrai**   **faux**

3. La veste jaune est très chère.   **vrai**   **faux**

4. Elle est trop petite pour
   Jean-Claude.   **vrai**   **faux**

5. Frédéric achète des
   chaussures noires.   **vrai**   **faux**

6. Les chaussures sont en solde.   **vrai**   **faux**

7. Elles sont démodées.   **vrai**   **faux**

Nom _____

Classe _____ Date _____ _____

Discovering
FRENCH
Nouveau!

B L E U

Unité 6
Leçon 18

Video Activities

18.2 Activité 3. Comment trouves-tu ce pull?

Counter 43:45–44:58

People in the video are looking at specific people or things. Starting with 1 and ending with 10, number the words below in the order in which they are mentioned in the video segment.

a. _____ blouson

b. _____ chapeau

c. _____ CD

d. _____ garçons

e. _____ sculpture

f. _____ chaîne

g. _____ chemise

h. _____ filles

i. _____ monument

j. _____ voiture

18.3 Activité 4. Quel objet?

Counter 44:59–45:25

As you watch the video, fill in the blank in each exchange below with **ce** or **cette,** as appropriate.

1. —Quel café?

   —_____ café-ci.

2. —Quelle glace est-ce que tu veux?

   —_____ glace-ci.

3. —Quelle cravate?

   —_____ cravate-ci.

4. —Quel polo désirez-vous?

   —_____ polo bleu.

Nom _____

Classe _____ Date _____

Discovering
FRENCH
Nouveau!

B L E U

18.4 Activité 5. Quelle veste désirez-vous?

Counter 45:26–46:09

Which clothes do you want? After you watch the video segment, fill in the sentences below with **ce, cette,** or **ces,** as appropriate.

1. —Je désire _____ veste bleue.

2. —Je désire _____ blouson jaune.

3. —Je désire _____ chaussettes vertes.

4. —Je désire _____ tee-shirt orange.

 ## 18.5 Activité 6. Un grand magasin

Counter 46:10–47:34

A. Now it's your turn to visit the Bon Marché department store in Paris! Starting with 1 and ending with 5, number the departments of the store in the order in which they appear in the **Vignette culturelle.**

_____ Jeux/Jouets

_____ Livres

_____ Parfumerie

_____ Supermarché

_____ Vêtements

B. Question personnelle: Would you like to go shopping at the Bon Marché? If so, what department(s) would you visit and what would you buy there? If not, why not?

Réponse: _____

Nom _____

Classe _____ Date _____

Discovering **FRENCH** *Nouveau!*

B L E U

Unité 6
Leçon 18
Video Activities

Activité 7. Un jeu: Bon Marché!

Imagine you are shopping in the **rayon des vêtements** of Le Bon Marché. Prepare your shopping list by drawing nine different clothing articles in the card below. *Do not show your card to anyone!*

Form a group with three or four classmates. The first student names one item he or she is buying. Another student asks *which one?* in French. The first student answers *this one!*, in French, marking an **X** through the clothing item on his or her card. If other students in the group have the same article, they also mark an **X** through it on their cards. Play continues with a different student saying what he or she is buying and so on, until someone has a row of **X**'s (vertical, horizontal or diagonal) and says **Bon Marché!**

▶ ÉLÈVE 1: **J'achète une cravate.**

ÉLÈVE 2: **Quelle cravate?**

ÉLÈVE 1: **Cette cravate-ci.**

ÉLÈVE 2: **J'achète un blouson.**

ÉLÈVE 3: **Quel blouson?**

ÉLÈVE 2: **Ce blouson-ci, etc.**

Bon Marché!

MODULE 18 Rien n'est parfait!

Video 3, DVD 2
Counter 42:15–42:44

Cet après-midi, Frédéric et Jean-Claude vont acheter des vêtements. Ils vont acheter ces vêtements dans un grand magasin. Ce magasin s'appelle «Le Bon Marché».

18.1 Dialogue: Rien n'est parfait!
Counter 42:45–43:44

Frédéric et Jean-Claude regardent les pulls.

FRÉDÉRIC: Comment trouves-tu ce pull?
JEAN-CLAUDE: Quel pull?
FRÉDÉRIC: Ce pull bleu.
JEAN-CLAUDE: Il est chouette.
FRÉDÉRIC: C'est vrai, il est très chouette.
JEAN-CLAUDE: Il est aussi très cher.

Maintenant, Frédéric et Jean-Claude regardent les vestes.

FRÉDÉRIC: Quelle veste est-ce que tu préfères?
JEAN-CLAUDE: Je préfère cette veste jaune. Elle est très élégante et elle n'est pas très chère.
FRÉDÉRIC: Oui, mais elle est trop grande pour toi!
JEAN-CLAUDE: Dommage!

Frédéric est au rayon des chaussures. Quelles chaussures est-ce qu'il va acheter?

JEAN-CLAUDE: Alors, quelles chaussures est-ce que tu achètes?
FRÉDÉRIC: J'achète ces chaussures noires. Elles sont très confortables . . . et elles ne sont pas chères. Regarde, elles sont en solde.
JEAN-CLAUDE: C'est vrai, elles sont en solde . . . mais elles ne sont plus à la mode.
FRÉDÉRIC: Hélas, rien n'est parfait!

18.2 Mini-scenes: Listening— Comment trouves-tu ce pull?
Counter 43:45–44:58

Do you remember how Frédéric and Jean-Claude pointed out specific articles of clothing? Listen again.

FRÉDÉRIC: Comment trouves-tu ce pull?
JEAN-CLAUDE: Je préfère cette veste jaune.
FRÉDÉRIC: J'achète ces chaussures noires.

Frédéric and Jean-Claude used the following words:

ce pull   [screen card]
cette veste   [screen card]
ces chaussures [screen card]

Now watch these scenes as people point things out to their friends.

—Dis, Stéphanie! Regarde ce blouson!
—Regarde ce chapeau.
—Qu'est-ce que tu penses de cette chemise?
—Regarde cette chaîne!
—Tu veux écouter ce CD?
—Regarde cette voiture!
—Regarde cette sculpture!
—Regardez ce monument!
—Eh! Regarde ces filles là-bas!
—Eh! Regarde ces garçons.

18.3 Mini-scenes: Listening— Quel café?
Counter 44:59–45:25

—Tu veux aller dans ce café?
—Quel café?
—Ce café-ci.
—D'accord.

—Quelle glace est-ce que tu veux?
—Cette glace-ci.

—Regarde cette cravate.
—Quelle cravate?
—Cette cravate-ci.
—Quelle horreur!

—Quel polo désirez-vous?
—Ce polo bleu.

Discovering
FRENCH
Nouveau!

BLEU

Unité 6
Leçon 18

Videoscripts

18.4 Mini-scenes: Speaking—
Quelle veste désirez-vous?

Counter 45:26–46:09

Now it's your turn to speak. Imagine that you are shopping in a French department store. The salesperson will ask you which item you want. Ask for the one you see on the screen, giving its color.

—Quelle veste désirez-vous? [screen card]
—Cette veste bleue.

—Quel blouson désirez-vous? [screen card]
—Ce blouson jaune.

—Quelles chaussettes désirez-vous? [screen card]
—Ces chaussettes vertes.

—Quel tee-shirt désirez vous? [screen card]
—Ce tee-shirt orange.

18.5 Vignette culturelle:
Un grand magasin

Counter 46:10–47:34

Aujourd'hui, nous allons visiter un grand magasin. Ce grand magasin s'appelle le «Bon Marché». Il est situé rue de Sèvres, à Paris. Entrons. Au rez-de-chaussée, il y a le rayon de la parfumerie. Voulez-vous essayer ce parfum? Voici le rayon des livres. Allons au rayon des vêtements. Ici, nous sommes au rayon des jeux, et des jouets. Au Bon Marché, il y a aussi un supermarché.

Discovering FRENCH *Nouveau*

B L E U

LEÇON 18   Rien n'est parfait!

PE AUDIO

CD 3, Track 24
Compréhension orale, p. 266

Cet après-midi, Frédéric et Jean-Claude vont acheter des vêtements. Ils vont acheter ces vêtements dans un grand magasin. Ce magasin s'appelle Le Bon Marché.

Scène 1

Frédéric et Jean-Claude regardent les pulls.

FRÉDÉRIC: Regarde! Comment trouves-tu ce pull?
JEAN-CLAUDE: Quel pull?
FRÉDÉRIC: Ce pull bleu.
JEAN-CLAUDE: Il est chouette.
FRÉDÉRIC: C'est vrai, il est très chouette.
JEAN-CLAUDE: Il est aussi très cher.
FRÉDÉRIC: Combien est-ce qu'il coûte?
JEAN-CLAUDE: Deux cents euros.
FRÉDÉRIC: Deux cents euros! Quelle horreur!

Scène 2

Maintenant, Frédéric et Jean-Claude regardent les vestes.

FRÉDÉRIC: Quelle veste est-ce que tu préfères?
JEAN-CLAUDE: Je préfère cette veste jaune. Elle est très élégante et elle n'est pas très chère.
FRÉDÉRIC: Oui, mais elle est trop grande pour toi!
JEAN-CLAUDE: Dommage!

Scène 3

Frédéric est au rayon de chaussures. Quelles chaussures est-ce qu'il va acheter?

JEAN-CLAUDE: Alors, quelles chaussures est-ce que tu achètes?
FRÉDÉRIC: J'achète ces chaussures noires. Elles sont très confortables . . . et elles ne sont pas chères. Regarde, elles sont en solde.

JEAN-CLAUDE: C'est vrai, elles sont en solde . . . mais elles ne sont plus à la mode.
FRÉDÉRIC: Hélas, rien n'est parfait!

CD 3, Track 25
Écoutez et répétez. p. 266

You will now hear a paused version of the dialog. Listen to the speaker and repeat right after he or she has completed the sentence.

Grammaire—Les verbes *acheter* et *préférer*

CD 3, Track 26
Écoutez et répétez. p. 268

Repeat the sentences after the speaker.

J'achète une veste. #
Je préfère la veste bleue. #

Tu achètes une cravate. #
Tu préfères la cravate jaune. #

Il achète un imper. #
Il préfère l'imper gris. #

Nous achetons un jean. #
Nous préférons le jean noir. #

Vous achetez un short. #
Vous préférez le short blanc. #

Elles achètent un pull. #
Elles préfèrent le pull rouge. #

Prononciation

CD 3, Track 27
Les lettres «e» et «è», p. 273

Écoutez: chemise   chaussette   chère

Practice pronouncing "e" within a word:

• /ə/ (as in je)

Unité 6
Leçon 18
Audioscripts

Discovering
FRENCH
Nouveau!

B L E U

Répétez: chemise # regarder # Denise # Renée # petit # venir #

Note that in the middle of a word the / ə / is sometimes silent.

Répétez: acheter # achetons # amener # samedi # rarement # avenue #

- / ɛ / (as in elle)

Répétez: chaussette # veste # quelle # cette # rester # professeur # raquette #

Now practice pronouncing "è" within a word:

/ ɛ / (as in elle)

Répétez: chère # père # mère # achète # amènent # espère # deuxième #

À votre tour!

CD 3, Track 28

1. La bonne réponse, p. 274

Listen to the conversation. *Écoutez la conversation entre Alice et Jérôme.*

ALICE: Je vais à la soirée de Delphine, et toi?

JÉRÔME: Moi aussi.
ALICE: Tu amènes une copine?
JÉRÔME: Oui, Christine.
ALICE: Qu'est-ce que vous allez apporter?
JÉRÔME: Nous allons acheter des pizzas.
ALICE: Qu'est-ce que tu vas mettre?
JÉRÔME: Mon pull jaune et mon blouson marron.

CD 3, Track 29

2. Créa-dialogue, p. 274

Listen to some sample *Créa-dialogues.* *Écoutez les conversations.*

Modèle: —Comment trouves-tu cette fille?
—Quelle fille?
—Cette fille-là!
—Eh bien, je pense qu'elle est jolie.

Maintenant, écoutez le dialogue numéro 1.

—Comment trouves-tu ces livres?
—Quels livres?
—Ces livres-là!
—Eh bien, je pense qu'ils sont intéressants.

....

WORKBOOK AUDIO

Section 1. Acheter et préférer

CD 10, Track 9

A. Écoutez et répétez. p. 157

The verbs "acheter" *(to buy)* and "préférer" *(to prefer)* are useful to know. Repeat the sentences in your Workbook after the speaker.

J'achète une veste. # Je préfère la veste bleue. #

Tu achètes une cravate. # Tu préfères la cravate jaune. #

Il achète un imper. # Il préfère l'imper gris. #

Nous achetons un jean. # Nous préférons le jean noir. #

Vous achetez un chemisier. # Vous préférez le chemisier blanc. #

Elles achètent un pull. # Elles préfèrent le pull rouge. #

Section 2. Ce et quel

CD 10, Track 10

B. Écoutez et répétez. p. 157

You use demonstrative adjectives like "ce" *(this)* to point out people or things. You use interrogative adjectives like "quel" *(which)* to ask questions about people or things.

Repeat the nouns in your Workbook with their corresponding demonstrative and interrogative adjectives.

First, let's use the word "le blouson".

ce blouson #
ce blouson-ci #
quel blouson? #

Now let's use "la veste".

cette veste #
cette-veste-ci #
quelle veste? #

Now with "l'imper".

cet imper #
cet imper-ci #
quel imper? #

Now with plural nouns like "les chaussures".

ces chaussures #
ces chaussures-ci #
quelles chaussures? #

And now with plural nouns beginning with a vowel sound, like "les affiches".

ces affiches #
ces affiches-ci #
quelles affiches? #

CD 10, Track 11

C. Écoutez et parlez. p. 157

Imagine that you are walking around a French shopping mall. Point out the following objects to your French friend.

Modèle: une casquette #
Regarde cette casquette.

Commençons.

1. un pull # Regarde ce pull.
2. une guitare # Regarde cette guitare.
3. des vestes # Regarde ces vestes.
4. un vélo # Regarde ce vélo.
5. des tee-shirts # Regarde ces tee-shirts.
6. des lunettes # Regarde ces lunettes de soleil.
7. un ordinateur # Regarde cet ordinateur.
8. des appareils-photo # Regarde ces appareils-photo.

CD 10, Track 12

D. Écoutez et parlez. p. 158

Now you will hear your French friend telling you what she is going to do. Ask her to be more specific.

Modèle: Je vais acheter une veste. #
Quelle veste?

Commençons.

1. Je vais acheter un blouson. #
Quel blouson?
2. Je vais regarder des photos. #
Quelles photos?
3. Je vais écouter un CD. #
Quel CD?
4. Je vais acheter une affiche. #
Quelle affiche?
5. Je vais acheter des affiches. #
Quelles affiches?

Section 3. Conversations

CD 10, Track 13

E. La réponse logique, p. 158

You will hear a series of short questions, each one read twice. In your Workbook, circle the letter (a, b, or c) corresponding to the most logical answer.

Commençons.

1. Tu vas acheter ce tee-shirt? #
2. Qu'est-ce que tu vas porter demain? #
3. Qui est-ce que tu vas amener à la boum? #
4. Qu'est-ce que tu vas apporter au pique-nique? #
5. Qu'est-ce que tu espères faire ce week-end?

Now check your answers. You should have circled 1-a, 2-b, 3-c, 4-a, and 5-b.

Discovering
FRENCH
Nouveau!

BLEU

Unité 6
Leçon 18
Audioscripts

Section 4. Dictée

CD 10, Track 14

F. Écoutez et écrivez. p. 158

You will hear a short dialogue spoken twice. First, listen carefully to what the people are saying. The second time you hear the dialogue, fill in the missing words.

Écoutez.

—Quels vêtements est-ce que tu vas mettre pour le pique-nique?
—Ce jean et cette chemise bleue.
—Et quelles chaussures est-ce que tu vas porter?
—Ces tennis.

Listen again and fill in the missing words.

LESSON 18 QUIZ

Part I: Listening

CD 15, Track 10

A. Questions et réponses

You will hear your French friend Julien ask you six questions. Listen carefully to each question and select the MOST LOGICAL answer on your test sheet. Circle the corresponding letter (a, b, or c). You will hear each question twice.

Let's begin.

1. *You and Julien are discussing next Saturday's picnic. He asks:*
   Qui est-ce que tu vas amener au pique-nique?

2. *You and Julien are talking about the party next Friday night. He asks:*
   Qu'est-ce que tu vas apporter à la boum?

3. *You and Julien are talking about summer plans. He asks:*
   Qu'est-ce que tu espères faire en juillet?

4. *You have stopped by Julien's house after school. He turns to you and asks:*
   Qu'est-ce que tu mets?

5. *Now you and Julien are talking about school. He asks:*
   Quelle classe est-ce que tu préfères?

6. *This afternoon you and Julien are shopping for clothes together. He asks:*
   Tu vas acheter cette chemise?

Nom _____

Classe _____ Date _____

QUIZ 18

Part I: Listening

A. Questions et réponses (30 points)

You will hear your French friend Julien ask you six questions. Listen carefully to each question and select the MOST LOGICAL answer on your test sheet. Circle the corresponding letter (a, b, or c). You will hear each question twice.

1. You and Julien are discussing next Saturday's picnic.
   You reply:
   a. Des sandwichs.
   b. Ma mobylette.
   c. Ma copine Élodie.

2. You and Julien are talking about the party next Friday night.
   You reply:
   a. Un copain.
   b. Mes amis.
   c. Ma guitare et des CD.

3. You and Julien are talking about summer plans.
   You reply:
   a. Je voudrais voyager.
   b. Non, je vais travailler.
   c. Oui, je reste chez moi.

4. You have stopped by Julien's house after school.
   You reply:
   a. Un portable.
   b. Un CD de musique africaine.
   c. Mes livres.

5. Now you and Julien are talking about school.
   You reply:
   a. La classe d'anglais.
   b. Oui, c'est une classe intéressante.
   c. Non, je ne suis pas dans cette classe.

6. This afternoon you and Julien are shopping for clothes together.
   You reply:
   a. Oui, c'est vrai.
   b. Oui, elle est géniale.
   c. Non, ce n'est pas ma chemise.

Nom _____

Classe _____ Date _____ _____

Discovering
FRENCH *Nouveau!*

BLEU

Unité 6
Leçon 18
Lesson Quiz

Part II: Writing

B. Les verbes (20 points)

Complete the following sentences with the appropriate form of the verb in parentheses.

1. (acheter)   Qu'est-ce que vous _____?

2. (préférer) Mon père _____ rester à la maison.

3. (amener)   Philippe et Marc _____ leurs copines au pique-nique.

4. (espérer)   Robert _____ visiter Paris.

5. (mettre)   Je _____ ma veste rouge.

C. Questions et réponses (30 points)

In the following mini-dialogues, complete each question with the appropriate form of **quel** and each answer with the appropriate form of **ce**.

1. —_____ ordinateur est-ce que tu vas acheter?

   —Je vais acheter _____ ordinateur japonais.

2. —_____ sandales est-ce que tu vas mettre?

   —Je vais mettre _____ sandales blanches.

3. —_____ casquette est-ce que tu préfères?

   —Je préfère _____ casquette rouge et bleue.

D. Expression personnelle (20 points)

Answer the following questions in French, using complete sentences.

• What do you prefer to do on weekends?

_____

• What do you hope to do this summer?

_____

Nom _____

Classe _____ Date _____

Discovering
FRENCH
Nouveau!

B L E U

Unité 6
Leçon 19

Workbook TE

LEÇON 19 Un choix difficile

LISTENING ACTIVITIES

Section 1. Les verbes en -ir

A. Écoutez et répétez.

Je choisis une casquette.
Tu choisis un blouson.
Il choisit une chaîne hi-fi.
Nous choisissons des CD.
Vous choisissez des vêtements.
Ils choisissent une voiture.

Section 2. Les comparaisons

B. Répétez.

plus grand que	Pierre est plus grand que Marc.
moins grand que	Pierre est moins grand que Jacques.
aussi grand que	Pierre est aussi grand que Nicolas.

C. Compréhension orale

Modèle: Sophie   [–]   Mélanie
    Sophie est moins grande que Mélanie.

1. la veste   [+]   le blouson
2. les tennis   [=]   les baskets
3. la casquette   [–]   le chapeau

4. Isabelle   [=]   Stéphanie
5. mon chien   [+]   mon chat
6. mes copains   [–]   que moi

URB
p. 69

Discovering French, Nouveau! Bleu

Unité 6, Leçon 19
Workbook

163

Unité 6
Leçon 19

Workbook TE

Nom _____

Classe _____ Date _____

Discovering
FRENCH
Nouveau!

B L E U

D. Questions et réponses

Modèle: [–]
Est-ce que la chemise est plus chère ou moins chère que le polo?
Elle est moins chère.

1. [+] Il est plus élégant.
2. [=] Elle est aussi longue.
3. [–] Il est moins grand.
4. [+] Elle est plus jeune.
5. [=] Il est aussi gentil.
6. [–] Il est moins amusant.

Section 3. Conversations

E. La réponse logique

1. a. Mardi.
   b. À dix heures.
   c. Elle ne finit pas.

2. a. Oui, elle est trop longue.
   b. Non, je préfère la veste jaune.
   c. Oui, je porte une veste bleue.

3. a. J'étudie le français.
   b. Je n'étudie pas.
   c. Je veux réussir à l'examen.

4. a. Je veux maigrir.
   b. Je veux grossir.
   c. Je mange une pizza.

Section 4. Dictée

F. Écoutez et écrivez.

—Qu'est-ce que tu _choisis_ ? Le hamburger ou la salade?

—Je _choisis_ la salade.

—Pourquoi?

—Parce que je veux _maigrir_ .

—J'espère que tu vas _réussir_ .

URB
p. 70

164

Unité 6, Leçon 19
Workbook

Discovering French, Nouveau! Bleu

Nom _____

Classe _____ Date _____

Discovering
FRENCH
Nouveau!

BLEU

Unité 6
Leçon 19
Workbook TE

WRITING ACTIVITIES

A 1. Au Bon Marché

The people below are shopping at Le Bon Marché. Say what each one is choosing, using the appropriate form of **choisir.**

1. Tu *choisis une raquette de tennis* _____.

2. Vous *choisissez des lunettes de soleil* _____.

3. Je *choisis un pantalon* _____.

4. Nous *choisissons des chaussures* _____.

5. M. Voisin *choisit un chapeau* _____.

6. Mme Lamy *choisit une jupe* _____.

7. Isabelle et Marthe *choisissent un imper(méable)* _____.

2. Oui ou non?

Read about the following people. Then describe a LOGICAL conclusion by completing the second sentence with the *affirmative* or *negative* form of the verb in parentheses.

▶ Alice fait beaucoup de jogging *Elle ne grossit pas* _____. (grossir?)

1. Nous étudions. *Nous réussissons* _____ à l'examen. (réussir?)

2. Vous êtes riches. *Vous choisissez* _____ des vêtements chers. (choisir?)

3. Marc regarde la télé. *Il ne finit pas* _____ la leçon. (finir?)

4. Mes cousins mangent beaucoup. *Ils ne maigrissent pas* _____. (maigrir?)

5. Vous faites beaucoup de sport. *Vous ne grossissez pas* _____. (grossir?)

6. Les élèves n'écoutent pas le prof. *Ils ne réussissent pas* _____ à l'examen. (réussir?)

URB
p. 71

Discovering French, Nouveau! Bleu

Unité 6, Leçon 19
Workbook

165

Nom _____

Classe _____ Date _____

B 3. Descriptions

Roger is describing certain people and things. Complete each description with the appropriate forms of the underlined adjectives.

1. Isabelle a beaucoup de <u>beaux</u> vêtements.

   Aujourd'hui elle porte une _belle_ jupe, un _beau_ chemisier et des _belles_ chaussures.

   Elle va acheter un _bel_ imperméable et des _beaux_ pulls.

2. Mes cousins habitent dans une <u>vieille</u> ville.

   Dans cette ville, il y a un très _vieil_ hôtel.

   Il y a aussi des _vieilles_ maisons, un _vieux_ musée et des _vieux_ quartiers.

3. Cet été, je vais acheter une <u>nouvelle</u> veste.

   Je vais aussi acheter un _nouveau_ maillot de bain, des _nouveaux_ pantalons et des _nouvelles_ chemises.

   Si j'ai beaucoup d'argent *(money)*, je vais aussi acheter un _nouvel_ appareil-photo.

C 4. Fifi et Nestor

Look at the scene and complete the comparisons, using the adjectives in parentheses.

(grand)	▶ Fifi _est moins grand que_	Nestor.
(sympathique)	1. Fifi _est moins sympathique que_	Nestor.
(méchant)	2. Fifi _est plus méchant que_	Nestor.
(grande)	3. Mme Paquin _est plus grande que_	Catherine.
(jeune)	4. Mme Paquin _est moins jeune que_	Catherine.

Nom _____

Classe _____ Date _____

BLEU

Unité 6
Leçon 19

Workbook TE

5. Opinions

Compare the following by using the suggested adjectives. Express your personal opinions.

▶ un imper / cher / un manteau

Un imper est moins (aussi, plus) cher qu'un manteau.

1. une chemise / chère / une veste

   Une chemise est moins chère qu'une veste.

2. une moto / rapide / une voiture

   Une moto est plus (moins, aussi) rapide qu'une voiture.

3. un chat / intelligent / un chien

   Un chat est plus (moins, aussi) intelligent qu'un chien.

4. le Texas / grand / l'Alaska

   Le Texas est moins grand que l'Alaska.

5. la Californie / jolie / la Floride

   La Californie est plus (moins, aussi) jolie que la Floride.

6. les filles / sportives / les garçons

   Les filles sont aussi (plus, moins) sportives que les garçons.

7. la cuisine italienne / bonne / la cuisine américaine

   La cuisine italienne est meilleure (moins bonne, aussi bonne) que la cuisine américaine.

8. les Royals / bons / les Yankees

   Les Royals sont meilleurs (moins bons, aussi bons) que les Yankees.

URB
p. 73

Discovering French, Nouveau! Bleu

Unité 6, Leçon 19
Workbook

167

Nom _____

Classe _____ Date _____

6. Communication: En français ! (sample answers)

Make four to six comparisons of your own involving familiar people, places, or things.

▶ Ma soeur est plus jeune que mon frère. Elle est aussi intelligente que lui.

▶ Notre maison est moins grande que la maison des voisins.

Ma mère est plus jeune que mon père.

Notre voiture est aussi grande que la voiture des voisins.

Mon chien est plus grand que mon chat. Il est aussi mignon que lui.

Mon école est plus vieille que l'école de ma cousine.

Mes bottes sont plus élégantes que mes chaussures.

Nom _____

Classe _____ Date _____ _____

Discovering
FRENCH
Nouveau!

BLEU

Unité 6
Leçon 19
Activités pour tous TE

LEÇON 19 Un choix difficile

A

Activité 1 Choisissez le verbe

First, circle the correct verb in each question. Then, fill in the blanks with the correct forms of the verbs in the responses.

1. —Vous (*finissez*) / *choisissez* à quelle heure?

   —Nous _finissons_ à trois heures.

2. —Tu manges trop! Tu vas *réussir* / (*grossir!*)

   —Mais non! Je ne _grossis_ pas.

3. —Ils (*choisissent*) / *réussissent* leurs vêtements pour la fête?

   —Oui. Et vous, vous _choisissez_ aussi vos vêtements?

4. —Tu (*choisis*) / *finis* le pantalon vert ou bleu?

   —J'aime le bleu, alors je _choisis_ le pantalon bleu.

5. —En général, tu *finis* / (*réussis*) aux examens de français?

   —Oui, et ma copine _réussit_ aussi.

Activité 2 En ville

You are showing your new Francophone friend around town and he is asking all kinds of questions. Making your selections from the box, fill in the blanks to complete your conversation. Each selection can be used only once.

—C'est un _nouvel_ hôtel?
—Oui, il est nouveau.

—C'est une _vieille_ église?
—Non, elle est assez nouvelle.

—Ce sont de _vieux_ restaurants?
—Non, ils sont assez nouveaux.

—Quels _beaux_ magasins!
—Oui, et les rues sont belles aussi, n'est-ce pas?

—Et quelle _belle_ bibliothèque municipale!

belle
beaux
vieux
vieille
nouvel

Activité 3 Des comparaisons

Circle the most logical terms.

1. Des chaussettes coûtent *plus* / *aussi* / (*moins*) cher qu'une veste.
2. Une cassette vidéo est *plus* / *aussi* / (*moins*) moderne qu'un DVD.
3. Un tee-shirt est *plus* / (*aussi*) / *moins* confortable qu'un sweat.
4. Une comédie est (*plus*) / *aussi* / *moins* amusante qu'un documentaire.
5. Un champion de tennis est (*plus*) / *aussi* / *moins* sportif qu'un champion de jeux d'ordinateur.

Unité 6 Leçon 19
Activités pour tous TE

Nom _____

Classe _____ Date _____

Discovering FRENCH *Nouveau!*

B L E U

B

Activité 1 Choisissez le verbe.

Choose the verb that completes each statement.

1. Moi, je *grossis /* (*choisis*) */ maigris* le pantalon noir.
2. Michèle étudie toujours. C'est pour ça qu'elle (*réussit*) */ finit / maigrit* aux examens.
3. Vous *choisissez /* (*finissez*) */ réussissez* vos devoirs cet après-midi?
4. Nous (*choisissons*) */ finissons / grossissons* un DVD pour ce soir.
5. Est-ce que tu *choisis / finis /* (*réussis*) en maths?

Activité 2 En ville

Fill in the blanks with the correct forms of the adjectives to complete the short dialogues.

beau   bel   belle   beaux   belles

1. —Comment trouves-tu ce blouson?

   —C'est un _beau_ blouson.

   —Et ces polos?

   —Ils sont _beaux_ aussi.

2. —Tu aimes cette voiture?

   —Oui, c'est une _belle_ voiture.

   —Et ces motos?

   —Ah oui, elles sont _belles_.

nouveau   nouvel   nouvelle   nouveaux   nouvelles

3. —C'est un _nouvel_ immeuble?

   —Oui, il y a vingt _nouveaux_ appartements.

4. —Tu aimes ma _nouvelle_ ceinture?

   —Oui, et j'aime tes _nouvelles_ chaussures aussi.

vieux   vieil   vieille   vieilles

5. —J'aime ce _vieil_ immeuble.

   —Oui. Ces _vieux_ bâtiments sont beaux.

6. —Le _vieux_ Nice est un quartier touristique.

   —Oui, les rues sont petites et _vieilles_.

Activité 3 Plus ou moins?

Fill in the blanks with **plus, aussi,** or **moins.**

1. Ton sac coûte 30 €. Mon sac coûte 45 €. Mon sac est _plus_ cher que ton sac.
2. Ta maison a cinq chambres. Mon appartement a trois chambres. Mon appartement est _moins_ grand que ta maison.
3. Nos grands-pères ont 76 ans. Mon grand-père est _aussi_ vieux que ton grand-père.
4. Marie parle toujours en classe. Jeanne n'aime pas parler. Jeanne est _plus_ timide que Marie.
5. Je joue au foot. Tu joues aux cartes. Je suis _plus_ sportif que toi.

Nom _____

Classe _____ Date _____ _____

Discovering
FRENCH
Nouveau!

B L E U

Unité 6
Leçon 19
Activités pour tous TE

C

Activité 1 Choisissez le verbe. Answers will vary.

Read the sentences below then write logical conclusions using the helping verbs **aller,**
vouloir, or **pouvoir** with a main verb selected from the box. Some of your conclusions can
be negative.

do not use helping words

Modèle: Je vais réussir à l'examen.

1. Je vais au cinéma avec Sylvie. Je _choisis le film_____ .

2. Ils étudient beaucoup. Ils _vont réussir à l'examen_____ .

3. Elle veut les deux robes. Elle _ne peut pas choisir_____ .

4. Ma soeur travaille beaucoup. Elle _veut réussir_____ .

5. Il est quatre heures. Les classes _vont finir_____ .

> **choisir**
> **finir**
> **réussir**

Activité 2 Mes cadeaux d'anniversaire

You are showing your Francophone friend three new things you received for your birthday.
Complete each sentence with an appropriate form of **beau, nouveau,** or **vieux.**

—C'est ton _nouvel_____ appareil-photo?

—Oui. C'est un cadeau de mes grands-parents.

—Et cette _nouvelle_____ veste? Elle est _belle_____ !

—Ça, c'est un cadeau de ma tante.

—J'aime cette veste avec ton _vieux_____ jean.

—Oui, et mes ~~vieilles~~ _vieux_____ baskets!

—Tu as aussi un _nouvel_____ ordinateur?

—Oui, ça, c'est un cadeau de mes parents. Génial, non?

Activité 3 Des comparaisons

Write sentences comparing the following items. Answers will vary.

1. une veste et une paire de chaussettes (cher)

   Une veste ~~coûte~~ est plus cher qu'une paire de chaussettes.

2. une voiture et une moto (grand)

   Une voiture est plus grande qu'une moto.

3. les films d'action et les documentaires (amusant)

   Les films d'action sont plus amusants que les documentaires.

4. le français et l'anglais (facile)

   Le français est moins facile que l'anglais.

URB
p. 77

Discovering French, Nouveau! Bleu

Unité 6, Leçon 19
Activités pour tous

101

Discovering
FRENCH
Nouveau!

BLEU

LEÇON 19 Un choix difficile, pages 276–277

Objectives

Communicative Functions and Topics
To describe actions
To describe people and things (new, beautiful, old)
To express comparisons
To introduce an opinion
To decide what to choose

Linguistic Goals
To use regular *-ir* verbs
To use comparisons
To pronounce the letters *"ill"*

Cultural Goals
To learn about how French young people buy clothes

Motivation and Focus

❏ Have students describe what is happening in the photos on pages 276–277. Talk about where they prefer to do their clothes shopping: small stores/boutiques or department stores. Ask about occasions for wearing formal clothes. What types of occasions are formal? What types of clothing are appropriate? Where can you buy formal clothing?

❏ Do SETTING THE SCENE, page 276 of the TE, to introduce **Audio** or **Video** 19.1. As an alternative, read **Videoscript** 19.1, page 92, or **Audioscript** CD 3, Tracks 30–31, page 94.

Presentation and Explanation

❏ *Lesson Opener:* Dramatize the text or replay the **Audio.** Ask students to read the conversations silently and then summarize what is happening.

❏ *Note culturelle:* Have students read *Les jeunes et la mode* on page 276. Encourage them to compare shopping habits of French and American young people. Play the **Video** for 19.4, Vignette culturelle: Dans un centre commercial, or read the **Videoscript** on page 93 to present information about a French commercial center.

❏ *Grammar A:* Present regular *-ir* verbs, page 278. Play **Audio** CD 3, Tracks 32–33. Point out endings and have students repeat. Use **Overhead Transparency** 39 to introduce other *-ir* verbs.

❏ *Grammar B:* Model describing people and things using **Overhead Transparency** 40 with the adjectives *beau, nouveau,* and *vieux.* Point out the placement of the adjectives before the nouns in the examples on page 279.

❏ *Grammar C:* Present the constructions used in comparisons on page 280. Model examples using students and objects in the class. Introduce the expression *à mon avis. . .* , page 281, to talk about personal opinions.

❏ *Prononciation:* Explain the pronunciation of the letters *"ill"* on page 281. Play **Audio** CD 3, Track 34, asking students to listen for the sound. Replay and have students repeat.

Guided Practice and Checking Understanding

❏ Follow the suggestions in **Overhead Transparencies,** pages A99–A103, with Transparencies 16 and 38–40 to practice comparisons, *-ir* verbs, and adjectives. You may also use WARM-UP AND REVIEW: TELLING TIME, page 278 of the TE, and Transparency 6.

❏ Play **Audio** CD 10, Tracks 15–20 or read **Audioscript** pages 95–97, and have students do **Workbook** Listening Activities A–F (pages 163–164).

❏ Use the questions in *Compréhension* on page 277 to check students' understanding of the opening text. Students can do pages 88–90 in the **Video Activities** as they watch **Video** Module 19, or listen as you read **Videoscript** pages 92–93.

❑ Use the COMPREHENSION Activity, pages 280–281 of the TE, to monitor understanding of comparatives.

Independent Practice

❑ Do the activities on pages 278–281. Assign Activities 1–4 and 6–7 for homework. Model and have students repeat Activities 5 and 8 before arranging them in pairs for PAIR PRACTICE.
❑ Use **Communipak** *Échange* 3, page 150, *Tête à tête* 2–3, pages 153–156, or **Video Activities** page 91 for pair practice in making comparisons.
❑ Have students do the activities in **Activités pour tous**, pages 99–101.

Monitoring and Adjusting

❑ Students can do the Writing Activities in the **Workbook** (pages 165–168).
❑ Monitor students' use of *-ir* verbs and adjectives as they do the practice activities. Point out grammar and vocabulary boxes as needed. Use the TEACHING STRATEGIES on pages 278 and 281 of the TE.

Assessment

❑ For formal assessment of the lesson, use Quiz 19 on pages 98–99. The **Test Generator** can be used to modify test items to meet a particular class's needs.

Reteaching

❑ Redo activities from the **Workbook** as appropriate to help with items that students find difficult.
❑ Reteach *-ir* verbs, comparisons, and vocabulary with **Teacher to Teacher** pages 20–21.

Extension and Enrichment

❑ To challenge students, introduce the SUPPLEMENTARY VOCABULARY, page 278 of the TE.

Summary and Closure

❑ Use Transparency S16 and the activities on pages A27–A28 of **Overhead Transparencies** to help students summarize what they have learned about comparisons and *-ir* verbs.
❑ Do PORTFOLIO ASSESSMENT on page 283 of the TE.

End-of-Lesson Activities

❑ *À votre tour!:* Have students do Activities 1–2. They can check their own answers, listening to **Audio** CD 3, Tracks 35–36 as needed. Do Activity 3 in small groups. Have students do Activity 4 for homework. Have students write their personal responses to Activity 5.

Discovering
FRENCH
Nouveau

BLEU

LEÇON 19 Un choix difficile, pages 276–277

Block Schedule (3 Days to Complete)

Objectives

Communicative Functions and Topics

To describe actions
To describe people and things (new, beautiful, old)
To express comparisons
To introduce an opinion
To decide what to choose

Linguistic Goals

To use regular *-ir* verbs
To use comparisons
To pronounce the letters *"ill"*

Cultural Goals

To learn about how French young people buy clothes

Day 1

Motivation and Focus

❑ Have students describe what is happening in the photos on pages 276–277. Talk about where they prefer to do their clothes shopping: small stores/boutiques or department stores. Ask about occasions for wearing formal clothes. What types of occasions are formal? What types of clothing are appropriate? Where can you buy formal clothing?

❑ Do SETTING THE SCENE, page 276 of the TE, to introduce **Audio** CD 3, Tracks 30–31 or **Video** 19.1. As an alternative, read **Videoscript** 19.1, page 92, or **Audioscript** page 94.

Presentation and Explanation

❑ *Lesson Opener:* Dramatize the text or replay the **Audio.** Ask students to read the conversations silently and then summarize what is happening.

❑ *Note culturelle:* Have students read *Les jeunes et la mode* on page 276. Encourage them to compare shopping habits of French and American young people. Play the **Video** for 19.4, Vignette culturelle: Dans un centre commercial, or read the **Videoscript** on page 97 to present information about a French commercial center.

❑ *Grammar A:* Present regular *-ir* verbs, page 278. Play **Audio** CD 3, Tracks 32–33. Point out endings and have students repeat. Use **Overhead Transparency** 39 to introduce other *-ir* verbs.

❑ *Grammar B:* Model describing people and things using **Overhead Transparency** 40 with the adjectives *beau, nouveau,* and *vieux.* Point out the placement of the adjectives before the nouns in the examples on page 279.

❑ *Grammar C:* Present the constructions used in comparisons on page 280. Model examples using students and objects in the class. Introduce the expression *à mon avis*. . . , page 281, to talk about personal opinions.

❑ *Prononciation:* Explain the pronunciation of the letters *"ill"* on page 281. Play **Audio** CD 3, Track 34, asking students to listen for the sound. Replay and have students repeat.

Guided Practice and Checking Understanding

❑ Follow the suggestions in **Overhead Transparencies,** pages A99–A103, with Transparencies 16 and 38–40 to practice comparisons, *-ir* verbs, and adjectives. You may also use WARM-UP AND REVIEW: TELLING TIME, page 278 of the TE, and Transparency 6.

❑ Play **Audio** CD 10, Tracks 15–20 or read **Audioscript** pages 95–97, and have students do **Workbook** Listening Activities A–F (pages 163–164).

Discovering
FRENCH
Nouveau!

BLEU

Unité 6
Leçon 19

Block Scheduling
Lesson Plans

Day 2

Motivation and Focus

☐ Use the questions in *Compréhension* on page 277 to check students' understanding of the opening text. Students can do pages 88–90 in the **Video Activities** as they watch **Video** Module 19, or listen as you read **Videoscript** pages 92–93.

☐ Use the COMPREHENSION Activity, pages 280–281 of the TE, to monitor understanding of comparatives.

Independent Practice

☐ Do the Activities on pages 278–281. Assign Activities 1–4 and 6–7 for homework. Model and have students repeat Activities 5 and 8 before arranging them in pairs for PAIR PRACTICE.

☐ Use **Communipak** *Échange* 3, page 150, *Tête à tête* 2–3, pages 153–156, or **Video Activities** page 91 for pair practice in making comparisons.

☐ Have students do the activities in **Activités pour tous**, pages 75–77.

Monitoring and Adjusting

☐ Students can do the Writing Activities in the **Workbook** (pages 165–168).

☐ Monitor students' use of *-ir* verbs and adjectives as they do the activities. Point out grammar and vocabulary boxes as needed. Use TEACHING STRATEGIES on pages 278 and 281 of the TE.

Day 3

End-of-Lesson Activities

☐ *À votre tour!:* Have students do Activities 1–2. They can check their own answers, listening to the **Audio** CD 3, Tracks 35–36 as needed. Do Activity 3 in small groups. Have students do Activity 4 for homework. Have students write their personal responses to Activity 5.

☐ Use **Block Scheduling Copymasters**, pages 145–152.

Reteaching (as needed)

☐ Redo activities from the **Workbook** to help with items that students find difficult.

☐ Reteach *-ir* verbs, comparisons, and vocabulary with **Teacher to Teacher** pages 20–21.

Extension and Enrichment (as desired)

☐ To challenge students, introduce the SUPPLEMENTARY VOCABULARY, page 278 of the TE.

☐ For expansion activities, direct students to www.classzone.com.

Summary and Closure

☐ Use Transparency S16 and the activities on pages A27–A28 of **Overhead Transparencies** to help students summarize what they have learned about comparisons and *-ir* verbs.

☐ Do PORTFOLIO ASSESSMENT on page 283 of the TE.

Assessment

☐ For formal assessment of the lesson, use Quiz 19 on pages 98–99. The **Test Generator** can be used to modify test items to meet a particular class's needs.

Nom _____

Classe _____ Date _____

LEÇON 19   Un choix difficile, pages 276–277

Materials Checklist

- **Student Text**
- **Audio** CD 3, Tracks 30–31
- **Video 3** or **DVD 2;** Counter 48:25–49:35

Steps to Follow

- Read *Un choix difficile: Scènes 1–2* (pp. 276–277). Look at the photographs for each scene.
- Read the questions in *Compréhension* (p. 277) before you watch the video or DVD, or listen to the audio.
- Watch **Video 3** or **DVD 2;** Counter 48:25–49:35, or listen to **Audio** CD 3, Tracks 30–31. Repeat everything you hear.
- Read *Note culturelle* (p. 276).
- Answer the questions in *Compréhension* (p. 276). Write your answers in complete sentences on a separate sheet of paper.

If You Don't Understand . . .

- Watch the **Video** or **DVD** in a quiet place. Try to stay focused. If you get lost, stop the **Video** or **DVD**. Replay it and find your place.
- Listen to the **CD** in a quiet place. Try to stay focused. If you get lost, stop the **CD**. Replay it and find your place.
- Repeat aloud with the audio. Try to sound like the people on the recording.
- Say aloud anything you write. Make sure you understand everything you say.
- Write down any questions so that you can ask your teacher or your partner later.

Self-Check

Answer the following questions in complete sentences on a separate sheet of paper.

1. Est-ce que les jeunes Français aiment être à la mode?
2. Est-ce qu'ils dépensent 50% de leur budget pour les vêtements?
3. En France, est-ce qu'il y a des boutiques spécialisées dans la mode des jeunes?
4. En France, quelles sont les boutiques spécialisées dans la mode des jeunes?

Answers

1. Oui, les jeunes Français aiment être à la mode.   2. Non, ils dépensent 30% de leur budget pour les vêtements.   3. Oui, en France il y a des boutiques spécialisées dans la mode des jeunes.   4. Les boutiques spécialisées dans la mode des jeunes sont Zara, Mango et Etam.

Nom _____

Classe _____ Date _____

Discovering FRENCH *Nouveau!*

B L E U

Unité 6
Leçon 19

Absent Student
Copymasters

A. Les verbes réguliers en *-ir,* page 278
Vocabulaire: Verbes réguliers en *-ir,* pages 278–279

Materials Checklist

- **Student Text**
- **Audio** CD 3, Tracks 32–33; CD 10, Tracks 15, 19–20
- **Workbook**

Steps to Follow

- Study *Les verbes réguliers en –ir* (p. 278). Copy the present conjugation of these verbs on a separate sheet of paper.
- Listen to **Audio** CD 3, Tracks 32–33. Repeat everything you hear.
- Do Activity 1 in the text (p. 278). Write the answers in complete sentences.
- Study *Vocabulaire: Verbes réguliers en –ir* (p. 278). Write out the present conjugation of **choisir, grossir, maigrir,** and **réussir**.
- Do Activities 2–3 in the text (p. 278–279). Write the answers on a separate sheet of paper.
- Do Writing Activities A, 1–2 in the **Workbook** (page 165).
- Do Listening Activities A, E–F in the **Workbook** (page 163). Use **Audio** CD 10, Tracks 15, 19–20.

If You Don't Understand . . .

- Listen to the **CDs** in a quiet place. Try to stay focused. If you get lost, stop the **CDs**. Replay them and find your place.
- Repeat aloud with the audio. Try to sound like the people on the recording.
- Reread the activity directions. Put the directions in your own words.
- Read the model several times. Be sure you understand it.
- Say aloud everything that you write. Make sure you understand what you are sayinig.
- When writing a sentence, ask yourself, "What do I mean? What am I trying to say?"
- Write down any questions so that you can ask your teacher or your partner later.

Self-Check

Complete the following sentences with the appropriate form of **choisir, réussir,** or **finir.**

1. À quelle heure . . . le film? (finir)
2. Aller au film? Aller au concert? Qu'est-ce que tu . . . ? (choisir)
3. Est-ce que vous . . . à vos classes? (réussir)
4. Nous . . . notre travail à quelle heure? (finir)
5. Elle . . . quel voyage? (choisir)
6. Il . . . parce qu'il travaille. (réussir)

Answers

1. À quelle heure finit le film? 2. Qu'est-ce que tu choisis? 3. Est-ce que vous réussissez à vos classes? 4. Nous finissons notre travail à quelle heure? 5. Elle choisit quel voyage? 6. Il réussit parce qu'il travaille.

Discovering
FRENCH
Nouveau!

B L E U

B. Les adjectifs *beau, nouveau* et *vieux,* page 279

Materials Checklist

- **Student Text**
- **Workbook**

Steps to Follow

- Study *Les adjectifs **beau**, **nouveau**, et **vieux*** (p. 279). Copy the chart on a separate sheet of paper. Underline the masculine singular and plural endings. Circle the feminine singular and plural endings.
- Do Activity 4 in the text (p. 279). Write complete sentences on a separate sheet of paper. Underline the adjective in each sentence, for example, "***Regarde le <u>beau</u> pantalon!***"
- Do Activity 5 in the text (p. 279). Write the parts for both speakers on a separate sheet of paper. Read both parts aloud.
- Do Writing Activity B, 3 in the **Workbook** (page 166).

If You Don't Understand . . .

- Reread the activity directions. Put the directions in your own words.
- Read the model several times. Be sure you understand it.
- Say aloud everything that you write. Be sure you understand what you are saying.
- When writing a sentence, ask yourself, "What do I mean? What am I trying to say?"
- Write down any questions so that you can ask your teacher or your partner later.

Self-Check

Write complete sentences using the correct form of **beau, nouveau,** or **vieux.** Check placement and agreement. Underline the adjectives.

1. vieux / voiture / être / derrière le garage
2. beau / maison / être / devant le garage
3. nouveau / stylo / être / sous la table
4. nouveau / veste / être / sur la chaise
5. vieux / imper / être / à la maison
6. vieux / pulls / être / à la mode
7. nouveau / vélos / être / dans le garage
8. nouveau / robes / être / chez moi

Answers

1. La <u>vieille</u> voiture est derrière le garage.   2. La <u>belle</u> maison est devant le garage.   3. Le <u>nouveau</u> stylo est sous la table.   4. La <u>nouvelle</u> veste est sur la chaise.   5. Le <u>vieil</u> imper est à la maison.   6. Les <u>vieux</u> pulls sont à la mode.   7. Les <u>nouveaux</u> vélos sont dans le garage.   8. Les <u>nouvelles</u> robes sont chez moi.

Nom _____

Classe _____ Date _____

Discovering
FRENCH *Nouveau!*

B L E U

Unité 6
Leçon 19

Absent Student
Copymasters

C. La comparaison avec les adjectifs, pages 280–281

Materials Checklist

- **Student Text**
- **Audio** CD 3, Tracks 34–36; CD 10, Tracks 16–18
- **Video 3** or **DVD 2**; Counter 49:36–51:55
- **Workbook**

Steps to Follow

- Watch **Video 3** or **DVD 2**; Counter 49:36–51:55. Repeat everything you hear.
- Study *La comparaison avec les adjectifs* (p. 280).
- Copy the model sentences on a separate sheet of paper. Underline the comparisons, for example, "*Cet imper est plus cher que ce manteau.*"
- Do Activity 6 in the text (p. 280). Write your answers in complete sentences on a separate sheet of paper.
- Do Activities 7–8 in the text (p. 281). Write the answers in complete sentences.
- Read the list of words in *Prononciation: Les lettres «ill»* in the text (p. 281). Listen to **Audio** CD 3, Track 34. Repeat what you hear.
- Do Writing Activities C, 4–5, and 6 in the **Workbook** (pages 166–168).
- Do Listening Activities B–D in the **Workbook** (pp. 163–164). Use **Audio** CD 10, Tracks 16–18.
- Do Activities 1–5 of *À votre tour!* in the text (pp. 282–283). Use **Audio** CD 3, Tracks 35–36 with Activities 1–2.

If You Don't Understand . . .

- Reread the explanation. Put the explanation in your own words.
- Watch the **Video** or **DVD** in a quiet place. Try to stay focused. If you get lost, stop the **Video** or **DVD**. Replay it and find your place.
- Listen to the **CD** in a quiet place. Try to stay focused. If you get lost, stop the **CD**. Replay it and find your place.
- Read the models several times. Copy the model. Say aloud everything that you write. Listen and be sure you understand what you are saying.
- Listen once without repeating. Then replay and repeat aloud with the audio. Try to sound like the people on the recording. Imitate their accents. Pause the **CD** if you can't keep up.
- Write down any questions so that you can ask your teacher or your partner later.

Self-Check

Write comparisons in complete sentences using the expressions indicated below. Make sure the adjective agrees in gender and number with the noun or pronoun it modifies.

1. mon vélo / plus grand / ton vélo
2. Jean / moins sportif / Louis
3. ta robe / aussi élégant / ma robe
4. l'appartement / moins cher / la maison
5. la voiture française / aussi cher / voiture italienne
6. Brigitte / plus blond / Barbara
7. le chocolat / bon / la vanille

Answers

1. Mon vélo est plus grand que ton vélo. 2. Jean est moins sportif que Louis. 3. Ta robe est aussi élégante que ma robe. 4. L'appartement est moins cher que la maison. 5. La voiture française est aussi chère que la voiture italienne. 6. Brigitte est plus blonde que Barbara. 7. Le chocolat est meilleur que la vanille.

Discovering
FRENCH
Nouveau

B L E U

LEÇON 19 Un choix difficile

Faire des achats

Find out if a family member wants to buy something new. Have him or her choose from among the following items.

- First, explain your assignment.
- Then, model the pronunciation of the words below each image. Point to the picture as you model each answer.
- Ask the question, **Est-ce que tu veux acheter . . .** adding the words below the picture. Point again to the pictures.
- When you have an answer, complete the sentence at the bottom of the page.

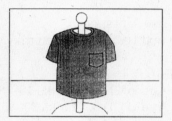

un nouveau tee-shirt?

une nouvelle casquette?

un nouvel ordinateur?

_____ veut acheter _____.

Nom _____

Classe _____ Date _____

Discovering FRENCH *Nouveau!*

B L E U

Unité 6
Leçon 19

Family Involvement

Les comparaisons

Ask a family member to compare the following pairs in order to determine who is more athletic and who is taller.

- First, explain your assignment.
- Then, model the pronunciation of the words. Point to the picture as you model each answer.
- Ask the questions, one at a time, pointing to the pictures.
- After you get an answer for each question, write it up in a sentence in the space that follows.

Qui est plus sportive . . . Suzanne ou Alice?

Suzanne   Alice

Qui est plus grand . . . Pierre ou Marc?   **Qui est moins grand . . . Pierre ou Jacques?**

1.

Pierre   Marc
plus grand que

2.

Pierre   Jacques
moins grand que

1. _____

2. _____

Nom _____

Classe _____ Date _____

B L E U

MODULE 19 Un choix difficile

Video 3, DVD 2

19 Activité 1. Une occasion importante
Counter 47:47–48:24

Delphine is about to attend an important event.
What is it? Watch the video and find out. If a
statement below is true, circle **vrai.** If it is false,
circle **faux.**

1. Delphine va aller au mariage de sa cousine. **vrai** **faux**

2. Elle va acheter une nouvelle robe pour cette occasion. **vrai** **faux**

3. Elle va au marché aux puces avec sa copine Véronique. **vrai** **faux**

19.1 Activité 2. Un choix difficile
Counter 48:25–49:35

Delphine is hesitating between two dresses. Watch and listen to the video and then draw a
line from what Véronique says on the left to Delphine's responses on the right. (*Note:* Some
sentences have been shortened.)

Véronique

Delphine

1. Bon, alors, quelle robe est-ce que tu choisis?

2. C'est vrai, elle est plus jolie . . .

3. Bon, écoute, essaie-la!

4. Pourquoi?

5. Et si tu grossis?

a. Mais non, elle n'est pas trop petite.

b. Parce que j'ai un mois pour maigrir.

c. Eh bien, finalement je choisis la robe rouge. Elle est plus jolie que la robe jaune.

d. C'est vrai, la robe rouge est plus petite, mais ce n'est pas grave.

e. Toi, tais-toi!

Nom _____

Classe _____ Date _____

Discovering
FRENCH
Nouveau!

BLEU

Unité 6
Leçon 19
Video Activities

19.2 Activité 3. Préférences

Watch the four scenes on the video which compare different people and things. Then, circle the letter of the completion to each statement below.

Scène 1

1. —Je vais acheter les chaussures . . .   a. blanches   b. noires
2. —Elles sont plus . . .   a. belles   b. confortables

Scène 2

3. —Je préfère le chapeau . . .   a. gris   b. vert
4. —Il est plus . . .   a. élégant   b. joli

Scène 3

5. —Je vais acheter . . .   a. la mini-chaîne   b. le baladeur
6. —Il/Elle est moins . . .   a. bon marché   b. cher (chère)

Scène 4

7. —Je préfère la classe . . .   a. d'anglais   b. d'espagnol
8. —Le prof est plus . . .   a. intéressant   b. sympa

19.3 Activité 4. Comparaisons

How expensive are things in the department store? As you watch the video segment, choose the appropriate word from the list to the right to complete the sentences below. (*Note:* The first item has been done for you.)

plus	aussi	moins

▶ La veste bleue est _moins_____ chère que la veste jaune.

1. Les chaussures noires sont _____ chères que les chaussures blanches.

2. Le vélo vert est _____ cher que le vélo rouge.

3. Le compact-disc est _____ cher que la cassette.

Nom _____

Classe _____ Date _____

🌐 19.4 Activité 5. Dans un centre commercial

Counter 51:56–53:19

A. As you watch the **Vignette culturelle** about a **centre commercial,** indicate where each conversation is taking place by marking an **X** in the appropriate column.

	dans un magasin de sport	dans un magasin de vêtements
Conversation 1		
Conversation 2		
Conversation 3		
Conversation 4		

B. After watching the **Vignette culturelle,** list similarities and differences between Les Quatre Temps shopping center and an American shopping mall with which you are familiar.

Similarities

1. _____

2. _____

3. _____

Differences

1. _____

2. _____

3. _____

C. Question personnelle: If you could go shopping at Les Quatre Temps, which stores would you visit? Why?

Réponse: _____

_____

Nom _____

Classe _____ Date _____

Discovering
FRENCH
Nouveau!

B L E U

Unité 6
Leçon 19

Video Activities

Activité 6. Une présentation de collections *(A fashion show)*

With a classmate, take turns playing the roles of a fashion designer and a store buyer. First, the designer draws several clothing outfits. Then, he or she shows them to the buyer, giving the name, color, price, and so on of each item of clothing. The buyer then comments on the designs, comparing them to each other. The designer responds to the buyer, trying to convince him or her to buy the designs. Then switch roles.

▶ DESIGNER: **Voici une jolie robe noire. Elle coûte cent euros. Et voici une jupe . . .**

    BUYER: **La robe est jolie, mais elle est plus courte que la jupe . . .**

DESIGNER: **La jupe est aussi moins chère que la robe . . .**

MODULE 19   Un choix difficile

Video 3, DVD 2 Counter 47:47–48:24

Dans un mois, Delphine va aller au mariage de sa cousine. Elle va acheter une nouvelle robe pour cette occasion. Pour cela, elle va dans un magasin de vêtements avec sa copine Véronique. Il y a beaucoup de jolies robes dans ce magasin.

19.1 Dialogue: Un choix difficile
Counter 48:25–49:35

Delphine hésite entre une robe rouge et une robe jaune. Quelle robe est-ce qu'elle va choisir? Ah là là, le choix n'est pas facile.

VÉRONIQUE: Bon, alors, quelle robe est-ce que tu choisis?

DELPHINE: Eh bien, finalement je choisis la robe rouge. Elle est plus jolie que la robe jaune.

VÉRONIQUE: C'est vrai, elle est plus jolie . . . mais la robe jaune est moins chère et . . . elle est plus grande. Regarde. La robe rouge est trop petite pour toi.

DELPHINE: Mais non, elle n'est pas trop petite.

VÉRONIQUE: Bon, écoute, essaie-la!

DELPHINE: C'est vrai, la robe rouge est plus petite, mais ce n'est pas grave.

VÉRONIQUE: Pourquoi?

DELPHINE: Parce que j'ai un mois pour maigrir.

VÉRONIQUE: Et si tu grossis?

DELPHINE: Toi, tais-toi!

19.2 Mini-scenes: Listening— Comparaisons Counter 49:36–51:10

Did you notice which expressions Véronique and Delphine used to compare the two dresses? Watch again.

DELPHINE: Eh bien, finalement je choisis la robe rouge. Elle est plus jolie que la robe jaune.

VÉRONIQUE: . . . mais la robe jaune est moins chère et . . . elle est plus grande.

To compare people or things, French people use the following constructions:

plus grand que: *Pierre est **plus grand que** Marc.*
[screen card]

moins grand que: *Pierre est **moins grand que** Jacques.*
[screen card]

aussi grand que: *Pierre est **aussi grand que** Nicolas.*
[screen card]

Now watch the following scenes.

JEAN-CLAUDE: Alors, quelles chaussures est-ce que tu vas acheter?

FRÉDÉRIC: Je vais acheter les chaussures noires.

JEAN-CLAUDE: Pourquoi?

FRÉDÉRIC: Parce qu'elles sont plus confortables que les chaussures blanches.

STÉPHANIE: Quel chapeau est-ce que tu préfères?

DOMINQUE: Je préfère le chapeau vert.

STÉPHANIE: Pourquoi?

DOMINQUE: Parce qu'il est plus joli que le chapeau gris.

CÉLINE: Tu vas acheter le baladeur CD ou la mini-chaîne?

TRINH: Je vais acheter le baladeur.

CÉLINE: Ah bon! Pourquoi?

TRINH: Parce qu'il est moins cher que la mini-chaîne.

NATHALIE: Tu préfères la classe d'anglais ou la classe d'espagnol?

YVONNE: Je préfère la classe d'anglais.

NATHALIE: Ah bon! Pourquoi?

YVONNE: Parce que le prof d'anglais est plus mignon . . . et plus sympa.

19.3 Mini-scenes: Speaking—Comparaisons Counter 51:11–51:55

Now it's your turn to speak. Imagine that you're shopping in a French department store with a friend. Answer your friend's questions about the prices of the following objects.

—Est-ce que la veste bleue est plus chère ou moins chère que la veste jaune? [screen card]
—Elle est moins chère.

—Et les chaussures noires? Est-ce qu'elles sont plus chères ou moins chères que les chaussures blanches? [screen card]
—Elles sont plus chères.

—Et le vélo vert? Est-ce qu'il est plus cher ou moins cher que le vélo rouge? [screen card]
—Il est aussi cher.

—Et le compact-disc? Est-ce qu'il est plus cher ou moins cher que la cassette?
—Il est plus cher.

19.4 Vignette culturelle: Dans un centre commercial Counter 51:56–53:19

Aujourd'hui nous allons visiter un centre commercial. Ce centre commercial s'appelle «Les Quatre Temps». Il est situé dans le quartier de la Défense, à l'ouest de Paris. C'est le plus grand centre commercial d'Europe.

Entrons aux Quatre Temps! C'est en réalité une petite ville sur deux étages.

Il y a une poste. Il y a des cinémas. Il y a des restaurants. Il y a surtout beaucoup de magasins de mode. Au total, il y a 250 magasins. Entrons dans quelques magasins.

—Pardon, monsieur . . . qu'est-ce que vous vendez dans ce magasin?
—Des costumes pour hommes, des vestes, des pantalons, des chemises.
—Merci.

—Pardon, madame.
—Bonjour, madame.
—Qu'est-ce que vous vendez dans ce magasin?
—Des chaussures et des sacs.
—Merci.

—Bonjour! Qu'est-ce que vous allez acheter?
—Je vais acheter une robe.
—Et vous?
—Une veste.

—Qu'est-ce que vous allez acheter?
—Un vélo, des chaussures de tennis.
—Et moi, une raquette.

LEÇON 19 Un choix difficile

PE AUDIO

CD 3, Track 30
Compréhension orale, p. 276

Dans un mois, Delphine va aller au mariage de sa cousine. Elle va acheter une nouvelle robe pour cette occasion. Pour cela, elle va dans un magasin de vêtements avec sa copine Véronique. Il y a beaucoup de jolies robes dans ce magasin.

Delphine hésite entre une robe jaune et une robe rouge. Quelle robe est-ce que Delphine va choisir? Ah là là, le choix n'est pas facile.

Scène 1

VÉRONIQUE: Bon, alors, quelle robe est-ce que tu choisis?

DELPHINE: Eh bien, finalement je choisis la robe rouge. Elle est plus jolie que la robe jaune.

VÉRONIQUE: C'est vrai, elle est plus jolie . . . mais la robe jaune est moins chère et elle est plus grande. Regarde. La robe rouge est trop petite pour toi.

DELPHINE: Mais non, elle n'est pas trop petite.

VÉRONIQUE: Bon, écoute, essaie-la!

Scène 2

Delphine sort de la cabine d'essayage.

DELPHINE: C'est vrai, la robe rouge est plus petite, mais ce n'est pas grave.

VÉRONIQUE: Pourquoi?

DELPHINE: Parce que j'ai un mois pour maigrir.

VÉRONIQUE: Et si tu grossis?

DELPHINE: Toi, tais-toi!

CD 3, Track 31
Écoutez et répétez. p. 276

You will now hear a paused version of the dialog. Listen to the speaker and repeat right after he or she has completed the sentence.

Grammaire: Les verbes réguliers en -*ir*

CD 3, Track 32
Écoutez et répétez. p. 278

Repeat the sentences after the speaker.

Je finis à deux heures. #

Tu finis à une heure. #

Elle finit à cinq heures. #

Nous finissons à midi. #

Vous finissez à une heure.

Ils finissent à minuit. #

Vocabulaire: Verbes réguliers en -*ir*

CD 3, Track 33
Écoutez et répétez. p. 278

choisir #   Quelle veste choisis-tu? #

finir #   Les classes finissent à midi. #

grossir #   Marc grossit parce qu'il mange beaucoup. #

maigrir #   Je maigris parce que je mange peu. #

réussir #   Tu vas réussir parce que tu travailles! #

réussir à un examen #   Nous réussissons à nos examens. #

Discovering
FRENCH
Nouveau!

B L E U

Unité 6
Leçon 19
Audioscripts

Prononciation

CD 3, Track 34

Les lettres «ill», p. 281

Écoutez: maillot

In the middle of a word, the letters "ill" usually represent the sound /j/ like the "y" of *yes*.

Répétez: maillot # travaillez # oreille # vieille # fille # famille # juillet #

En juillet, Mireille va travailler pour sa vieille tante. #

At the end of a word, the sound /j/ is sometimes spelled il.

Répétez: appareil-photo # vieil # travail #

Mon oncle a un vieil appareil-photo. #

Exception: The letters ill are pronounced /il/ in the following words:

Répétez: ville # village # mille # Lille #

À votre tour!

CD 3, Track 35

1. La bonne réponse, p. 282

Listen to the conversation. *Écoutez la conversation entre François et Stéphanie.*

FRANÇOIS: Tu aimes cette veste verte?
STÉPHANIE: Oui, mais elle est très chère.
FRANÇOIS: Combien est-ce qu'elle coûte?
STÉPHANIE: 300 euros.
FRANÇOIS: Et qu'est-ce que tu penses de cette robe rouge?
STÉPHANIE: À mon avis, elle est moins jolie.
FRANÇOIS: Alors, qu'est-ce que tu vas choisir?
STÉPHANIE: La veste bleue. Elle est meilleur marché et elle est aussi élégante.

CD 3, Track 36

2. Créa-dialogue, p. 282

Listen to some sample *Créa-dialogues.* *Écoutez les conversations.*

Modèle: —Tu choisis la voiture rouge ou la voiture noire?
—Je choisis la voiture rouge.
—Pourquoi?
—Parce qu'elle est plus petite et moins chère.

Maintenant, écoutez le dialogue numéro 1.

—Tu achètes la chaîne hi-fi ou le baladeur?
—J'achète la chaîne hi-fi.
—Pourquoi?
—Parce qu'elle est meilleure et plus grande.

WORKBOOK AUDIO

Section 1. Les verbes en *-ir*

CD 10, Track 15

A. Écoutez et répétez. p. 163

Some French regular verbs end in -ir, like "finir" (to finish) and "choisir" (to choose). Repeat the sentences in your Workbook after the speaker.

Je choisis une casquette. #

Tu choisis un blouson. #

Il choisit une chaîne hi-fi. #

Nous choisissons des CD. #

Vous choisissez des vêtements. #

Ils choisissent une voiture. #

Section 2. Les comparaisons

CD 10, Track 16

B. Répétez. p. 163

To compare people or things, the French use the constructions you see in your Workbook. Repeat the comparisons after the speaker.

Unité 6
Leçon 19

Audioscripts

Discovering
FRENCH
Nouveau!

BLEU

plus grand que # Pierre est plus grand que Marc. #

moins grand que # Pierre est moins grand que Jacques. #

aussi grand que # Pierre est aussi grand que Nicolas. #

CD 10, Track 17

C. Compréhension orale, p. 163

Now you will hear sentences in which people or things are compared. Listen carefully. If you hear "plus," write a plus-sign. If you hear "moins," write a minus-sign. If you hear "aussi," write an equals-sign.

Modèle: Sophie est moins grande que Mélanie.

Did you hear "moins grande"? You should have written a minus-sign.

Commençons.

1. La veste est plus chère que le blouson. #
2. Les tennis sont aussi confortables que les baskets. #
3. La casquette est moins jolie que le chapeau. #
4. Isabelle est aussi sympathique que Stéphanie. #
5. Mon chien est plus intelligent que mon chat. #
6. Mes copains sont moins sportifs que moi. #

Now let's check your answers.

You should have written a plus-sign for comparisons 1 and 5, a minus-sign for comparisons 3 and 6, and an equals-sign for comparisons 2 and 4.

CD 10, Track 18

D. Questions et réponses, p. 164

Now it is your turn to make comparisons. Answer the questions you hear according to the comparison signs in your Workbook.

Modèle: Est-ce que la chemise est plus chère ou moins chère que le polo?

Since you see a minus-sign, you would answer: Elle est moins chère. #

Commençons.

1. Est-ce que le pantalon est plus élégant ou moins élégant que le jean? #
   Il est plus élégant.
2. Est-ce que la robe est plus longue ou moins longue que la jupe? #
   Elle est aussi longue.
3. Est-ce que le salon est plus grand ou moins grand que la salle à manger? #
   Il est moins grand.
4. Est-ce que ta soeur est plus jeune ou moins jeune que ta copine? #
   Elle est plus jeune.
5. Est-ce que ton oncle est plus gentil ou moins gentil que ta tante? #
   Il est aussi gentil.
6. Est-ce que le prof d'anglais est plus amusant ou moins amusant que le prof de français? #
   Il est moins amusant.

Section 3. Conversations

CD 10, Track 19

E. La réponse logique, p. 164

You will hear a series of short questions, each one read twice. In your Workbook, circle the letter (a, b, or c) corresponding to the most logical answer.

Commençons.

1. À quelle heure finit la boum? #
2. Tu vas choisir cette veste bleue? #
3. Pourquoi est-ce que tu étudies? #
4. Pourquoi est-ce que tu manges moins? #

Now check your answers. You should have circled 1-b, 2-b, 3-c and 4-a.

Section 4. Dictée

CD 10, Track 20

F. Écoutez et écrivez. p. 164

You will hear a short dialogue spoken twice. First listen carefully to what the people are saying. The second time you hear the dialogue, fill in the missing words.

Écoutez.

—Qu'est-ce que tu choisis? Le hamburger ou la salade?
—Je choisis la salade.

—Pourquoi?
—Parce que je veux maigrir.
—J'espère que tu vas réussir.

Listen again and fill in the missing words.

LESSON 19 QUIZ

Part I: Listening

CD 15, Track 11

A. Questions et réponses

You will hear your French friend Antoine ask you six questions. Select the MOST LOGICAL response and circle the corresponding letter (a, b, or c). You will hear each question twice.

Let's begin.

1. *You and Antoine are at the shopping mall looking at jackets. He asks:*
   Pourquoi est-ce que tu choisis le blouson noir?

2. *You and Antoine have stopped at a fast food place. He asks:*
   Pourquoi est-ce que tu ne manges pas de frites?

3. *You and Antoine are talking about your classmate Paul. He asks:*
   Est-ce que Paul va réussir à l'examen?

4. *The conversation turns to Élodie. He asks:*
   Qu'est-ce que tu penses d'Élodie?

5. *Now you and Antoine are at school between classes. He asks:*
   Tu préfères l'anglais ou l'espagnol?

6. *Antoine has one last question. He asks:*
   Tu es bon en français?

Nom _____

Classe _____ Date _____

Discovering
FRENCH
Nouveau!

BLEU

QUIZ 19

Part I: Listening

A. Questions et réponses (30 points)

You will hear your French friend Antoine ask you six questions. Select the MOST LOGICAL response and circle the corresponding letter (a, b, or c). You will hear each question twice.

1. You and Antoine are at the shopping mall looking at jackets.
   You reply:
   a. Parce que je vais au cinéma.
   b. Parce qu'il est trop grand.
   c. Parce qu'il est plus beau que le blouson marron.

2. You and Antoine have stopped at a fast food place.
   You reply:
   a. Parce que je n'ai pas soif.
   b. Parce que je ne veux pas grossir.
   c. Parce que je n'aime pas ce restaurant.

3. You and Antoine are talking about your classmate Paul.
   You reply:
   a. C'est vrai, il a un bon prof.
   b. Bien sûr, il étudie beaucoup!
   c. Oui, il va acheter un livre à la librairie.

4. The conversation turns to Élodie.
   You reply:
   a. Elle est moins amusante que sa soeur.
   b. Elle va au lycée Carnot.
   c. Bien sûr, je suis son copain.

5. Now you and Antoine are at school between classes.
   You reply:
   a. Oui, je parle anglais!
   b. L'anglais, parce que c'est plus facile!
   c. J'ai une classe à trois heures.

6. Antoine has one last question.
   You reply:
   a. Oui, c'est difficile.
   b. Il n'est pas mauvais.
   c. Oui, mais ma copine est meilleure que moi.

Nom _____

Classe _____ Date _____ _____

Discovering
FRENCH Nouveau!
BLEU

Unité 6
Leçon 19
Lesson Quiz

Part II: Writing

B. Les verbes (25 points)

Complete each of the following sentences with the appropriate form of the verb in parentheses.

1. (finir)   Les classes _____ à trois heures.

2. (choisir) Qu'est-ce que tu _____?

3. (réussir) Céline _____ toujours à ses examens.

4. (grossir) Vous mangez, mais vous ne _____ pas.

5. (maigrir) Nous _____.

C. Les vêtements (25 points)

Complete each of the following sentences with the appropriate form of the adjective in parentheses.

1. (nouveau) J'aime tes _____ collants.

2. (vieux)   Tu portes tes _____ chaussures.

3. (beau)   Les chaussures italiennes qu'il porte sont très _____.

4. (vieux)   Qui veut mon _____ ordinateur?

5. (beau)   Nathalie a une _____ jupe.

D. Expression personnelle (20 points)

Compare yourself to other people, using the elements below. Use complete sentences.

• je / sportif / mes copains

_____

• je / bon en maths / ma copine

_____

• je / intelligent / le prof

_____

Nom _____

Classe _____ Date _____

Discovering FRENCH *Nouveau!*

BLEU

Unité 6
Leçon 20

WorkbookTE

LEÇON 20   Alice a un job

LISTENING ACTIVITIES

Section 1. Le pronom *on*

A. Compréhension orale

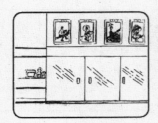

a. _6_   b. _7_   c. _1_

d. _5_   e. _3_   f. _2_   g. _4_

B. Questions et réponses

Qu'est-ce qu'on vend ici?

On vend des ordinateurs.

1.   2.   3.

1. On vend des vélos.
2. On vend des chaussures.
3. On vend des livres.

Discovering French, Nouveau! Bleu

Unité 6, Leçon 20
Workbook

169

URB
p. 101

C. Questions et réponses

Modèle: —Vous parlez anglais?
          —**Bien sûr, on parle anglais.**

1. . . . on joue au baseball. 2. . . . on joue aux jeux vidéo. 3. . . . on mange des hamburgers. 4. . . . on regarde la télé. 5. . . . on va au concert. 6. . . . on a des ordinateurs.

Section 2. L'impératif

D. Compréhension orale

		Modèle	1	2	3	4	5	6	7	8
A: statement		✓	✓		✓			✓		
B: suggestion				✓		✓	✓		✓	✓

E. Parlez.

Modèle: Tu dois écouter le professeur
          Écoute le professeur.

1. Écoute ce CD. 2. Regarde cette photo. 3. Achète cette casquette. 4. Travaille.
5. Finis ce livre.

Modèle: Nous aimons jouer au foot.
          Jouons au foot.

6. Regardons la télé. 7. Jouons aux jeux vidéo. 8. Visitons Paris. 9. Faisons une promenade.
10. Allons au cinéma.

Section 3. Conversations

F. La réponse logique

1. a. Un copain.
   b. Ma tante Victoire.
   c. Le musée Picasso.

2. a. À mon oncle.
   b. Notre Dame.
   c. La France.

3. a. Oui, je suis riche.
   b. Oui, j'ai 20 euros.
   c. Oui, prête-moi 10 euros, s'il te plaît.

4. a. Oui, j'ai faim.
   b. Oui, je mange une pizza.
   c. Non, je suis au restaurant.

5. a. L'école.
   b. Ma montre.
   c. Le bus.

6. a. J'ai besoin d'argent.
   b. Je vais faire une promenade.
   c. Je vais en ville.

URB
p. 102

170

Unité 6, Leçon 20
Workbook

Discovering French, Nouveau! Bleu

Nom _____

Classe _____ Date _____

Discovering FRENCH *Nouveau!*

BLEU

Unité 6
Leçon 20

Workbook TE

Section 4. Dictée

G. Écoutez et écrivez.

You will hear a short dialogue spoken twice. First listen carefully to what the people are saying. The second time you hear the dialogue, fill in the missing words.

Écoutez.

—Qu'est-ce qu' _on_____ fait?

—J'ai _envie_____ d'aller au cinéma, mais je n'ai pas d' _argent_____.

—De _combien_____ est-ce que tu as _besoin_____ ?

—De dix euros.

—Tiens, voilà dix euros.

URB
p. 103

Discovering French, Nouveau! Bleu

Unité 6, Leçon 20
Workbook

171

Nom _____

Classe _____ Date _____

WRITING ACTIVITIES

A 1. Où?

Say where one usually does the activities suggested in parentheses. Choose one of the places from the box. Be logical!

▶ (étudier) On étudie à l'école.

1. (nager) On nage à la piscine.

2. (dîner) On dîne au restaurant.

3. (jouer au foot) On joue au foot au stade.

4. (acheter des vêtements) On achète des vêtements dans les grands magasins.

5. (parler français) On parle français en France.

6. (parler espagnol) On parle espagnol au Mexique.

- **au Mexique**
- **en France**
- **au stade**
- **à la piscine**
- **à l'école**
- **au restaurant**
- **dans les grands magasins**

B 2. Jobs d'été

The following students have jobs as salespeople this summer. Say what each one is selling.

1.   2.   3.   4.   5.   6.

▶ Caroline vend des maillots de bain.

1. Nous vendons des livres.

2. Vous vendez des CD.

3. Éric et Pierre vendent des vélos.

4. Tu vends des guitares.

5. Je vends des pantalons.

6. Corinne vend des sandwichs.

URB
p. 104

172
Unité 6, Leçon 20
Workbook

Discovering French, Nouveau! Bleu

Nom _____

Classe _____ Date _____ _____

Discovering
FRENCH *Nouveau!*

BLEU

Unité 6
Leçon 20

WorkbookTE

3. Pourquoi?

Explain why people do certain things by completing the sentences with the appropriate form of the verbs in the box. Be logical!

• **attendre**	• **répondre**
• **entendre**	• **vendre**
• **perdre**	• **rendre**

À vendre
INSTRUMENTS
DE MUSIQUE

1. Olivier _vend_ son vélo parce qu'il a besoin d'argent.

2. Nous _perdons_ le match parce que nous ne jouons pas bien.

3. Vous _répondez_ correctement aux questions du prof parce que vous êtes de bons élèves.

4. Tu n'_entends_ pas parce que tu n'écoutes pas.

5. Je _rends_ souvent visite à mes voisins parce qu'ils sont sympathiques.

6. Martine et Julie _attendent_ leurs copains parce qu'elles ont un rendez-vous avec eux.

C 4. Oui ou non?

Tell a French friend to do or not to do the following things according to the situation. Be logical.

▶ (téléphoner) _Ne téléphone pas_ à Sophie. Elle n'est pas chez elle.

▶ (inviter) _Invite_ Jean-Paul. Il est très sympathique.

1. (acheter) _N'achète pas_ cette veste. Elle est trop longue.

2. (choisir) _Choisis_ ce tee-shirt. Il est joli et bon marché.

3. (attendre) _Attends_ tes copains. Ils vont venir dans cinq minutes.

4. (mettre) _Ne mets pas_ ce pantalon. Il est moche et démodé.

5. (aller) _Va_ au cinéma. Il y a un très bon film.

6. (venir) _Viens_ chez moi. J'organise une boum.

7. (apporter) _Apporte_ tes CD. Nous allons danser.

8. (manger) _Ne mange pas_ la pizza. Tu vas grossir.

Nom _____

Classe _____ Date _____

5. Au choix *(Your choice)* (sample answers)

Your friends have asked your advice. Tell them what to do, choosing one of the suggested options. If you wish, you may explain your choice.

▶ aller au théâtre ou au cinéma?

Allez au cinéma. C'est plus amusant (moins cher)!

(Allez au théâtre. C'est plus intéressant!)

1. regarder le film ou le match de baseball?

Regardez le film (le match de baseball).

2. dîner à la maison ou au restaurant?

Dînez à la maison (au restaurant).

3. organiser une boum ou un pique-nique?

Organisez une boum (un pique-nique).

4. étudier le français ou l'espagnol?

Étudiez le français (l'espagnol).

6. Suggestions

It is Saturday. You and your friends are wondering what to do. Suggest that you do the following things together.

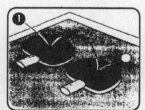

▶ Jouons au basket.

1. Jouons au ping-pong.

2. Regardons la télé.

3. Faisons une promenade à vélo.

4. Allons à la plage.

5. Dînons au restaurant.

6. Allons au cinéma.

Nom _____

Classe _____ Date _____

Discovering FRENCH *Nouveau!*

B L E U

Unité 6
Leçon 20
Workbook TE

7. Communication (sample answers)

Describe three things that you would like to do or buy, and say how much money you need to do so.

▶ J'ai envie d'acheter un baladeur.

J'ai besoin de cinquante dollars.

1. J'ai envie d'aller au cinéma.

   J'ai besoin de sept dollars.

2. J'ai envie d'acheter une casquette.

   J'ai besoin de dix dollars.

3. J'ai envie d'acheter des bottes.

   J'ai besoin de quatre-vingts dollars.

les 300 films de la semaine
cinéscope
Du mercredi 27 février au mardi 5 mars

Le Club 20 Ans
à la mode américaine

1er, 2ème ÉTAGES

URB p. 107

Discovering French, Nouveau! Bleu

Unité 6, Leçon 20
Workbook 175

Nom _____

Classe _____ Date _____

Discovering FRENCH *Nouveau!*

B L E U

Unité 6
Leçon 20
Activités pour tous TE

LEÇON 20 Alice a un job

A

Activité 1 Où est-on?

People are eating local foods: match the capital cities on the right with the foods on the left.

_b_ 1. On mange des croissants.   a. On est à Tokyo.

_e_ 2. On mange des tacos.   b. On est à Paris.

_a_ 3. On mange du sushi.   c. On est à Rome.

_c_ 4. On mange des spaghettis.   d. On est à Washington.

_d_ 5. On mange des hot dogs.   e. On est à Mexico.

Activité 2 Quelques activités

Making your selections from the box, fill in the blanks with the correct conjugated verbs.

| perds | rends visite | réponds | perdons | attendez | entendez |

1. Le téléphone sonne. Tu _réponds_ ?

2. Je _rends visite_ à mes grands-parents.

3. Est-ce que vous _entendez_ bien la radio?

4. Est-ce que nous gagnons ou nous _perdons_ ?

5. Ah, non! C'est la troisième fois que je _perds_ mes clés.

6. Qui est-ce que vous _attendez_ ?

Activité 3 Allez!

Change the following statements to imperatives by crossing out words or letters.

Modèle: Tu écoutes le prof. > ~~Tu~~ écoute~~s~~ le prof!

1. ~~Nous~~ faisons une promenade.   4. ~~Tu~~ achètes le livre.

2. ~~Vous~~ gagnez le match.   5. ~~Tu~~ regardes le tableau.

3. ~~Nous~~ attendons le bus.   6. ~~Tu~~ prépares le dîner.

Nom _____

Classe _____ Date _____

Discovering
FRENCH
Nouveau!

B L E U

B

Activité 1 Les endroits

Determine whether the following statements are generally true or false and circle **Vrai** or **Faux**.

1. Au musée, on regarde des films. — Vrai **(Faux)**

2. Dans un grand magasin, on peut acheter des vêtements. — **(Vrai)** Faux

3. Dans un centre commercial, on peut visiter beaucoup de magasins. — **(Vrai)** Faux

4. Aux grands magasins, on peut dépenser trop d'argent. — **(Vrai)** Faux

5. À la bibliothèque, on vend des livres. — Vrai **(Faux)**

Activité 2 Quelques activités

Read the questions and look at the pictures on the left. Fill in the blanks on the right to complete the answers with the correct verb form and vocabulary.

1. —Qu'est-ce que tu vends?

   —Je _vends_ mon _appareil-photo_.

2. —À qui est-ce que vous rendez visite ce week-end?

   —Nous _rendons visite_ à nos _grands-parents_.

3. —Qui perd?

   —Les joueurs de notre _école_ _perdent_ maintenant.

4. —Qu'est-ce que vous attendez?

   —Nous _attendons_ le _bus_. Eux,

   ils _attendent_ un _copain_.

5. —Où est-ce que vous allez attendre?

   —Nous allons _attendre_ _à la maison_.

Activité 3 Allez!

Rewrite the following statements to make imperatives.

Modèle: Tu écoutes le prof. > Écoute le prof!

1. Nous rendons visite aux copains.
   Rendons visite aux copains!

2. Vous gagnez le match.
   Gagnez le match!

3. Nous attendons Dominique.
   Attendons Dominique!

4. Tu fais tes devoirs.
   Fais tes devoirs!

5. Tu vas aux grands magasins.
   Va aux grands magasins!

6. Tu regardes le tableau.
   Regarde le tableau!

URB
p. 110

104

Unité 6, Leçon 20
Activités pour tous

Discovering French, Nouveau! Bleu

C

Activité 1 Des questions answers will vary

Answer the following questions using **on**.

1. Est-ce que toi et tes copains, vous allez à l'école le samedi?

   Non, le samedi, on ne va pas à l'école.

2. Est-ce que vous allez à la bibliothèque municipale le samedi?

   Oui, le samedi, on va à la bibliothèque.

3. Est-ce que vous faites souvent des promenades à vélo?

   Non, on ne fait pas beaucoup de promenades à vélo.

4. Est-ce que vous trouvez le français difficile?

   Oui, on trouve le français difficile!

Activité 2 Quelques activités

Fill in each blank with the appropriate form of one of the verbs in the box.

attendre	entendre	perdre	rendre visite	répondre	vendre

1. Allons-y! Les copains attendent .

2. Je vends mon vieux vélo demain.

3. Est-ce que tu perds souvent ton parapluie?

4. J' entends le téléphone! Tu vas répondre ?

5. Tu attends le train? Voilà! Il arrive maintenant.

6. L'été, nous rendons visite à nos grands-parents.

Activité 3 Allez!

You are babysitting. Tell the children to do or not to do the following.

Modèle: Alain, ne mange pas trop!

1. Ludovic répond au téléphone. Ludovic, ne répond pas au téléphone!

2. Claire et Inès jouent avec l'ordinateur. Claire et Inès, ne jouez pas avec l'ordinateur!

3. Monique n'attend pas son frère. Monique, attend ton frère!

4. Sylvie ne vient pas là. Sylvie, viens là!

5. Bernard et Serge vont dans le jardin. Bernard et Serge, n'allez pas dans le jardin!

LEÇON 20 Alice a un job, pages 284–285

Objectives

Communicative Functions and Topics
To talk about where to go shopping, what you need, what you like
To use money-related expressions and find out prices
To give advice and indicate approval
To give commands

Linguistic Goals
To use regular -re verbs and the verb *payer*
To use the pronoun *on* and the imperative
To pronounce the letters *"an"* and *"en"*

Cultural Goals
To learn about the ways in which young people earn money

Motivation and Focus

❏ Have students preview the photos on pages 284–285. Encourage comments about the jobs pictured. Compare the jobs in the photos to local jobs that young people have.

❏ Use WARM-UP AND REVIEW, page 284 of the TE, with **Overhead Transparency** 20 to practice vocabulary.

Presentation and Explanation

❏ *Lesson Opener:* Together, read the introductory paragraph, page 284. Play **Video** 20.1 or **Audio** CD 3, Tracks 37–38, or model the opening conversation, pausing to check comprehension. Ask students to read the dialogue and discuss its content.

❏ *Note culturelle:* Ask students to read *L'argent des jeunes*, page 285. Compare work opportunities for French and American young people.

❏ *Vocabulaire:* Introduce money vocabulary on page 286. Model using the words and expressions. Have students create other questions and sentences using the vocabulary.

❏ *Grammar A:* Explain the pronoun *on* on page 288. Show how it is used in general statements with third-person singular verb forms.

❏ *Grammar B:* Present regular -re verbs on page 290. Play **Audio** CD 3, Tracks 39–40. Introduce other -re verbs with **Overhead Transparency** 41.

❏ *Grammar C:* Model giving commands using the imperative on page 291. Point out affirmative and negative forms.

❏ *Prononciation:* Explain the pronunciation of *"an"* and *"en"* on page 293. Play **Audio** CD 3, Track 11 and have students repeat the words and sentences.

Guided Practice and Checking Understanding

❏ Use the activities on **Overhead Transparencies** pages A104–A105 and Transparencies 16 and 41 to practice -re verbs.

❏ Check listening comprehension with **Workbook** Listening Activities A–G (pages 169–171). Play **Audio** CD 10, Tracks 21–27 or read **Audioscript** pages 133–135 for the activities.

❏ Play **Video** Module 20 or read **Videoscript** pages 130–131 as students complete **Video Activities** pages 124–128.

Independent Practice

❏ Model the activities on pages 286–293. Assign Activities 3–5, 8–11 and 14 for homework. Model and have students practice Activities 1–2, 6–7, 12–13, and 15 as PAIR PRACTICE.

❏ Use any of the following for pair practice: **Communipak** *Tu as la parole* 1–6, pages 142–143, or *Conversations* 2–8, pages 144–147; or **Video Activities** page 129.

❏ Have students do the activities in **Activités pour tous**, pages 103–105.

Discovering
FRENCH
Nouveau!

BLEU

Unité 6
Leçon 20

Lesson Plans

Monitoring and Adjusting

❑ Assign the Writing Activities in the **Workbook** (pages 172–175).
❑ Monitor use of *-re* verbs and the imperative as students work on practice activities. Point out grammar and vocabulary boxes, pages 286–291. Explain information in LANGUAGE NOTES and PRONUNCIATION NOTES, pages 289–293 of the TE. Use TEACHING STRATEGIES on page 290 of the TE to explain verb endings.

End-of-Lesson Activities

❑ *À votre tour!:* Have students prepare Activities 1–2 on page 294 and then do them as PAIR PRACTICE. They can use **Audio** CD 3, Tracks 42–43 to check their responses. Assign Activities 3–4 for homework. Have students practice writing advice in Activity 5, page 295.

Review

❑ Have students review the information they learned in this unit by completing the *Tests de contrôle* activities on pages 296–297. Encourage students to use the page references in the **Review . . .** tabs to verify/clarify grammar and vocabulary.

Reteaching

❑ Redo appropriate activities from the **Workbook.**
❑ Assign the **Video** for review or for make-up work.

Assessment

❑ Use Quiz 20 on pages 136–137 after students have completed the lesson. Administer Unit Test 6 (Form A or B) on pages 166–174 of **Unit Resources** as a comprehensive assessment of the unit. You may also do any or all of the **Performance Tests** for the unit.
❑ Use Comprehensive Test 2 (Form A or B) on pages 197–220 of **Unit Resources** to assess Units 4–6.

Extension and Enrichment

❑ Play the GAME: DRILLING WITH DICE, pages 292–293 of the TE, for more practice with verb forms.

Summary and Closure

❑ As pairs of students present any of the **Communipak** activities for this unit, have the rest of the class summarize functions and structures that have been learned.
❑ Do PORTFOLIO ASSESSMENT on page 295 of the TE.

End-of-Unit Activities

❑ *Entracte 6:* Use the suggestions in the TE margins to read and discuss the selections on pages 300–305.
❑ *Reading and Culture Activities:* Assign **Workbook** activities (pages 177–179).

LEÇON 20   Alice a un job, page 284

Block Schedule (5 Days to Complete – including Unit Test)

Objectives

Communicative Functions and Topics
To talk about where to go shopping, what you need, what you like
To use money-related expressions and find out prices
To give advice and indicate approval
To give commands

Linguistic Goals
To use regular -*re* verbs and the verb **payer**
To use the pronoun **on** and the imperative
To pronounce the letters *"an"* and *"en"*

Cultural Goals
To learn about the ways in which young people earn money

Block Schedule

Change of Pace To practice the imperative and the expressions *avoir besoin de*, and *avoir envie de*, have groups of three students write and act out a dialogue based on activity 13 on page 292. The first student will play a character wondering whether he or she should do certain things. The second student will be the angel who gives her good advice. The third student will play the role of the devil and give the first student bad advice. ■

Day 1

Motivation and Focus

❏ Have students preview the photos on pages 284–285. Encourage comments about the jobs pictured. Compare the jobs in the photos to local jobs that young people have.

❏ Use WARM-UP AND REVIEW, page 284 of the TE, with **Overhead Transparency** 20 to practice vocabulary.

Presentation and Explanation

❏ *Lesson Opener:* Together, read the introductory paragraph, page 284. Play **Video** 20.1 or **Audio** CD 3, Tracks 37–38, or model the opening conversation, pausing to check comprehension. Ask students to read the dialogue and discuss its content.

❏ *Note culturelle:* Ask students to read *L'argent des jeunes*, page 285. Compare work opportunities for French and American young people.

❏ *Vocabulaire:* Introduce money vocabulary on page 286. Model using the words and expressions. Have students create other questions and sentences using the vocabulary.

❏ *Grammar A:* Explain the pronoun **on** on page 288. Show how it is used in general statements with third-person singular verb forms.

❏ *Grammar B:* Present regular -*re* verbs on page 290. Play **Audio** CD 3, Tracks 39–40. Introduce other -*re* verbs with **Overhead Transparency** 41.

❏ *Grammar C:* Model giving commands using the imperative on page 291. Point out affirmative and negative forms.

❏ *Prononciation:* Explain the pronunciation of *"an"* and *"en"* on page 293. Play **Audio** CD 3, Track 41 and have students repeat the words and sentences.

Discovering
FRENCH
Nouveau!

BLEU

Unité 6
Leçon 20

Block Scheduling
Lesson Plans

Guided Practice and Checking Understanding

❑ Use the activities on **Overhead Transparencies** pages A104–A105 and Transparencies 16 and 41 to practice *-re* verbs.

❑ Check listening comprehension with **Workbook** Listening Activities A–G (pages 169–171). Play **Audio** CD 10, Tracks 21–27 or read **Audioscript** pages 133–135 for the activities.

Day 2

Motivation and Focus

❑ Play **Video** Module 20 or read **Videoscript** pages 130–131 as students complete **Video Activities** pages 124–128.

Independent Practice

❑ Model the activities on pages 286–293. Assign Activities 3–5, 8–11 and 14 for homework. Model and have students practice Activities 1, 2, 6, 7, 12–13, and 15 as PAIR PRACTICE.

❑ Use any of the following for pair practice: **Communipak** *Tu as la parole* 1–6, pages 142–143, or *Conversations* 2–8, pages 144–147; or **Video Activities** page 129.

❑ Have students do the activities in **Activités pour tous**, pages 103–105.

Monitoring and Adjusting

❑ Assign the Writing Activities in the **Workbook** (pages 172–175).

❑ Monitor use of *-re* verbs and the imperative as students work on practice activities. Point out grammar and vocabulary boxes, pages 286–291. Explain information in LANGUAGE NOTES and PRONUNCIATION NOTES, pages 289–293 of the TE. Use TEACHING STRATEGIES on page 290 of the TE to explain verb endings.

Day 3

End-of-Lesson Activities

❑ *À votre tour!:* Have students prepare Activities 1–2 on page 294 and then do them as PAIR PRACTICE. They can use the **Audio** CD 3, Tracks 42–43 to check their responses. Assign Activities 3–4 for homework. Have students practice writing advice in Activity 5, page 295.

Review

❑ Have students review the information they learned in this unit by completing the *Tests de contrôle* activities on pages 296–297. Encourage students to use the page references in the **Review . . .** tabs to verify/clarify grammar and vocabulary.

Reteaching (as needed)

❑ Redo appropriate activities from the **Workbook**.

❑ Assign the **Video** for review or for make-up work.

Extension and Enrichment

❑ Play the GAME: DRILLING WITH DICE, pages 292–293 of the TE, for more practice with verb forms.

❑ Use **Block Scheduling Copymasters**, pages 153–160.

❑ For expansion activities, direct students to www.classzone.com.

Summary and Closure

❏ As pairs of students present any of the **Communipak** activities for this unit, have the rest of the class summarize functions and structures that have been learned.
❏ Do PORTFOLIO ASSESSMENT on page 295 of the TE.

Assessment

❏ Use Quiz 20 on pages 136–137 after students have completed the lesson. The **Test Generator** can be used to adjust the quiz to meet the class's specific needs.

Day 4

End-of-Unit Activities

Note: These activities may be done at the end of the unit, or at any time that seems appropriate during the unit.

❏ Administer Unit Test 6 (Form A or B) on pages 166–174 of **Unit Resources** as a comprehensive assessment of the unit.
❏ Do any or all of the **Performance Tests** for the unit.
❏ Use Comprehensive Test 2 (Form A or B) on pages 197–220 of **Unit Resources** to assess Units 4–6.

Day 5

Assessment

❏ Give Unit Test 6 (Form A or B) on pages 166–174.
❏ For assessment of specific language skills, select the appropriate **Performance Tests.** Any of the test questions can be modified using the **Test Generator.**

Notes

Nom _____

Classe _____ Date _____

Discovering
FRENCH
Nouveau!

B L E U

Unité 6
Leçon 20

Absent Student
Copymasters

LEÇON 20   Alice a un job, pages 284–285

Materials Checklist

- **Student Text**
- **Audio** CD 3, Tracks 37–38
- **Video 3** or **DVD 2;** Counter 54:15–55:10

Steps to Follow

- Read *Alice a un job* (p. 284).
- Read the *Compréhension* questions (p. 285) before you watch the **Video** or **DVD,** or listen to the **CD.**
- Watch **Video 3** or **DVD 2;** Counter 54:15–55:10, or listen to **Audio** CD 3, Tracks 37–38. Repeat everything you hear.
- Answer the *Compréhension* questions (p. 285). Write your answers in complete sentences on a separate sheet of paper.
- Read *Note culturelle* (p. 285).

If You Don't Understand . . .

- Watch the **Video** or **DVD** in a quiet place. Try to stay focused. If you get lost, stop the **Video** or **DVD.** Replay it and find your place.
- Listen to the **CD** in a quiet place. Try to stay focused. If you get lost, stop the **CD.** Replay it and find your place.
- Repeat aloud with the audio. Try to sound like the people on the recording.
- Say aloud anything you write. Make sure you understand everything you say.
- Write down any questions so that you can ask your teacher or your partner later.

Self-Check

Answers the following questions in complete sentences on a separate sheet of paper.

1. Est-ce que les jeunes Français travaillent dans les supermarchés, les boutiques ou les stations-service?
2. Est-ce que les jeunes Français dépendent de la générosité de leurs parents pour leur argent?
3. Quel est le montant en moyenne que reçoivent les jeunes Français de 15–17 ans?
4. Est-ce que les jeunes Français reçoivent de l'argent de leur famille pour des occasions spéciales?

Answers

occasions spéciales.
euros par mois.   4. Oui, les jeunes Français reçoivent de l'argent de leur famille pour des
argent.   3. Le montant en moyenne que reçoivent les jeunes Français de 15–17 ans est de 100
stations-service.   2. Oui, les jeunes Français dépendent de la générosité de leurs parents pour leur
1. Non, les jeunes Français ne travaillent pas dans les supermarchés, les boutiques ou les

Nom _____

Classe _____ Date _____

Vocabulaire: L'argent, pages 286–287

Materials Checklist

- **Student Text**

Steps to Follow

- Study *Vocabulaire: L'argent* (p. 286). Copy the words and the model sentences on a separate sheet of paper.
- Do Activity 1 in the text (p. 286). Write the parts for both speakers in complete sentences on a separate sheet of paper. Read both parts aloud.
- Do Activity 2 in the text (p. 287). Write the parts for all speakers on a separate sheet of paper. Be logical.
- Do Activities 3–4 in the text (p. 287). Write the answers in complete sentences.

If You Don't Understand . . .

- Reread the activity directions. Put the directions in your own words.
- Read the model several times. Be sure you understand it.
- Say aloud anything you write. Make sure you understand everything you say.
- When writing a sentence, ask yourself, "What do I mean? What am I trying to say?"
- Write down any questions so that you can ask your teacher or your partner later.

Self-Check

Answer the following questions according to the indications given in parentheses.

1. Est-ce que Jean a besoin de travailler? (oui)
2. Est-ce que Marise et Hélène ont envie d'aller au cinéma ce soir? (non)
3. C'est toi qui paies ce soir? (oui)
4. Combien d'argent est-ce que vous gagnez par mois? (1 000 euros)
5. Est-ce que nous dépensons trop d'argent? (non)
6. Tu as des billets et des pièces dans ta poche? (oui)

Answers

et des pièces dans ma poche.

1. **Oui,** Jean a besoin de travailler. / **Oui,** il a besoin de travailler.   2. **Non,** elles n'ont pas envie d'aller au cinéma ce soir. / **Non,** Marise et Hélène n'ont pas envie d'aller au cinéma ce soir.   3. **Oui,** c'est moi qui paie ce soir.   4. Je gagne 1 000 euros par mois.   5. **Non,** vous ne dépensez pas trop d'argent. / **Non,** nous ne dépensons pas trop d'argent.   6. **Oui,** j'ai des billets

Nom _____

Classe _____ Date _____

Discovering
FRENCH
Nouveau!

B L E U

Unité 6
Leçon 20
Absent Student
Copymasters

A. Le pronom *on,* page 288
Vocabulaire: Expression pour la conversation, page 289

Materials Checklist

- **Student Text**
- **Audio** CD 10, Tracks 21–23
- **Video 3** or **DVD 2;** Counter 55:11–58:13
- **Workbook**

Steps to Follow

- Study *Le pronom* **on** (p. 288). Copy the model sentences. Underline *on*.
- Watch **Video 3** or **DVD 2;** Counter 55:11–58:13. Repeat everything you hear.
- Do Activity 5 in the text (p. 288). Write the answers in complete sentences.
- Study *Vocabulaire: Expression pour la conversation* (p. 289).
- Do Activities 6 and 7 in the text (p. 289). Write the parts for both speakers on a separate sheet of paper. Read both parts aloud.
- Do Activity 8 in the text (p. 289). Write the answers in complete sentences.
- Do Writing Activity A, 1 in the **Workbook** (page 172).
- Do Listening Activities A–C in the **Workbook** (pp. 169–170). Use **Audio** CD 10, Tracks 21–23.

If You Don't Understand . . .

- Watch the **Video** or **DVD** in a quiet place. Try to stay focused. If you get lost, stop the **Video** or **DVD**. Replay it and find your place.
- Listen to the **CD** in a quiet place. Try to stay focused. If you get lost, stop the **CD**. Replay it and find your place.
- Reread the activity directions. Put the directions in your own words.
- Read the model several times. Be sure you understand it.
- Say aloud anything you write. Make sure you understand everything you say.
- When writing a sentence, ask yourself, "What do I mean? What am I trying to say?"
- Write down any questions so that you can ask your teacher or your partner later.

Self-Check

Answer the following questions according to the indications given in parentheses.

1. Est-ce qu'on va au cinéma ce soir? (non / rester à la maison)
2. À quelle heure est-ce qu'on dîne? (8 heures)
3. Est-ce qu'on va jouer au tennis demain? (non / au football)
4. Qu'est-ce qu'on va mettre pour aller au concert? (une veste / un jean)
5. Est-ce qu'on va acheter des vêtements aujourd'hui? (non / des CD)
6. Pourquoi est-ce qu'on va mettre un imper? (il pleut)

Answers

1. Non, on va rester à la maison. 2. On dîne à huit heures. 3. Non, on va jouer au football. 4. On va mettre une veste et un jean. 5. Non, on va acheter des CD. 6. On va mettre un imper parce qu'il pleut.

Nom _____

Classe _____ Date _____

B. Les verbes réguliers en –re, pages 290–291

Materials Checklist

- **Student Text**
- **Audio** CD 3, Tracks 39–40
- **Workbook**

Steps to Follow

- Listen to **Audio** CD 3, Tracks 39–40. Repeat everything you hear.
- Study *Les verbes réguliers en -re* (p. 290). Copy the conjugation of **vendre** on a separate sheet of paper.
- Study *Vocabulaire: Verbes réguliers en –re* (p. 290). Copy the list of –**re** verbs. Check meanings.
- Do Activity 9 in the text (p. 290). Write the answers on a separate sheet of paper. Underline the verb in each sentence.
- Do Activities 10–11 in the text (p. 291). Write the answers on a separate sheet of paper. Underline the verb in each sentence. Check meanings.
- Do Writing Activities B, 2–3 in the **Workbook** (pages 172–173).

If You Don't Understand . . .

- Listen to the **CD** in a quiet place. Try to stay focused. If you get lost, stop the **CD**. Replay it and find your place. Repeat what you hear. Try to sound like the people in the recording.
- Reread the activity directions. Put the directions in your own words.
- Read the model several times. Be sure you understand it.
- Say aloud everything that you write. Be sure you understand what you are saying.
- When writing a sentence, ask yourself, "What do I mean? What am I trying to say?"
- Write down any questions so that you can ask your teacher or your partner later.

Self-Check

Complete the following sentences using the correct form of **attendre, perdre, vendre, entendre, répondre à,** or **rendre visite à.** Underline the verb in each sentence.

1. Il . . . sa vieille voiture. Il va acheter une nouvelle voiture.
2. Je . . . toujours au tennis. Je n'aime pas ce sport!
3. Tu . . . ta copine? Elle est en retard?
4. Nous . . . un bruit mystérieux. C'est le chat qui gratte (*is scratching*)?
5. Cet été nous . . . visite à mes grands-parents.
6. Est-ce que vous . . . la question? Quelle est votre réponse?

Answers

1. Il <u>vend</u> sa vieille voiture. 2. Je <u>perds</u> toujours au tennis. 3. Tu <u>attends</u> ta copine? 4. Nous <u>entendons</u> un bruit mystérieux. 5. Cet été nous <u>rendons</u> visite à mes grands-parents. 6. Est-ce que vous <u>répondez</u> à la question?

Nom _____

Classe _____ Date _____

Discovering FRENCH *Nouveau!*

BLEU

Unité 6
Leçon 20

Absent Student
Copymasters

C. L'impératif, pages 291–293

Materials Checklist

- **Student Text**
- **Audio** CD 3, Tracks 41–43; CD 10, Tracks 24–27
- **Workbook**

Steps to Follow

- Study *L'impératif* (p. 291). Read *Learning about Language*. How is the imperative used? Copy the chart on a separate sheet of paper.
- Do Activities 12–14 in the text (p. 292). Write your answers in complete sentences on a separate sheet of paper. Underline the imperative verbs, for example, "***Apporte une pizza!***" Check the verb endings.
- Do Activity 15 in the text (p. 293). Write the parts for both speakers in complete sentences on a separate sheet of paper. Underline the imperative verbs. Check the verb endings.
- Read the list of words in *Prononciation: Les lettres «an» et «en»* in the text (p. 293). Listen to **Audio** CD 3, Track 41. Repeat everything you hear.
- Do Writing Activities C, 4–7 in the **Workbook** (pages 173–174).
- Do Listening Activities D–G in the **Workbook** (pages 170–171). Use **Audio CD** 10, Tracks 24–27.
- Do Activities 1–5 of *À votre tour!* in the text (pp. 294-295). Use **Audio CD** 3, Tracks 42–43 with Activities 1–2.

If You Don't Understand . . .

- Listen to the **CDs** in a quiet place. Try to stay focused. If you get lost, stop the **CDs**. Replay them and find your place.
- Listen once without repeating. Then replay and repeat aloud with the audio. Try to sound like the people on the recording. Imitate their sounds and accents. Pause the **CDs** if you can't keep up.
- Reread the activity directions. Put the directions in your own words.
- Read the model several times before beginning so you are certain what to do. Copy the model. Say aloud everything that you write. Listen and be sure you understand what you are saying.

Self-Check

Write one affirmative and one negative command using the following verbs and the person indicated in parentheses.

acheter / maillot de bain rose / (tu)

Achète le maillot de bain rose! N'achète pas le maillot de bain rose!

1. attendre / Jean / (nous)
2. finir / le travail / (vous)
3. faire / attention / (vous)

4. parler / plus fort / (tu)
5. venir / chez moi / (tu)
6. jouer / au tennis / (nous)

Answers

1. Attendons Jean! / N'attendons pas Jean! 2. Finissez le travail! / Ne finissez pas le travail! 3. Faites attention! / Ne faites pas attention! 4. Parle plus fort! / Ne parle pas plus fort! 5. Viens chez moi! /Ne viens pas chez moi! 6. Jouons au tennis! / Ne jouons pas au tennis!

LEÇON 20 Alice a un job

L'envie

Interview a family member. Find out what he or she feels like doing. Ask him or her to choose among the following activities.

- First, explain your assignment.
- Then, model the pronunciation of the words below each picture. Point to the picture as you model each answer.
- Ask the question, **Tu as envie de . . . ?**
- When you have an answer, complete the sentence at the bottom of the page.

dîner au restaurant?

jouer au tennis?

aller au cinéma?

faire une promenade?

_____ a envie de (d') _____ .

Nom _____

Classe _____ Date _____

Discovering
FRENCH *Nouveau!*

BLEU

Unité 6
Leçon 20

Family Involvement

Jouons!

Ask a family member what he or she wants to play. Have the family member suggest that you play one of the following games.

- First, explain your assignment.
- Then, model the pronunciation of the words below each picture. Point to the picture as you model each answer.
- Model the pronunciation of the answer, **Jouons . . .**
- Ask the question, **Tu veux jouer . . . ?**
- When you have an answer, write a sentence saying what you both are going to do.

au baseball?

au volley?

au tennis?

au basket?

Jouons _____ .

Discovering
FRENCH
Nouveau

BLEU

MODULE 20   Alice a un job

Video 3, DVD 2

20 Activité 1. Où travaille Alice?

Counter 53:31–54:14

Alice has a new job. Where does she work?
Watch the video to find out. If a statement
below is true, circle **vrai.** If it is false, circle
faux.

1. Alice travaille dans un magasin de matériel audio-visuel.   **vrai   faux**

2. Dans ce magasin, on vend toutes sortes de choses.   **vrai   faux**

3. On vend des ordinateurs et des calculatrices.   **vrai   faux**

4. Un jour son frère rend visite à Alice.   **vrai   faux**

20.1 Activité 2. Alice et Jérôme

Counter 54:15–55:10

What do Alice and Jérôme say to each other at the store where Alice works? Watch the
following scene on the video. Draw a line from each sentence below to the person who
says it on the video.

1. —Salut, ça va?

2. —C'est super!

Jérôme

3. —Tu es bien payée?

4. —Qu'est-ce que tu vas
faire avec ton argent?

5. —Je n'ai pas d'argent.

Alice

6. —Cherche un job!

Nom _____

Classe _____ Date _____

Discovering FRENCH *Nouveau!*

B L E U

Unité 6
Leçon 20

Video Activities

20.2 Activité 3. Qu'est-ce qu'on fait?

Watch the video, paying attention to the use of the word **on.** Circle the letter of the correct completion to each sentence below as you watch. The sentences are in the same order as you hear them in the video.

1. —On vend des . . .   a. jeux vidéo   b. ordinateurs   c. vêtements

2. —On vend des . . .   a. hamburgers   b. pizzas   c. sandwichs

3. —Bien sûr! On parle . . .   a. anglais   b. espagnol   c. français

20.3 Activité 4. Qu'est-ce qu'on vend ici?

What products do different stores sell? After you watch the video segment, draw a line from each sentence to the corresponding picture.

1. On vend des crêpes.

a.

2. On vend des chaussures.

b.

3. On vend des vélos.

c.

4. On vend les livres.

d.

Nom _____

Classe _____ Date _____

Discovering
FRENCH
Nouveau!

BLEU

20.4 Activité 5. D'accord!

What are the people in the video going to do? As you watch the video, fill in each blank with the letter of the correct completion to each sentence. (*Note:* The sentences on the left appear in the same order you hear them on the video.)

1. On dîne _____.

2. D'accord! _____!

3. Allons _____.

4. Regardons _____.

5. Achetons _____.

6. Allons _____.

7. Faisons _____.

a. au cinéma

b. une promenade

c. des glaces

d. à sept heures et demie

e. au café

f. Dansons

g. « La Roue de la fortune »

Nom _____

Classe _____ Date _____

Discovering
FRENCH *Nouveau!*

B L E U

Unité 6
Leçon 20

Video Activities

20.5 Activité 6. On joue au tennis?

People are inviting you to do things and you agree. After you watch the video segment, fill in each blank with the correct form of the appropriate verb from the box. (*Note:* Some verbs are used more than once. The first item has been done for you.)

visiter	dîner	faire	jouer	aller	regarder

▶ D'accord! *Jouons* _____ au tennis.

1. D'accord, _____ au volley.

2. D'accord, _____ une promenade en ville.

3. D'accord, _____ au cinéma.

4. D'accord, _____ au restaurant.

5. D'accord, _____ aux jeux vidéo.

20.6 Activité 7. Au magasin hi-fi

Listen and watch the **Vignette culturelle** as Alice shows products she sells in the hi-fi store.
Mark an **X** next to each item she mentions as you hear it.

a. _____ le casque

b. _____ le CD

c. _____ des chaînes hi-fi

d. _____ un lecteur de DVD

e. _____ une calculatrice

f. _____ une mini-chaîne

g. _____ un ordinateur

h. _____ une pile

i _____ la radio

j. _____ un DVD

k. _____ une télé

l. _____ une console de jeux vidéo

m. _____ un baladeur

n. _____ le tuner

o. _____ le plateau CD

p. _____ l'amplificateur

q. _____ les enceintes

Nom _____

Classe _____ Date _____ _____

Discovering FRENCH *Nouveau!*

BLEU

Unité 6
Leçon 20

Video Activities

 Activité 8. J'ai un job!

Now you have a sales job—either real or imaginary! Fill in the chart on the left with information about your job. When you have finished, use the **Phrases utiles** to interview a classmate to find out about his or her job. Record the information in the chart on the right. Your partner will interview you and record the appropriate information on his or her paper.

Le job de mon/ma camarade

Nom: _____

Job: _____

Compagnie: _____

Produits qu'il/elle vend: _____

_____

Salaire: _____ par l'heure

Avec son argent il/elle va . . . _____

_____

Mon job

Nom: _____

Job: _____

Compagnie: _____

Produits que je vends: _____

_____

Salaire: _____ par l'heure

Avec mon argent je vais . . . _____

_____

«» | ***Phrases utiles***

Comment t'appelles-tu?

Combien est-ce que tu
  gagnes par heure?

Quel est ton job?

Où est-ce que tu travailles?

Qu'est-ce que tu as envie de
  faire avec ton argent?

Qu'est-ce que tu vends?

URB
p. 129

BLEU

MODULE 20   Alice a un job

Video 3, DVD 2   Counter 53:31–54:14

Alice a un nouveau job. Elle travaille dans un magasin de matériel audio-visuel. Dans ce magasin, on vend toutes sortes de choses: des baladeurs, des chaînes hi-fi, des radiocassettes/CD, des lecteurs de DVD. Un jour son cousin Jérôme lui rend visite.

20.1 Dialogue: Alice a un job
Counter 54:15–55:10

JÉRÔME: Salut, ça va?
ALICE: Oui, ça va.
JÉRÔME: Et ce nouveau job?
ALICE: C'est super.
JÉRÔME: Qu'est-ce qu'on vend dans ton magasin?
ALICE: Eh bien, tu vois, on vend toutes sortes de matériel audio-visuel . . . Moi, je vends des mini-chaînes.
JÉRÔME: Tu es bien payée?
ALICE: Non, on n'est pas très bien payé, mais on a des réductions sur l'équipement stéréo et sur les CD et les DVD.
JÉRÔME: Qu'est-ce que tu vas faire avec ton argent?
ALICE: Je ne sais pas . . . J'ai envie de voyager cet été.
JÉRÔME: Tu as de la chance. Moi aussi, j'ai envie de voyager, mais je n'ai pas d'argent.
ALICE: Écoute, Jérôme, si tu as besoin d'argent, fais comme moi.
JÉRÔME: Comment?
ALICE: Cherche un job!

20.2 Mini-scenes: Listening— Qu'est-ce qu'on vend?
Counter 55:11–55:59

*Did you notice how Alice and Jérôme used the pronoun **on**? Watch again.*

JÉRÔME: Qu'est-ce qu'on vend dans ton magasin?
ALICE: Eh bien, tu vois, on vend toutes sortes de matériel audio-visuel.

*French people use the pronoun **on** to mean "one, you, they, or people, in general."* [screen card]

*Listen for **on** as you watch the following dialogues.*

—Qu'est-ce qu'on vend ici?
—On vend des vêtements.

—Qu'est-ce qu'on vend ici?
—On vend des pizzas.

—Est-ce qu'on parle français à Dakar?
—Bien sûr! On parle français!

20.3 Mini-scenes: Speaking— Qu'est-ce qu'on vend ici?
Counter 56:00–56:43

Now, it's your turn to speak. Use the illustrations to answer the question **Qu'est-ce qu'on vend ici?** *What is sold here?*

—Qu'est-ce qu'on vend ici? [screen card]
—On vend des chaussures.

—Qu'est-ce qu'on vend ici? [screen card]
—On vend des vélos.

—Qu'est-ce qu'on vend ici? [screen card]
—On vend des crêpes.

—Qu'est-ce qu'on vend ici? [screen card]
—On vend des livres.

*In conversation, French people often use **on** instead of **nous**, meaning we. Listen for **on** as you watch the following dialogues.*

20.4 Mini-scenes: Listening— On dîne?
Counter 56:44–57:19

—Dis, Maman. À quelle heure est-ce qu'on dîne?
—On dîne à sept heures et demie.
—Salut.
—Salut.

—On danse?
—D'accord! Dansons!

—Qu'est-ce qu'on fait samedi?
—Allons au cinéma!

—Qu'est-ce qu'on regarde?
—Regardons «La Roue de la fortune».

—On achète des glaces?
—C'est une bonne idée! Achetons des glaces!

—On va au café?
—D'accord! Allons au café!

—On fait une promenade?
—Bonne idée! Faisons une promenade.

20.5 Mini-scenes: Speaking— On joue au tennis?
Counter 57:20–58:13

Now, it's your turn to speak. French friends are inviting you to do certain things with them. Accept the invitations.

—On joue au tennis? [screen cue]
—D'accord! Jouons au tennis!

—On joue au volley? [screen cue]
—D'accord, jouons au volley.

—On fait une promenade en ville? [screen cue]
—D'accord, faisons une promenade en ville.

—On va au cinéma? [screen cue]
—D'accord, allons au cinéma.

—On va au restaurant? [screen cue]
—D'accord. Allons au restaurant.

—On joue aux jeux vidéo? [screen cue]
—D'accord. Jouons aux jeux vidéo.

20.6 Vignette culturelle: Au magasin hi-fi
Counter 58:14–1:00

ALICE: Bonjour!
CHRISTOPHE: Bonjour!
ALICE: Je vais vous montrer les différentes choses qu'on vend dans le magasin où je travaille.
CHRISTOPHE: D'accord!
ALICE: Venez! Ça, c'est une radio. Ça, c'est un baladeur. Ici on met le CD. Ça, c'est une pile. Et ça, c'est le casque. Ça, c'est un lecteur de DVD. Ça, c'est un DVD. Ça, c'est une console de jeux-vidéo. Ici, c'est le rayon des chaînes hi-fi.
CHRISTOPHE: Et qu'est-ce que c'est, ça?
ALICE: C'est une mini-chaîne.
CHRISTOPHE: Est-ce que tu peux nous expliquer les différents éléments de la chaîne?
ALICE: Mais oui. Ça, c'est l'amplificateur. Ça, le tuner. Voilà le plateau CD. Et voici les enceintes.
CHRISTOPHE: Et combien coûte cette mini-chaîne?
ALICE: Sept cent soixante euros.
CHRISTOPHE: Ah, merci.
ALICE: Au revoir.
CHRISTOPHE: Au revoir.

LEÇON 20 Alice a un job

PE AUDIO

CD 3, Track 37
Compréhension orale, p. 284

Alice a un nouveau job. Elle travaille dans un magasin de matériel audio-visuel. Dans ce magasin, on vend toutes sortes de choses: des baladeurs, des chaînes hi-fi, des radiocassettes/CD, des lecteurs de DVD…

Un jour son cousin Jérôme lui rend visite.

JÉRÔME: Salut, ça va?
ALICE: Oui, ça va.
JÉRÔME: Et ce nouveau job?
ALICE: C'est super.
JÉRÔME: Qu'est-ce qu'on vend dans ton magasin?
ALICE: Eh bien, tu vois, on vend toutes sortes de matériel audio-visuel . . . Moi, je vends des mini-chaînes.
JÉRÔME: Tu es bien payée?
ALICE: Non, on n'est pas tres bien payé, mais on a des réductions sur l'équipment stéréo et sur les CD et les DVD.
JÉRÔME: Qu'est-ce que tu vas faire avec ton argent?
ALICE: Je ne sais pas . . . J'ai envie de voyager cet été.
JÉRÔME: Tu as de la chance. Moi aussi, j'ai envie de voyager, mais je n'ai pas d'argent.
ALICE: Écoute, Jérôme, si tu as besoin d'argent, fais comme moi.
JÉRÔME: Comment?
ALICE: Cherche un job!

CD 3, Track 38
Écoutez et répétez. p. 284

You will now hear a paused version of the dialog. Listen to the speaker and repeat right after he or she has completed the sentence.

Grammaire: Les verbes réguliers en -re

CD 3, Track 39
Écoutez et répétez. p. 290

Repeat the sentences with vendre.

Je vends ma raquette. #

Tu vends ton scooter. #

Il vend son ordinateur. #

Nous vendons nos livres. #

Vous vendez vos CDs. #

Elles vendent leur voiture. #

Vocabulaire: Verbes réguliers en -re

CD 3, Track 40
Écoutez et répétez. p. 290

Repeat these sentences containing -re verbs.

attendre #   Pierre attend Michèle au café. #

entendre #   Est-ce que tu entends la radio? #

perdre #   Jean-Claude perd le match. #

rendre visite à #   Je rends visite à mon oncle. #

répondre à #   Nous répondons à la question du prof. #

vendre #   À qui vends-tu ton vélo? #

Prononciation

CD 3, Track 41
Les lettres «an» et «en», p. 293

Écoutez: enfant

The letters "an" and "en" represent the nasal vowel / ã /. Be sure not to pronounce the sound "n" after the vowel.

Répétez: / ã / # enfant # an # manteau # collants # grand # élégant #

André mange un grand sandwich.

/ã/ # enfant # en # argent # dépenser #
attends # entend # vend # envie #

Vincent dépense rarement son argent. #

À votre tour!

CD 3, Track 42

1. La bonne réponse, p. 294

Listen to the conversation. *Écoutez la conversation entre Anne et Jean-François.*

ANNE: Est-ce que tu rends visite à tes cousins ce week-end?

JEAN-FRANÇOIS: Non, je reste ici.

ANNE: Tu veux aller dans les boutiques avec moi?

JEAN-FRANÇOIS: Écoute! Je n'ai besoin de vêtements.

ANNE: Est-ce que tu as envie d'aller au cinéma?

JEAN-FRANÇOIS: Bonne idée! Il y a un nouveau film au Majestic.

ANNE: Et après, qu'est-ce qu'on fait?

JEAN-FRANÇOIS: Eh bien, allons au restaurant!

CD 3, Track 43

2. Créa-dialogue, p. 294

Listen to some sample *Créa-dialogues.* *Écoutez les conversations.*

Modèle: —Qu'est-ce qu'on fait samedi?
—Allons au cinéma.
—Je n'ai pas envie d'aller au cinéma.
—Eh bien, rendons visite à nos amis. D'accord?
—Oui, c'est une bonne idée!

Maintenant, écoutez le dialogue numéro 1.

—Qu'est-ce qu'on fait?
—Étudions.
—Je n'ai pas envie d'étudier.
—Eh bien, regardons la télé. D'accord?
—Oui, c'est une bonne idée!

WORKBOOK AUDIO

Section 1. Le pronom *on*

CD 10, Track 21

A. Compréhension orale, p. 169

In conversation, French people often use the pronoun "on" instead of "nous". Note that "on" is followed by the il/elle form of the verb. Listen.

En classe, on parle français.
"In class, we speak French."

Now, you will hear people telling you what they do, using "on" instead of "nous". Listen carefully and write the number of the sentence under the corresponding activity.

Modèle: 1. On dîne. #

You would write the number "one" under picture "c".

Commençons.

2. On va au café. #
3. On mange des glaces. #
4. On écoute de la musique. #
5. On fait une promenade. #
6. On va au cinéma. #
7. On regarde la télé. #

Now check your answers. You should have marked a-6, b-7, d-5, e-3, f-2 and g-4.

CD 10, Track 22

B. Questions et réponses, p. 169

The pronoun "on" is also used to refer to people in general. Listen.

"Qu'est-ce qu'on vend ici?"
This means "What do they sell here?"

At a computer store, one might answer: "On vend des ordinateurs."

Answer the questions you hear according to the illustrations in your Workbook.

Commençons.

1. Qu'est-ce qu'on vend ici? #
   On vend des vélos.
2. Qu'est-ce qu'on vend ici? #
   On vend des chaussures.
3. Qu'est-ce qu'on vend ici? #
   On vend des livres.

CD 10, Track 23

C. Questions et réponses, p. 170

Now, a French person will ask whether people do certain things in the United States. In their questions they will use "vous". Answer them, using "on".

Modèle: Vous parlez anglais? #
   Bien sûr, on parle anglais.

Commençons.

1. Vous jouez au baseball? #
   Bien sûr, on joue au baseball.
2. Vous jouez aux jeux vidéo? #
   Bien sûr, on joue aux jeux vidéo.
3. Vous manger des hamburgers? #
   Bien sûr, on mange des hamburgers.
4. Vous regardez la télé? #
   Bien sûr, on regarde la télé.
5. Vous allez aux concerts? #
   Bien sûr, on va aux concerts.
6. Vous avez des ordinateurs? #
   Bien sûr, on a des ordinateurs.

Section 2. L'impératif

CD 10, Track 24

D. Compréhension orale, p. 170

When we want to make a suggestion or tell someone what to do, we use the imperative. For example, if you want to play tennis, you might say to your friends: "Play tennis with me." or "Let's play tennis."

In French you would say:

"Joue au tennis avec moi." or
"Jouez au tennis avec moi." or
"Jouons au tennis."

Note that in French as in English you do not use subject pronouns when you use the imperative.

Now, you will hear people talking. Can you tell whether they are making a statement or telling people what to do? Listen carefully. If you hear a subject pronoun, they are making a statement. Check Row A. If you do not hear a subject pronoun, they are making a suggestion or telling someone what to do. Check Row B.

Modèle: Vous regardez la télé. #

Since you heard the subject pronoun "vous", you know the person is making a statement. You would check Row A.

Commençons.

1. Tu parles bien français. #
2. Étudiez. #
3. Nous jouons au foot. #
4. Faisons une promenade. #
5. Écoutez le professeur. #
6. Vous dînez au restaurant. #
7. Allons au cinéma. #
8. Attends ton copain. #

Now check your answers. You should have marked Row A for items 1, 3 and 6. You should have marked Row B for items 2, 4, 5, 7 and 8.

CD 10, Track 25

E. Parlez. p. 170

Now, it is your turn to tell people what you would like them to do, using the imperative. First you will speak to one person.

Modèle: Tu dois écouter le professeur. #
   Écoute le professeur.

Commençons.

1. Tu dois écouter ce CD. #
   Écoute ce CD.
2. Tu dois regarder cette photo.#
   Regarde cette photo.
3. Tu dois acheter cette casquette.#
   Achète cette casquette.
4. Tu dois travailler.# Travaille.
5. Tu dois finir ce livre.# Finis ce livre.

Now you will suggest to a group of friends to do what you all like to do.

Modèle: Nous aimons jouer au foot. #
Jouons au foot.

Commençons.

6. Nous aimons regarder la télé. #
Regardons la télé.
7. Nous aimons jouer aux jeux vidéo. #
Jouons aux jeux vidéo.
8. Nous aimons visiter Paris. #
Visitons Paris.
9. Nous aimons faire une promenade. #
Faisons une promenade.
10. Nous aimons aller au cinéma. #
Allons au cinéma.

Section 3. Conversations

CD 10, Track 26

F. La réponse logique, p. 170

You will hear a series of short questions, each one read twice. In your Workbook, circle the letter (a, b, or c) corresponding to the most logical answer.

Commençons.

1. Qu'est-ce que tu vas visiter? #
2. À qui est-ce que tu rends visite? #
3. Tu as besoin d'argent? #

4. Tu as envie d'une pizza? #
5. Qu'est-ce que tu attends? #
6. Pourquoi est-ce que tu vends ta mobylette? #

Now check your answers. You should have circled 1-c, 2-a, 3-c, 4-a, 5-c, and 6-a.

Section 4. Dictée

CD 10, Track 27

G. Écoutez et écrivez. p. 171

You will hear a short dialogue spoken twice. First listen carefully to what the people are saying. The second time you hear the dialogue, fill in the missing words.

Écoutez.

—Qu'est-ce qu'on fait?
—J'ai envie d'aller au cinéma, mais je n'ai pas d'argent.
—De combien est-ce que tu as besoin?
—De dix euros.
—Tiens, voilà dix euros.

Listen again and fill in the missing words.

LESSON 20 QUIZ

Part I: Listening

CD 15, Track 12

A. Questions et réponses

You will hear your French friend Alice ask you six questions. Listen carefully to each question. Then select the MOST LOGICAL response and circle the corresponding letter (a, b, or c). You will hear each question twice.

Let's begin.

1. *Alice is short of cash. She asks:*
Combien d'argent as-tu?
2. *You and Alice are making weekend plans. Alice asks:*

Qu'est-ce que tu as envie de faire samedi?

3. *You and Alice are walking around the mall. Alice asks:*
Qu'est-ce qu'on vend dans ce magasin?

4. *It is Saturday afternoon. Alice is talking to you on the phone. She asks:*
Qu'est-ce qu'on fait?

5. *You and Alice are at a café. Alice asks:*
Tu attends Mélanie?

6. *Alice has a problem and wants some advice. She says:*
J'ai besoin de gagner de l'argent. Qu'est-ce que je peux faire?

Nom _____

Classe _____ Date _____

QUIZ 20

Part I: Listening

A. Questions et réponses (30 points)

You will hear your French friend Alice ask you six questions. Listen carefully to each question and select the MOST LOGICAL answer on your test sheet. Circle the corresponding letter (a, b, or c). You will hear each question twice.

1. Alice is short of cash.
   You reply:
   a. Vingt euros.
   b. Je n'ai pas de job.
   c. C'est toi qui paie.

2. You and Alice are making weekend plans.
   You reply:
   a. Oui, je travaille samedi après-midi.
   b. Non, je n'ai pas besoin d'argent.
   c. Je voudrais aller au cinéma.

3. You and Alice are walking around the mall.
   You reply:
   a. C'est très bon marché.
   b. Des bottes et des chaussures.
   c. Elle vend des appareils-photo.

4. It is Saturday afternoon. Alice is talking to you on the phone.
   You reply:
   a. Ils travaillent.
   b. Je fais un match.
   c. Allons au musée!

5. You and Alice are at a café.
   You reply:
   a. Oui, elle arrive dans cinq minutes.
   b. Oui, j'invite Mélanie à la boum.
   c. Oui, elle rend visite à un copain.

6. Alice has a problem and wants some advice.
   You reply:
   a. Achète un portable.
   b. Cherche un job!
   c. Non, je n'ai pas d'argent.

Nom _____

Classe _____ Date _____ _____

Discovering
FRENCH
Nouveau!
BLEU

Unité 6
Leçon 20

Lesson Quiz

Part II. Writing

B. Activités (25 points)

Complete each of the following sentences with the appropriate form of the verb in parentheses.

1. (vendre)   Madame Moulin _____ des portables.

2. (entendre)   Est-ce que vous _____ la question?

3. (répondre)   Les bons élèves _____ au professeur.

4. (attendre)   J'_____ mes parents.

5. (rendre)   Tu _____ visite à tes grands-parents.

C. Conseils *(Advice)* (25 points)

Read what your friends want to do, and give them some good advice. Complete each sentence with the appropriate AFFIRMATIVE or NEGATIVE IMPERATIVE form of the verb in parentheses.

▶ Tu as besoin d'argent   Travaille _____! (travailler)

1. Tu veux avoir un «A».   _____ à l'examen!   (réussir)

2. Tu veux être à l'heure *(on time)*.   _____ ton copain!   (attendre)

3. Tu veux maigrir.   _____ la pizza!   (manger)

4. Tu veux étudier.   _____ au cinéma!   (aller)

D. Expression personnelle (20 points)

Describe two things that you and your friends DO on weekends and one thing that you DO NOT DO. Use the subject **on.**

UNITÉ 6
Le shopping

CULTURAL CONTEXT: Buying clothes

FUNCTIONS:

- talking about clothes
- discussing shopping plans
- buying clothes
- talking about money

RELATED THEMES:

- clothing and accessories
- adjectives used to describe clothing
- shops that sell clothing
- numbers from 100 to 1000

 **POUR** *COMMUNIQUER* **Communicative Expressions and Thematic Vocabulary**

Nom _____

Classe _____ Date _____

UNITÉ 6   Interviews

In this section you will be interviewed by different people who want to get to know you better. If you wish, you may write the answers to the interview questions in the space provided.

Interview 1

I am doing a survey on what color clothing people wear. Please answer my questions.

- **De quelle couleur est ta chemise / ton tee-shirt?**
- **De quelle couleur est ton pantalon / ta jupe?**
- **De quelle couleur sont tes chaussures?**
- **De quelle couleur sont tes chaussettes?**

Couleurs de vêtements
- Chemise/tee shirt _____
- Pantalon/jupe _____
- Chaussures _____
- Chaussettes _____

Interview 2

I am working for a French teenage fashion magazine and am interested in what you like to wear.

- **En général, est-ce que tu préfères porter une chemise ou un tee-shirt quand tu vas à l'école?**
- **Est-ce que tu préfères mettre des tennis ou des chaussures?**
- **Quand il fait froid, est-ce que tu préfères porter un blouson ou un manteau?**
- **Combien de casquettes as-tu?**

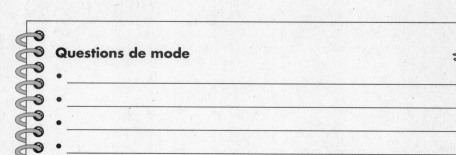

Questions de mode
- _____
- _____
- _____
- _____

Discovering
FRENCH
Nouveau!

B L E U

Interview 3

I want to buy some clothes, but since I am new in town, I need your advice. Tell me about your favorite clothing store.

- **Comment s'appelle ce magasin?**
- **Est-ce qu'il est cher ou bon marché?**
- **Est-ce qu'on vend des survêtements dans ce magasin?**
- **Est-ce qu'on vend des chaussures?**

Magasin de vêtements

- _____
- _____
- _____
- _____

Interview 4

I have just moved to your neighborhood and I would like to know more about it.

- **Quel magasin vend des CD?**
- **Quel magasin vend des vêtements de sport?**
- **Quel magasin vend des chaussures bon marché?**
- **Dans quel restaurant est-ce qu'on mange bien?**

EN VILLE

- _____
- _____
- _____
- _____

Nom _____

Classe _____ Date _____

**Discovering
FRENCH
Nouveau!**

B L E U

Tu as la parole

Read the instructions on the cards below, and give your partner
the corresponding information in French. Take turns reading
your cards and listening to each other.

PRINTEMPS

TU AS LA PAROLE 1   **UNITÉ 6**

Name three things that you buy with your
allowance.

-
-
-

TU AS LA PAROLE 2   **UNITÉ 6**

Answer as if you have the following amounts
of money to spend on clothes. Say what you
are going to buy in each case.

- **Avec 25 dollars, je vais acheter . . .**
- **Avec 50 dollars . . .**
- **Avec 100 dollars . . .**

TU AS LA PAROLE 3   **UNITÉ 6**

Describe what you do when you are invited to
a party or a picnic. Mention . . .

- what clothes you wear
- ▶ **Quand je vais à une boum
  (à un pique-nique), je mets . . .**
- what things you bring
- whom you bring along

Nom _____

Classe _____ Date _____

Discovering
FRENCH
Nouveau!

B L E U

Unité 6
Resources

Communipak

TU AS LA PAROLE 4   UNITÉ 6

Compare yourself to a friend of yours in terms of the following:

- size: who is taller?
- age: who is younger?
- sports: who is more athletic?

TU AS LA PAROLE 5   UNITÉ 6

Describe things you hope to do, achieve, or obtain in three of the following situations or circumstances.

▶ **Un jour, j'espère avoir une voiture de sport (aller en France, . . .).**

- **Ce soir** *(tonight)* . . .
- **Ce week-end** . . .
- **Pendant les vacances** . . .
- **En classe de français** . . .
- **Après** *(after)* **l'école** . . .
- **Dans cinq ans** . . .

TU AS LA PAROLE 6   UNITÉ 6

Look at the list and name two things you feel like doing right now and two things you do NOT feel like doing.

- eat
- study
- work
- speak French
- play ping-pong
- go to a movie
- go for a walk
- speak English
- visit a friend
- go home
- answer the teacher
- play video games

Nom _____

Classe _____ Date _____

Discovering FRENCH
Nouveau

BLEU

Side A

Conversations

Act out the following situations with your partner. Take turns:

- In the odd-numbered situations, you will be asking the questions.
- In the even-numbered situations, you will be answering your partner's questions.

CONVERSATION 1	**UNITÉ 6**

Brr! The weather has suddenly turned much colder. You and your partner plan to go downtown later on this afternoon. You don't want to freeze!

◆────────────────────◆

Ask your partner . . .

- if he/she has a hat
- if he/she is going to put on a sweater
- if he/she is going to wear a raincoat or a jacket

CONVERSATION 2

You and your partner are planning a camping trip. Your partner wants to make sure you have what you need.

Answer your partner's questions.

CONVERSATION 3	**UNITÉ 6**

Your friend has received money as a birthday present from an uncle. With the money he/she intends to buy clothes. You are curious about your partner's plans!

◆────────────────────◆

Ask your partner . . .

- how much money he/she has
- what clothes he/she is going to buy
- in which stores he/she is going to go

CONVERSATION 4

You have found a job as a salesperson in a store. Your partner is very interested.

Answer your partner's questions.

Nom _____

Classe _____ Date _____

Discovering
FRENCH
Nouveau!

B L E U

Unité 6
Resources

Communipak

Conversations

Act out the following situations with your partner. Take turns:

• In the odd-numbered situations, you will be asking the questions.
• In the even-numbered situations, you will be answering your partner's questions.

CONVERSATION 1

Brr! The weather has suddenly turned much colder. You and your partner plan to go downtown later on this afternoon. Your partner wants to make sure that neither of you gets too cold.

Answer your partner's questions.

CONVERSATION 2   **UNITÉ 6**

You are planning a camping trip with your partner and want to make sure you are both well equipped.

◆━━━━━━━━━━━━━━━━━━━━━━━━━━━━━━━◆

Ask your partner . . .

• if he/she is going to wear jeans or a jogging suit
• if he/she is going to wear boots or sneakers
• if he/she is going to bring his/her cell phone

CONVERSATION 3

You just received money as a birthday present from one of your uncles. With the money you intend to buy clothes. Your partner is curious about your plans.

Answer your partner's questions.

CONVERSATION 4   **UNITÉ 6**

Your friend has found a job as a salesperson in a store.

◆━━━━━━━━━━━━━━━━━━━━━━━━━━━━━━━◆

Ask your partner . . .

• in which store he/she is working
• what he/she sells
• how much he/she earns per hour **(par heure)**

Nom _____

Classe _____ Date _____

BLEU

Side A

Conversations

CONVERSATION 5   **UNITÉ 6**

You are a new student in this school and want to find out more about the students in your French class.

◆————————————————————————————◆

Ask your partner . . .

- if they **(on)** study a lot
- if they always speak French in class
- if they have lots of tests

CONVERSATION 6

Your partner is new in town and wants to know more about places to shop and eat. You have lived here for years.

Answer your partner's questions.

CONVERSATION 7   **UNITÉ 6**

It is Saturday afternoon and you are downtown with your friend. You have both finished your shopping.

◆————————————————————————————◆

Ask your partner . . .

- if he/she feels like going to a café
- if he/she feels like going to the movies
- what he/she feels like doing afterwards **(après)**
- if he/she needs money

CONVERSATION 8

You have met a new friend in school who does not know your family and is particularly curious about your brother.

Answer your partner as though you have a brother.

Nom _____

Classe _____ Date _____

Discovering
FRENCH *Nouveau!*

B L E U

Side B

Conversations

CONVERSATION 5

Your partner is a new student in this school and wants to know more about your French class.

Answer your partner's questions.

CONVERSATION 6	**UNITÉ 6**

You are new in town and want to know more about places to shop and eat . . .

◆ ——————————————————————————— ◆

Ask your partner . . .

- where they **(on)** sell records and cassettes
- where they sell inexpensive clothing
- in which restaurants one eats well

CONVERSATION 7

It is Saturday afternoon. You and your partner are downtown and have finished shopping. Your partner is wondering what you might both do next.

Answer your partner's questions.

CONVERSATION 8	**UNITÉ 6**

You have met a new friend in school, but you do not know his/her brother.

◆ ——————————————————————————— ◆

Ask your partner (who will answer as though he/she had a brother) . . .

- if he/she is younger than his/her brother
- if he/she is taller than he is
- if he/she is more or less athletic than he is
- if he/she is as nice

Nom _____

Classe _____ Date _____

Échanges

1 You think it's hard to guess how much something will cost and want to find out if your classmates are good at this.

- Bring to class a newspaper ad for clothing or a common item such as a TV set, a camera, or a bicycle. Cut off the price.

- Show the ad to five different students and ask each one how much they think the item costs. Note: **selon toi** = *in your opinion*.

- Record your classmates' answers.

Gagnant(e) *(winner)*:

> Dis, Cécile, selon toi, combien coûtent ces tennis?

> Quarante-cinq dollars.

NOMS	PRIX ESTIMÉ
▶ Cécile	$45
1	
2	
3	
4	
5	

- The winner is the one who made the closest guess.

Nom _____

Classe _____ Date _____

Discovering
FRENCH *Nouveau!*

B L E U

2 You and your classmates are going to the French
island of Martinique this spring on a school exchange.
This weekend, you all plan to go to the mall to buy
some accessories or clothing that you will want to
take along on the trip.

• Ask several classmates which three items they will buy.

• Ask them to rank these items in order of importance.

• Record their answers.

Dis, Alice, qu'est-ce que
tu vas acheter?

Je vais acheter un maillot de bain,
des tennis et des lunettes de soleil.

NOM	ACHATS		
► Alice	**1** maillot de bain	**2** tennis	**3** lunettes de soleil
	1	**2**	**3**
	1	**2**	**3**
	1	**2**	**3**
	1	**2**	**3**

• Then decide what is the most popular item.

L'achat le plus populaire est _____

Nom _____

Classe _____ Date _____

3 This weekend your classmates all have various plans (real or not). You want to find out what they are going to do!

- Interview five classmates about their plans.
- Ask them each where they will be going and what clothes they will wear. Record their answers below.
- Each one will select one of the places or events from the list below.

Où vas-tu ce week-end?

Qu'est-ce que tu vas porter?

- **la plage**
- **la campagne** (country)
- **un mariage**
- **un match de foot**
- **une boum**
- **un concert de rock**

Je vais à la plage.

Je vais porter
un maillot de bain
et des lunettes
de soleil.

NOM	ENDROIT/ÉVÉNEMENT	VÊTEMENTS
1		
2		
3		
4		
5		

Nom _____

Classe _____ Date _____

Discovering FRENCH *Nouveau!*

B L E U

Unité 6
Resources
Communipak

Tête à tête

1 Au grand magasin

a

■ Find out from your partner what the following items cost.

Combien coûte l'appareil-photo?

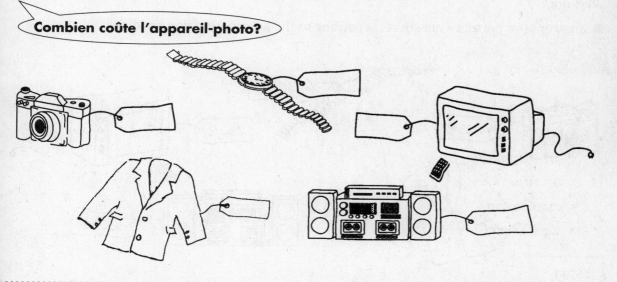

....

b

Now, look at the pictures below. You know how much these items cost in euros but your partner does not.

■ Answer your partner's questions according to the information you have.

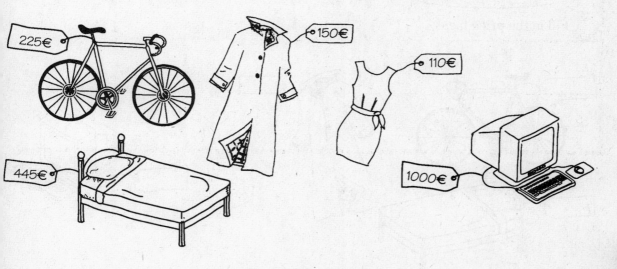

Nom _____

Classe _____ Date _____

Discovering
FRENCH
Nouveau!

BLEU

Élève B

Tête à tête

1 Au grand magasin

a

Look at the pictures below. You know how much these items cost in euros but your partner does not.

■ Answer your partner's questions according to the information you have.

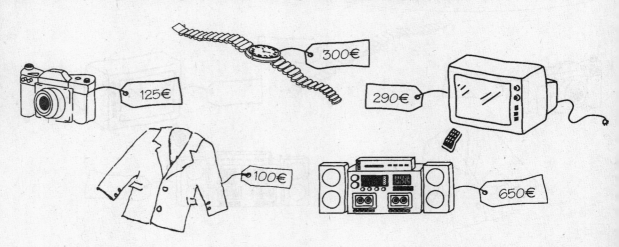

b

■ Now, find out from your partner what the following items cost.

Combien coûte la robe?

✎ Fill in the price tags

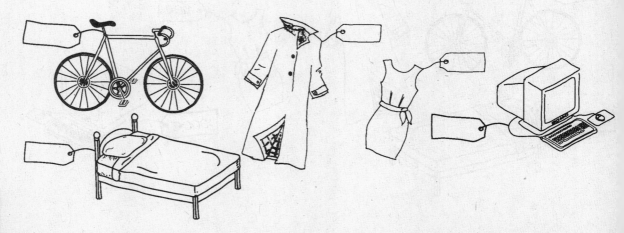

Discovering
FRENCH
Nouveau!

BLEU

Unité 6
Resources

Communipak

Tête à tête

2 Cadeaux d'anniversaire

 a

A lot of your friends have birthdays this month.

 Choose a present for them by drawing a line connecting each person to a different object.

■ Then answer your partner's questions.

 b

Your partner also has many friends who are having birthdays.

■ Find out what presents your partner is going to give them.

> **Qu'est-ce que tu vas acheter à [Alain] pour son anniversaire?**

Write this information in the gift box that has the right name.

Thomas

Carole

Damien

Cécile

 Jean-François

Tête à tête

2 Cadeaux d'anniversaire

Élève B

a

Your partner has many friends who are having birthdays.

■ Find out what presents your partner is going to give them.

> **Qu'est-ce que tu vas acheter à [Thomas] pour son anniversaire?**

 Write this information in the gift box that has the right name.

b

A lot of your friends also have birthdays this month.

 Choose a present for them by drawing a line connecting each person to a different object.

■ Then answer your partner's questions.

| Alain |  |

| Christine |  |

| Julien |  |

| Antoine |  |

| Sophie | |

Nom _____

Classe _____ Date _____

Discovering
FRENCH
Nouveau!

B L E U

Unité 6
Resources

Communipak

Tête à tête

Élève A

3 Comparaisons

a

You would like to compare various people and things.

■ Ask your partner for information.

> **Est-ce que [Sophie] est plus ou moins [grande] que [Claire]?**

 Record your partner's answers in the boxes below by writing the appropriate symbols:

+   −   =

- Sophie / grande / Claire? ☐

- Marc / élégant / Julien? ☐

- M. Duval / jeune / M. Lassalle? ☐

- les bottes / chères / les chaussures? ☐

- la jupe / longue / la robe? ☐

b

Now your partner wants to compare the following people and things, but does not have the information that you do.

■ Look at the illustrations and answer your partner's questions accordingly.

Thomas   **Richard**

Christine   Alice

Charlemagne   **Bijou**

Nom _____

Classe _____ Date _____

Discovering
FRENCH
Nouveau!

B L E U

Élève B

Tête à tête

3 Comparaisons

a

Your partner would like to compare the following people and things, but does not have the information that you do.

■ Look at the illustrations and answer your partner's questions accordingly.

Sophie   **Claire**

Marc   **Julien**

M. Duval   **M. Lassalle**

180 €   *180 €*

b

Now you want to compare various people and things.

■ Ask your partner for information.

> **Est-ce que [Thomas] est plus ou moins [riche] que [Richard]?**

 Record your partner's answers in the boxes below by writing the appropriate symbols.

+   –   =

- Thomas / riche / Richard?   ☐

- Christine / sportive / Alice?   ☐

- Charlemagne / gentil / Bijou?   ☐

- Les lunettes de soleil / chères / la ceinture?   ☐

- les baskets / grandes / les sandales?   ☐

Nom _____

Classe _____ Date _____

Discovering
FRENCH
Nouveau!

BLEU

Unité 6
Resources

Communipak

Communicative Expressions and Thematic Vocabulary

Pour communiquer
Shopping for clothes

Pardon . . .	*Excuse me . . .*
Vous désirez, (monsieur)?	*May I help you, (Sir)?*
Je cherche . . .	*I'm looking for . . .*
Quel est le prix de . . .?	*What is the price of . . .?*
Combien coûte . . .	*How much does . . . cost?*

Expressing opinions and making comparisons

Qu'est-ce que tu penses de [la robe rose]?	*What do you think of [the pink dress]?*
Comment tu trouves [la robe noire]?	*What do you think of [the black dress]?*

La robe rose est	plus belle que moins belle que aussi belle que	la robe noire.	The pink dress is	more beautiful than less beautiful than as beautiful as	the black dress.

Mots et expressions
Les magasins

un magasin	*store*	une boutique	*shop*
un grand magasin	*department store*		

L'argent

l'argent	*money*	une pièce	*coin*
un billet	*bill, paper money*		

Les vêtements et les accessoires

des baskets	*(hightop) sneakers*	des bottes	*boots*
un blouson	*jacket*	une casquette	*baseball cap*
un chapeau	*hat*	une ceinture	*belt*
un chemisier	*blouse*	des chaussettes	*socks*
des collants	*tights*	des chaussures	*shoes*
un imper(méable)	*raincoat*	une chemise	*shirt*
un jean	*jeans*	une cravate	*tie*
un jogging	*jogging suit*	une jupe	*skirt*
un maillot de bain	*bathing suit*	des lunettes	*glasses*
un manteau	*overcoat*	des lunettes de soleil	*sunglasses*
un pantalon	*pants*	une robe	*dress*
un polo	*polo shirt*	des sandales	*sandals*
un pull	*sweater*	une veste	*jacket*
un short	*shorts*		
un survêtement	*track suit*		
un sweat	*sweatshirt*		
un tee-shirt	*t-shirt*		
les tennis	*sneakers*		

La description

à la mode	*in style*	joli(e)	*pretty*
beau (belle)	*beautiful*	long(ue)	*long*
bon marché	*cheap*	meilleur(e)	*better*
cher (chère)	*expensive*	moche	*ugly*
chouette	*neat*	nouveau (nouvelle)	*new*
court(e)	*short*	pauvre	*poor*
démodé(e)	*out of style*	petit(e)	*small*
élégant(e)	*elegant*	riche	*rich*
génial(e)	*terrific*	vieux (vieille)	*old*
grand(e)	*big*		

Verbes réguliers en -er

chercher	*to look for*
coûter	*to cost*
dépenser	*to spend*
gagner	*to earn ; to win*
penser (que)	*to think (that)*
porter	*to wear*
trouver	*to find ; to think of*

Verbes avec changements orthographiques

acheter	*to buy*
amener	*to bring (a person)*
espérer	*to hope*
préférer	*to prefer*
payer	*to pay, to pay for*

Verbes réguliers en -ir

choisir	*to choose*
finir	*to finish*
grossir	*to gain weight*
maigrir	*to lose weight*
réussir	*to succeed*
réussir à un examen	*to pass an exam*

Verbes réguliers en -re

attendre	*to wait, to wait for*
entendre	*to hear*
perdre	*to lose, to waste*
rendre visite à	*to visit (a person)*
répondre à	*to answer*
vendre	*to sell*

Verbes irréguliers

avoir besoin de + *noun*	*to need*
avoir besoin de + *infinitive*	*to need to ; to have to*
avoir envie de + *noun*	*to want*
avoir envie de + *infinitive*	*to feel like, to want to*
mettre	*to put, to put on*

Les nombres de 100 à 1000

100	cent	300	trois cents	700	sept cents
101	cent un	400	quatre cents	800	huit cents
102	cent deux	500	cinq cents	900	neuf cents
200	deux cents	600	six cents	1000	mille

Expressions utiles

à mon avis	*in my opinion*
Eh bien!	*Well!*
C'est une bonne idée!	*That's a good idea!*

ce, cet, cette, ces	*this, that, these, those*	combien + *verb*	*how much*
quel, quelle, quels, quelles	*what, which*	combien de + *noun*	*how much, how many*
		trop + *adjective*	*too*

Nom _____

Classe _____ Date _____

Discovering FRENCH Nouveau!

BLEU

Unité 6 Resources

Activités pour tous
Reading TE

UNITÉ 6 Reading Comprehension

A

DÉPÔT-VENTE
PRÊT-À-PORTER FÉMININ
COUTURE ET CRÉATEURS - ACCESSOIRES DE MARQUES

DEPÓSITO-VENTA - ROPA DE CONFECCIÓN FEMENINA
COSTURA DE CREADORES - ACCESORIOS DE MARCAS

SALE ON CONSIGNMENT - WOMEN'S READY TO WEAR
DESIGN AND FASHION - BRAND NAME ACCESSORIES

CHANEL - SAINT LAURENT - HERMÈS - ESCADA - ETC.

Tenue de ville :
17, bd de Courcelles - 75008 PARIS
Métro : Villiers

01 42 25 86 07

Tenue de soirée:
119, bd Malesherbes - 75008 PARIS

01 45 61 19 47

Fax : 01 43 80 97 47

Compréhension

1. How many branches does this store have?

   one   (two)   three

2. The store at the **boulevard Malesherbes** specializes in . . .

   business attire   (evening attire)

3. What is the French word for "attire?"

   tenue

4. What expression means "ready-to-wear?"

   dépôt-vente   (prêt-à-porter)   couture

5. What expression means "sale on consignment?"

   dépôt-vente

Qu'est-ce que vous en pensez?

1. Judging by the zip codes, these stores are . . .

   (near each other.)   far from each other.

2. How do you say "brand" in French?

   couture   (marque)

3. What expression tells you that you can find designer clothes here?

   dépôt   vente   (couture)

URB
p. 159

Discovering French, Nouveau! Bleu

Unité 6, Resources
Activités pour tous Reading

107

Nom _____

Classe _____ Date _____ _____

B

Corinne Sarrut
Boutique - Mariage
Prêt à Porter Féminin
Accessoires Divers

4, rue du Pré Aux Clercs - 75007 PARIS
01 42 61 71 60

Les Deux
OURSONS
Pour Elle et Lui
Location jaquettes
Robes de soir
Chapeaux • Fourrures
Vente d'accessoires
Ouvert en août
Métro la Motte Picquet Grenelle
**106 bd de Grenelle
75015 PARIS
01 45 75 10 77**

jacadi
*Prêt-à-porter
enfant 0-12 ans
Chaussures, puériculture,
chambres d'enfant*
Vaycadi 17, rue Tronchet - 75008 PARIS
01 42 65 84 98
Métro : Madeleine, Havre-Caumartin

B E L D A M
TAILLES DU 40 AU 60
UN IMMEUBLE ENTIER
PRET A PORTER FÉMININ
FEMME FORTE

Métro : Porte d'Orléans
111, av. du Gén. Leclerc 75014 PARIS
01 45 40 47 72

Compréhension

1. Which store would someone go to in the following situations?

   a) If one just became a new aunt or uncle? <u>Jacadi</u>

   b) If one were looking for a wedding gown? <u>Corinne Sarrut</u>

   c) If a couple were going to a formal event? <u>Les Deux Oursons</u>

2. Does **Les Deux Oursons** rent or sell men's clothes only?

   yes   (no)

3. Does **Les Deux Oursons** rent or sell accessories?

   rent   (sell)

4. Does the store **Corinne Sarrut** sell men's clothes?

   yes   (no)

5. What are two sorts of items **Jacadi** sells?

   a) <u>chaussures</u>   b) <u>chambres d'enfant</u>

Qu'est-ce que vous en pensez?

1. Why do you think **Les Deux Oursons** mentions that it is **ouvert en août?**

   because August is the season for elegant parties

   (because many places are closed for vacation in August)

2. What do you think **divers** means?

   matching   (various)

3. Say the store name **Beldam** aloud. Why did the store choose that name?

   It sounds like <u>belle</u> [adjective]

   <u>dame</u> [noun].

Nom _____

Classe _____ Date _____

Discovering
FRENCH *Nouveau!*

BLEU

Unité 6 **Resources**

Activités pour tous TE
Reading

C

carte d'escompte -10%
12% détaxe
défilés de mode gratuits

10% Carte d'escompte 10% offerte avec ce coupon et votre passeport étranger au Welcome Service, R.d.C. Printemps de la Mode.

PRINTEMPS – 64, BD HAUSSMANN 75009 PARIS
METRO: HAVRE-CAUMARTIN – RER A: AUBER – RER E: HAUSSMANN-ST-LAZARE
OUVERT DU LUNDI AU SAMEDI DE 9H35 À 19H. NOCTURNE LE JEUDI JUSQU'À 22H.

Compréhension

1. What night is the store open late? _Thursday night (10 p.m.)_

2. How do you say "fashion" in French? _la mode_

3. How do you say "free" in French? _gratuit_

4. In order to get 10% off, what do you need to show along with this card?
   your passport

5. On what floor is the Welcome Service? _R.d.C. = rez-de-chaussée = ground floor_

Qu'est-ce que vous en pensez?

1. What kind of store is **Printemps?** _It's a department store._

2. What do you think **carte d'escompte** means? _It's a discount card._

3. What is a **défilé de mode?** _It's a fashion show._

URB
p. 161

Discovering French, Nouveau! Bleu

Unité 6, Resources
Activités pour tous Reading

109

Nom _____

Classe _____ Date _____

Discovering
FRENCH
Nouveau!

BLEU

Unité 6
Resources

Workbook TE
Reading and Culture Activities

UNITÉ 6 Reading and Culture Activities

A. Six boutiques

1.

PRIX SPECIAUX

JANVIER

Des exemples:

COSTUME pure laine	165€
VESTE pure laine	130€
BLAZER pure laine	125€
PULLOVER laine d'agneau	
«Fabriqué en Ecosse»	40€

ASTER hommes

2.
Les fameuses
CHEMISES Arrow

toutes tailles
toutes longueurs
Dépositaire
JOCKEY-CLUB
240 bis, bd Saint-Germain. M° Bac
167, rue de la Pompe
Près avenue Bugeaud

3.
LUNETTES

PETIT BATEAU®

EN VENTE CHEZ *TOUT POUR LA VUE*

6.
V de V
*ouvre
sa
boutique*

Maillots de bain, danse, jogging, ski
HOMMES - FEMMES - ENFANTS
4, rue de Sèvres PARIS 6ᵉ

4.
les cravates
JEAN **PATOU**
sont en vente à
MADELIOS
PLACE DE LA MADELEINE - PARIS

5.
**Chaussures
RALLYE**

VILLE - SPORT - MONTAGNE
ARCUS - TECNICA

14, rue Royale, Annecy   Tél. 04.50.45.09.88

- These six Paris shops are each advertising different things.
- Note that the ads have been numbered 1, 2, 3, 4, 5, and 6.
- Indicate where one would go to buy the following items by circling the number of the corresponding shop.

	BOUTIQUES					
a dress shirt	1	②	3	4	5	6
a jacket	①	2	3	4	5	6
a swimsuit	1	2	3	4	5	⑥
an elegant tie	1	2	3	④	5	6
a man's suit	①	2	3	4	5	6
a pair of new glasses	1	2	③	4	5	6
a ballet leotard	1	2	3	4	5	⑥
a pair of walking shoes	1	2	3	4	⑤	6

URB
p. 163

Discovering French, Nouveau! Bleu   **Workbook Reading and Culture Activities**   Unité 6

177

B. Les soldes

CORONER

PRET A PORTER - SPORTSWEAR

COLLECTION AUTOMNE - HIVER

-30% à -50%

BOUTIQUE HOMME	BOUTIQUE FEMME	BOUTIQUE SPORTSWEAR
CHEMISES à 20€	PULLS à 25€	JEANS à 25€
PULLS à 30€	PANTALONS à 30€	SWEAT SHIRTS à 20€
VESTES "NEW LOOK" à 69€	JUPES LAINAGE à 35€	PANTALONS NEWMAN à 30€
PANTALONS LAINAGES à 35€	ENSEMBLES à 45€	BLOUSONS à 45€
PANTALONS (forme large) à 40€		CHEMISES à 30€

353, Rue de Vaugirard, PARIS 15 ème
OUVERT DE 9 H 30 à 19 H 30 - SANS INTERRUPTION

1. As you were walking down the Boulevard Saint-Michel in Paris, you were handed this flyer announcing a special sale. Read it carefully and answer the following questions.

   • Comment s'appelle la boutique? _Coroner_____

   • Quelle est l'adresse de la boutique? _353, rue de Vaugirard_____

   • À quelle heure est-ce que la boutique ouvre *(open)*? _à 9 h 30_____

   • Combien coûtent les jeans? _25€_____

   Est-ce qu'ils sont chers ou bon marché? _Ils sont bon marché (chers)._____

URB
p. 164

178
Unité 6
Workbook Reading and Culture Activities

Discovering French, Nouveau! Bleu

Nom _____

Classe _____ Date _____

Discovering
FRENCH
Nouveau!

B L E U

Unité 6
Resources

Workbook TE
Reading and Culture Activities

2. You have decided to go shop at the Coroner. Imagine you have saved 100 euros to buy clothes. Make a list of what you are planning to buy and add up the total cost of your intended purchases.

Article	*Prix*
Answers will vary.	
Prix total:	

3. You have tried on the items and they all fit well. You will buy all the things on your list. Write out a check for the total amount.

Discovering French, Nouveau! Bleu

Workbook Reading and Culture Activities

Unité 6

179

URB
p. 165

Nom _____

Classe _____ Date _____

UNIT TEST 6 (Lessons 17, 18, 19, 20)

Part I. Listening Comprehension

1. The Logical Answer (20 points)

You will hear a series of ten questions. Listen carefully to each question and select the most logical answer on your test sheet. Circle the corresponding letter: a, b, or c. You will hear each question twice. First, listen to the model.

Modèle: [Qu'est-ce que tu achètes?]
    a. Cent euros.
    b. À la pharmacie.
    c. Des chaussures.

1. a. Au supermarché.
   b. Je dépense beaucoup.
   c. Dans une boutique avenue du Maine.

2. a. Ma veste jaune.
   b. Des lunettes.
   c. Un maillot de bain.

3. a. Il pleut.
   b. Il est démodé.
   c. Je vais à la plage.

4. a. Je fais une promenade.
   b. Oui, je fais attention.
   c. Je voudrais aller au cinéma.

5. a. Elle est géniale.
   b. Je suis d'accord.
   c. Non, elle est bleue.

6. a. Oui, elle est très jolie.
   b. Non, elle est trop courte.
   c. Non, elle est bon marché.

7. a. Ma cousine Carole.
   b. Des sandwichs au jambon.
   c. Je n'ai pas faim.

8. a. Vingt euros par jour.
   b. Je dépense beaucoup.
   c. Je n'aime pas perdre.

9. a. Ce monument.
   b. À ma tante Charlotte.
   c. J'aime voyager.

10. a. Non, je suis pauvre.
   b. C'est mille euros.
   c. C'est trop cher pour moi.

Part II. Language

2. The Right Number (6 points)

Use digits to write the numbers below in the corresponding boxes.

▶ | 29 | vingt-neuf.

1. | | cinq cent un

2. | | cent quatorze

3. | | mille deux cents

4. | | neuf cent soixante-quinze

5. | | huit cent vingt

6. | | trois mille

Nom _____

Classe _____ Date _____ _____

Discovering
FRENCH
Nouveau!

B L E U

Unité 6
Resources

Unit Test
Form A

3. The Right Item (12 points)

Write the names of six of the items shown in the illustrations below. With each one, be sure to use the appropriate article: **un**, **une**, or **des**.

1. _____   3. _____   5. _____

2. _____   4. _____   6. _____

4. The Right Verb (14 points)

Complete each of the following sentences with the appropriate form of the French verb that corresponds to the verb in parentheses.

1. (to finish)   La classe _____ à onze heures.

2. (to choose)   Nous _____ ces tee-shirts.

3. (to wait for)   Monsieur Rimbaud _____ le bus.

4. (to hear)   Est-ce que vous _____ bien?

5. (to answer)   Marc _____ à la lettre de sa cousine.

6. (to put on)   Je _____ ma veste verte.

7. (to buy)   Caroline _____ ses vêtements dans cette boutique.

5. The Right Comparison (10 points)

Complete the following comparisons by filling in the missing words.

1. Je n'ai pas beaucoup d'argent. Je vais acheter la chemise bleue parce qu'elle est _____ chère _____ la chemise verte.

2. Stéphanie va acheter le pull rouge parce qu'il est _____ joli _____ le pull orange.

3. Le manteau coûte 100 euros. L'imper coûte 100 euros aussi. Le manteau est _____ cher _____ l'imper.

4. Jean-Paul a 13 ans. Éric a 16 ans. Jean-Paul est _____ jeune _____ Éric.

5. À l'examen d'espagnol Marc a un "B" et à l'examen d'anglais il a un "A." Il est bon en espagnol, mais il est _____ en anglais.

URB
p. 167

Nom _____

Classe _____ Date _____

Discovering
FRENCH
Nouveau!

B L E U

6. The Right Choice (10 points)

Choose the words that complete the following sentences and circle the corresponding letter: a, b, or c.

1. _____ chemise verte est très jolie.
   a. Ce　　b. Cet　　c. Cette

2. Qui est _____ homme?
   a. ce　　b. cet　　c. cette

3. Je n'aime pas _____ chaussettes noires.
   a. ce　　b. cette　　c. ces

4. _____ est ta couleur préférée?
   a. Quel　　b. Quelle　　c. Quels

5. _____ copines est-ce que tu vas inviter?
   a. Quelle　　b. Quels　　c. Quelles

6. _____ élèves est-ce qu'il y a dans la classe?
   a. Comment　b. Combien　c. Combien d'

7. Est-ce que tu aimes ma _____ casquette?
   a. nouveau　b. nouvel　c. nouvelle

8. Ces sandales noires sont très _____.
   a. belle　　b. belles　　c. beaux

9. Mon grand-père a 50 ans. Il n'est pas très
   a. vieil　　b. vieille　　c. vieux

10. Au Pérou, _____ parle espagnol, n'est-ce pa
    a. ils　　b. on　　c. un

7. The Logical Choice (8 points)

Choose the logical completion for each of the following sentences and circle the corresponding letter: a, b, or c.

1. Thomas n'a pas beaucoup d'argent. Il est _____.
   a. pauvre
   b. très riche
   c. sympathique

2. Cette veste est moche. Elle n'est pas _____.
   a. longue
   b. belle
   c. vieille

3. Cette veste n'est pas assez longue. En fait (*as a matter of fact*), elle est trop _____ pour moi.
   a. courte
   b. chère
   c. bon marché

4. J'aime beaucoup cette chemise. Elle est très _____.
   a. chouette
   b. vieille
   c. pauvre

5. Marc _____ parce qu'il mange moins.
   a. perd
   b. grossit
   c. maigrit

6. Céline a besoin d'argent. Elle espère _____ un job.
   a. gagner
   b. trouver
   c. dépenser

7. Cette boutique _____ des vêtements très élégants.
   a. vend
   b. porte
   c. cherche

8. Dis, Alain, est-ce que tu as _____ d'aller au cinéma avec nous?
   a. soif
   b. besoin
   c. envie

Nom _____

Classe _____ Date _____ _____

Discovering FRENCH *Nouveau!*

B L E U

Unité 6
Resources

Unit Test
Form A

Part III. Written Expression

8. Composition (20 points)

Express your personal ideas, using only vocabulary and expressions that you know in French. Write five or six sentences.

Job d'été

You have a summer job in a clothing store. Describe your job. You may mention, for instance:

- what type of store you are going to work in
- what type of clothes you are going to wear for this job
- what clothes or accessories you are going to sell
- how much you are going to earn
- what you are going to do with your money

_____

_____

_____

_____

_____

_____

_____

Discovering
FRENCH
Nouveau!

B L E U

Nom _____

Classe _____ Date _____

UNIT TEST 6 (Lessons 17, 18, 19, 20)   FORM B

Part I. Listening Comprehension

1. The Logical Answer (20 points)

You will hear a series of ten questions. Listen carefully to each question and select the most logical answer on your test sheet. Circle the corresponding letter: a, b, or c. You will hear each question twice. First, listen to the model.

Modèle: [Qu'est-ce que tu achètes?]
    a. Cent euros.
    b. À la pharmacie.
    c. Des chaussures.

1. a. Je veux rester ici.
    b. Je n'ai pas d'argent.
    c. Je cherche une robe longue.

2. a. J'ai soif.
    b. Il fait froid.
    c. Il est moche.

3. a. Des bottes.
    b. Mon nouveau survêtement.
    c. Nous allons gagner le match.

4. a. Oui, je veux bien.
    b. Oui, c'est loin.
    c. Non, je préfère marcher.

5. a. Elles sont géniales.
    b. Je ne pense pas.
    c. Je ne suis pas d'accord avec toi.

6. a. Oui, je vais au supermarché.
    b. Non, il est trop court.
    c. Non, il est cher.

7. a. Mon nouveau CD.
    b. Ma copine Élisabeth.
    c. Je n'aime pas danser.

8. a. Parce qu'il pleut.
    b. Je vais à la bibliothèque.
    c. Je vais à la plage.

9. a. Non, il est vieux.
    b. Oui, il est démodé.
    c. Oui, c'est mon imperméable.

10. a. Mille.
    b. Je n'ai pas de billets.
    c. Deux cents euros.

Part II. Language

2. The Right Number (6 points)

Use digits to write the numbers below in the corresponding boxes.

▶ | 29 | vingt-neuf

1. | | sept cent dix

2. | | trois mille

3. | | cent soixante-six

4. | | mille huit cents

5. | | cinq cent vingt-quatre

6. | | quatre cent quatre-vingts

Nom _____

Classe _____ Date _____

3. The Right Item (12 points)

Write the names of six of the items shown in the illustrations below. With each one, be sure to use the appropriate article: **un**, **une,** or **des**.

1. _____   3. _____   5. _____

2. _____   4. _____   6. _____

4. The Right Verb (14 points)

Complete each of the following sentences with the appropriate form of the French verb that corresponds to the verb in parentheses.

1. (to finish)   Les élèves _____ l'examen.

2. (to choose)   Je _____ ce CD.

3. (to wait for)   Nous _____ nos copains au café.

4. (to hear)   Qu'est-ce que vous _____?

5. (to answer)   Je _____ au téléphone.

6. (to put on)   Françoise _____ son nouveau pull.

7. (to buy)   Qu'est-ce que tu _____?

5. The Right Comparison (10 points)

Complete the following comparisons by filling in the missing words.

1. Le Vermont est _____ grand _____ le Texas.

2. En hiver, il fait _____ chaud à Miami _____ à New York.

3. La jupe coûte 80 euros. La robe coûte 100 euros. La jupe est _____ chère _____ la robe.

4. Daniel et Martine ont eu un "A" en maths. Daniel est _____ intelligent _____ Martine.

5. Paul est bon en maths, mais Thomas n'est pas très bon. Paul est _____ en maths _____ Thomas parce qu'il étudie plus que lui.

Nom _____

Classe _____ Date _____ _____

6. The Right Choice (10 points)

Choose the words that complete the following sentences and circle the corresponding letter:
a, b, or c.

1. Combien coûte _____ ordinateur?
   a. ce   b. cet   c. cette

2. Je vais acheter _____ lunettes de soleil.
   a. ce   b. cette   c. ces

3. Qu'est-ce que tu penses de _____ chemise verte?
   a. ce   b. cet   c. cette

4. _____ chaussures est-ce que tu vas mettre?
   a. Quelle   b. Quels   c. Quelles

5. _____ est ta classe préférée?
   a. Quel   b. Quelle   c. Quels

6. _____ crayons est-ce que tu vas acheter?
   a. Comment   b. Combien
   c. Combien de

7. Je vais mettre mon _____ imperméable.
   a. vieux   b. vieil   c. vieille

8. Tes _____ sandales sont très élégantes.
   a. nouvel   b. nouveaux
   c. nouvelles

9. Alice porte une _____ robe.
   a. beau   b. bel   c. belle

10. À Bruxelles, _____ parle français, n'est-ce pas?
    a. on   b. un   c. ils

7. The Logical Choice (8 points)

Choose the logical completion for each of the following sentences and circle the corresponding letter: a, b, or c.

1. Je n'aime pas ce blouson. Il est très _____.
   a. chouette
   b. moche
   c. élégant

2. Je cherche des collants _____ parce que je n'ai pas beaucoup d'argent.
   a. chers
   b. nouveaux
   c. bon marché

3. Je ne peux pas mettre ce pantalon. Il est trop _____.
   a. beau
   b. court
   c. jeune

4. Marie-Christine n'est pas patiente. Elle n'aime pas _____.
   a. attendre
   b. entendre
   c. espérer

5. Stéphane _____ son argent en vêtements.
   a. vend
   b. achète
   c. dépense

6. Robert _____ sa copine à la boum.
   a. amène
   b. apporte
   c. espère

7. Tu _____ parce que tu manges trop.
   a. réponds
   b. grossis
   c. maigris

8. Si tu ne fais pas attention, tu vas _____ ton match.
   a. perdre
   b. attendre
   c. entendre

Nom _____

Classe _____ Date _____

Discovering
FRENCH
Nouveau!

BLEU

Unité 6
Resources

Unit Test
Form B

Part III. Written Expression

8. Composition (20 points)

Express your personal ideas, using only vocabulary and expressions that you know in French. Write five or six sentences.

Un bal masqué (*Costume ball*)

You are going to a Mardi Gras party where everyone is in costume. Describe what you and your friend (of the opposite sex) are going to wear. For example, you can indicate the articles of clothing, their color, size, and style. Use your imagination in describing your outfits.

_____

_____

_____

_____

_____

_____

_____

Part III. Cultural Awareness (Alternate)   **FORMS A and B**

8. Culture (20 points)

Choose the completion which best reflects the cultural information that you read about in this unit. Circle the corresponding letter: a, b, or c.

1. **Pierre Cardin** and **Christian Dior** are famous French . . .
   a. TV actors. b. rock artists. c. fashion designers.

2. **Le Bon Marché** is a well-known French . . .
   a. museum. b. department store. c. supermarket chain.

3. A French teenager would go to **le Marché aux Puces** if he/she were looking for . . .
   a. a pet. b. the latest CDs. c. old clothes.

4. A **boutique de soldes** is a shop that sells . . .
   a. very expensive jewelry.
   b. clothes at discounted prices.
   c. all types of electronic equipment.

5. A **grand magasin** is the French equivalent of a . . .
   a. department store.
   b. large shopping mall.
   c. library browsing room.

6. French people go to the **grandes surfaces** to . . .
   a. jog or roller skate.
   b. watch their favorite sport: tennis.
   c. buy food and all types of everyday products at good prices.

7. In general French teenagers . . .
   a. dress like their parents.
   b. want to be in style.
   c. are not interested in their personal appearance.

8. Most young French teenagers get their spending money . . .
   a. from their parents.
   b. by working after school.
   c. by working instead of going to school.

9. There are many French young people of Algerian origin. Their parents emigrated to France from . . .
   a. North Africa.
   b. South Africa.
   c. Asia.

10. The major religion of Algeria is . . .
    a. Catholicism.
    b. Islam.
    c. Judaism.

Nom _____

Classe _____ Date _____

Discovering
FRENCH
Nouveau!

BLEU

UNITÉ 6   Listening Comprehension Performance Test

Partie A. Conversations

This part of the Listening Comprehension Performance Test will let you see how well you understand spoken French. You will hear five short conversations. Look at your Listening Comprehension Performance Test Sheet and read the corresponding questions. After you have heard each conversation the second time, select the correct answer and mark the corresponding letter (a, b, c, or d) on your answer sheet.

1. Listen to the following conversation between a sales clerk and Caroline.
   What does Caroline want to buy?
   a. Sunglasses.
   b. A raincoat.
   c. A swimsuit.
   d. Shoes.

2. Listen to the following conversation between Béatrice and her brother Alain.
   From the conversation, what is the weather like?
   a. It is sunny.
   b. It is very nice.
   c. It is hot and muggy.
   d. It is cold and rainy.

3. Listen to the following conversation between Jean-Paul and Philippe.
   What is the problem with the blue jacket?
   a. It's too expensive.
   b. It's too long.
   c. It's too short.
   d. It's ugly.

4. Listen to the following conversation between Nathalie and Éric.
   What is their main topic of discussion?
   a. School life.
   b. Summer plans.
   c. Friends.
   d. Their allowance.

5. Listen to the following conversation between Pauline and Nicolas.
   What have they decided to do?
   a. To go to a movie.
   b. To go to the bank.
   c. To go for a bike ride.
   d. To go shopping.

Nom _____

Classe _____ Date _____ _____

Unité 6 Resources

Listening Comprehension
Performance Test

Discovering
FRENCH
Nouveau

BLEU

Partie B. Questions et réponses

This part of the Listening Comprehension Performance Test will let you see how well you can handle French questions. You will hear your French friend Michèle ask you five questions. Listen carefully. Then look at your Listening Comprehension Performance Test Sheet and select the MOST LOGICAL answer to each question. Mark the corresponding letter (a, b, c, or d) on your answer sheet. You will hear each question twice.

6. You and Michèle are walking through the mall.
   You reply:
   a. C'est cher.
   b. Il coûte cent euros.
   c. J'achète des livres.
   d. Je vends des vêtements.

7. It is Saturday afternoon and Michèle has come by your house.
   You reply:
   a. Oui, je vais aller nager.
   b. Oui, j'achète des vêtements.
   c. Non, je n'ai pas faim.
   d. Non, je n'aime pas cette boutique.

8. You and Michèle are shopping.
   You reply:
   a. Il est moche.
   b. Il est démodé.
   c. Il est chouette.
   d. Il est trop grand.

9. You and Michèle are in town walking along the street.
   You reply:
   a. Il fait froid.
   b. Je grossis.
   c. N'achète pas cette veste.
   d. Allons au café!

10. It is the weekend and Michèle has phoned you.
    You reply:
    a. Oui, j'ai des baskets.
    b. Oui, je vais perdre le match.
    c. Non, je n'ai pas besoin de chaussures.
    d. Non, je préfère rester à la maison.

Nom _____

Classe _____ Date _____

Discovering
FRENCH
Nouveau!

BLEU

Unité 6
Resources

Speaking Performance Test

UNITÉ 6   Speaking Performance Test

1. Conversations

In this part of the Speaking Performance Test, I will describe a situation and then ask you some related questions. In your answers, use the vocabulary and structures you have learned. Use your imagination.

CONVERSATION A   UNITÉ 6

Your friend Caroline is giving a birthday party, and you have been invited. I am going to ask you some questions about your plans for the party.

- Est-ce que tu vas mettre de beaux vêtements?
- Qu'est-ce que tu vas porter?
- Qu'est-ce que tu vas apporter à Caroline?
- Qui est-ce que tu vas amener avec toi?

CONVERSATION B   UNITÉ 6

I just heard that your friend Hélène has found a job at the new shopping center. I am going to ask you some questions about Hélène.

- Où est-ce qu'Hélène travaille?
- Qu'est-ce qu'elle vend?
- Combien est-ce qu'elle gagne par heure?
- Est-ce qu'elle aime travailler là-bas?

CONVERSATION C   UNITÉ 6

You asked me to go shopping with you Saturday afternoon. I have some questions about what you have in mind.

- Dans quel(s) magasin(s) est-ce que tu veux aller?
- Qu'est-ce que tu vas acheter?
- Qu'est-ce que tu as envie de faire après *(afterwards)*?
- À quelle heure allons-nous rentrer?

Nom _____

Classe _____ Date _____

BLEU

CONVERSATION D   UNITÉ 6

You have just asked me to go to a café with you. Fine, but first I have a few questions.

- Qui va payer? Moi ou toi?
- Qu'est-ce que tu vas choisir—un sandwich ou une pizza?
- Est-ce que tu as envie d'un café ou d'une limonade?
- Qu'est-ce qu'on va faire après *(afterwards)*?

CONVERSATION E   UNITÉ 6

A friend of yours told me you are selling your old bicycle. I may be interested, but first let me ask you a few questions.

- Pourquoi est-ce que tu vends ton vieux vélo?
- Est-ce qu'il marche bien?
- Quel est son prix?
- Qu'est-ce que tu vas faire avec l'argent?

CONVERSATION F   UNITÉ 6

You are in a clothing store where I am working as a salesperson. Decide what item of clothing you are going to buy and I will help you. Please answer my questions.

- Vous désirez, monsieur/mademoiselle?
- De quelle couleur?
- Combien d'argent voulez-vous dépenser?
- Qu'est-ce que vous pensez de ce pantalon/cette robe *[use article of clothing named by student]*?

Unité 6 Resources

Speaking Performance Test

Nom _____

Classe _____ Date _____

Discovering FRENCH *Nouveau!*

B L E U

Unité 6 Resources

Speaking Performance Test

2. Tu as la parole

In this part of the Speaking Performance Test, you have the opportunity to make three comments about a familiar topic. Use only the structures and vocabulary you know. Use your imagination.

TU AS LA PAROLE (A)   UNITÉ 6

Name THREE things that you can take to the beach. Use the list below as a guide or mention other items of your choice.

- sunglasses
- sandals
- a swimsuit

TU AS LA PAROLE (B)   UNITÉ 6

Name THREE items of clothing that you may want to give to your favorite uncle on his 40th birthday. Use the list below as a guide or mention other items of your choice.

- a tie
- a shirt
- a belt

TU AS LA PAROLE (C)   UNITÉ 6

Think of a boy you know—a friend or a classmate. Compare yourself to him in THREE different ways: For example . . .

- are you taller than he is?
- are you as nice as he is?
- are you better in French than he is?

Discovering
FRENCH
Nouveau!

B L E U

TU AS LA PAROLE (D)   UNITÉ 6

Tell your French friend Jean-Claude that he cannot wear his old tie to the prom. Give him THREE reasons. You may use the following suggestions or add your own.

- It's ugly.
- It's out of style.
- It's too short.

TU AS LA PAROLE (E)   UNITÉ 6

Your friends do not seem to know what to do this weekend. Make THREE suggestions. Use the list below as a guide or add other activities of your choice.

- Let's go to the movies.
- Let's play soccer.
- Let's go to the museum.

TU AS LA PAROLE (F)   UNITÉ 6

Your friend Éric needs money to buy a new bicycle. Tell him THREE things he might do. You may use the suggestions below as a guide or add your own ideas. For example, you could tell him . . .

- sell your old books (or CDs)
- look for a job **(un job)**
- work on Saturdays

Nom _____

Classe _____ Date _____

Discovering
FRENCH *Nouveau!*

B L E U

Unité 6
Resources
Reading Comprehension
Performance Test

UNITÉ 6 Reading Comprehension Performance Test

Read carefully the following flyer. Then read the questions. On your Answer Sheet, mark the correct answers by placing a check next to the corresponding letter.

GRAND CHOIX DE SHORTS, BERMUDAS, JEANS, MAILLOTS DE BAINS, HOMMES - FEMMES - ENFANTS

HOMME

POLO, 100% coton, à partir de .... **5€**
CHEMISE Mac Kay, 100% coton, le lot de 3 .... **12€**
COSTUME Roger Arloing, 100% polyester .... **90€**
PANTALON Roger Arloing, 100% coton .... **30€**
PANTALON D'ÉTÉ, 100% coton, à partir de .... **8€**

ENFANT

ENSEMBLE STYLE JEANS, 100% coton .... **12€**
CHEMISE STYLE ARMY 100% coton .... **6€**
SURVÊTEMENT BICOLORE SATINÉ,
100% polyester .... **24€**
TEE-SHIRT IMPRIMÉ, 100% coton .... **4€**
TEE-SHIRT + SHORT COULEUR,
l'ensemble .... **6€**

FEMME

PANTALON À PINCES, 100% coton,
à partir de .... **12€**
JUPE-CULOTTE COURTE,
65% polyester, 35% viscose, à partir de .... **15€**
TEE-SHIRT avec impression brodée .... **8€**
PULL MANCHES COURTES,
50% coton, 50% acrylique .... **8€**
JUPE GRANDE TAILLE,
100% polyester, à partir de .... **9€**
ENSEMBLE JUPE + CHEMISIER,
100% viscose, à partir de .... **27€**
CHEMISIER, 100% polyester, à partir de .... **9€**

1. What type of clothing is advertised in this flyer?
   a. Summer clothes.
   b. Winter clothes.
   c. Formal evening attire.

2. What is the most expensive item of women's clothing listed in the flyer?
   a. A short-sleeved sweater.
   b. A pair of pleated slacks.
   c. A matching skirt and blouse.

Read carefully the following ad from a Paris magazine. Then read the question. On your Answer Sheet, mark the correct answer by placing a check next to the corresponding letter.

3. To whom is this advertisement addressed?
   a. To people who like to dance.
   b. To people who want to lose weight.
   c. To people who want to learn water ballet.

Perdez jusqu'à 10 kilos en 23 jours.

Pour la première fois
en France,
il est maintenant possible
de perdre du poids
sous contrôle médical,
rapidement, sans pilules,
sans massages,
sans exercices,
sans avoir
faim.

Nom _____

Classe _____ Date _____

Read carefully the following flyer that was distributed in Paris. Then read the questions. On your Answer Sheet, mark the correct answers by placing a check next to the corresponding letter.

AU PRINCE DE GALLES

125, rue de Sèvres   Paris 6ᵉ

Soldes de printemps
sur tous nos articles

Cravates	~~16€~~	12€
Costumes	~~230€~~	183€
Pantalons	~~92€~~	69€
Imperméables	~~185€~~	137€
Manteaux	~~215€~~	168€

Cartes de crédit acceptées
10% d'escompte supplémentaire
avec paiement en traveller's chèques

4. What does this flyer announce?
   a. A sale.
   b. The arrival of spring fashions.
   c. The opening of a new boutique.

5. Which of the following types of clothing are *not* mentioned in the ad?
   a. Neckties.
   b. Raincoats.
   c. Dress shirts.

Read carefully the following clipping taken from a newspaper article in Paris. Then read the questions. On your Answer Sheet, mark the correct answers by placing a check next to the corresponding letter.

L'individu en question est un homme âgé de 30 à 35 ans. Il est petit, brun et porte une moustache. Il est généralement vêtu d'un costume bleu et porte un chapeau et des lunettes de soleil. Cet homme n'est pas armé, mais il peut être dangereux. Prière de signaler sa présence au poste de police le plus proche ou de téléphoner au 02.37.74.28.12.

6. Who is the person described in the article?
   a. A private detective.
   b. A person sought by the police.
   c. A famous actor traveling incognito.

7. What is distinctive about this person?
   a. He is shabbily dressed.
   b. He generally wears a hat and sunglasses.
   c. He has a false moustache.

Nom _____

Classe _____ Date _____

Discovering
FRENCH
Nouveau!

B L E U

Read the letter that Jean-Claude wrote to Nathalie. Then read the questions. On your Answer Sheet, mark the correct answers by placing a check next to the corresponding letter.

8. Why did Jean-Claude write to Nathalie?
   a. To invite her to his birthday party.
   b. To tell her about the clothes he bought.
   c. To ask her to go shopping with him.

9. What does Jean-Claude hope to buy?
   a. A raincoat.
   b. A jogging outfit.
   c. A basketball.

10. How did Jean-Claude get the money?
   a. It was a gift from his aunt.
   b. He earned it by working on weekends.
   c. He saved his allowance.

Chère Nathalie,

J'ai reçu 100 euros de ma tante pour mon anniversaire. Avec cet argent, je pense acheter des vêtements. J'ai envie d'un imperméable, mais c'est probablement trop cher. Alors, j'espère trouver un survêt et des baskets. Je vais aller dans les magasins samedi prochain. Est-ce que tu veux venir avec moi? J'ai besoin de tes conseils! Merci.

Je t'embrasse,
Jean-Claude

Nom _____

Classe _____ Date _____

UNITÉ 6   Writing Performance Test

A. Voyage à Nice (10 points)

You entered a contest and have just won the grand prize: a two-week trip to the French Riviera in July. Make a list of five items of clothing that you want to pack. Use the following list as a guide, or choose other items.

- a swimsuit
- sunglasses
- a baseball cap
- sandals
- shirts

- _____
- _____
- _____
- _____
- _____

B. Vêtements d'hiver (10 points)

The weather forecast is predicting a very cold winter this year. Make a list of five items of clothing that you will need. Use the items pictured as a guide, or choose other items.

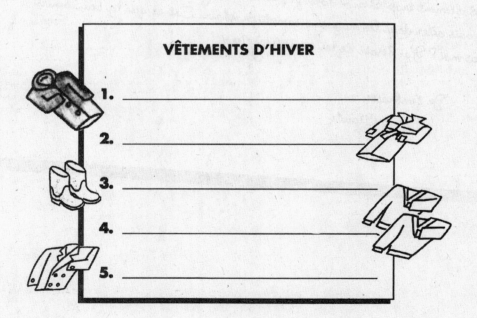

VÊTEMENTS D'HIVER

1. _____
2. _____
3. _____
4. _____
5. _____

Nom _____

Classe _____ Date _____

Discovering
FRENCH
Nouveau!

BLEU

Unité 6
Resources

Writing Performance Test

C. Comparaisons (20 points)

Complete the chart with the names of five friends and compare yourself to each of them in terms of the suggested characteristics.

Mes amis	Moi
Michael	Je suis plus jeune que lui.

► jeune

• grand

• sportif

• timide

• bon en français

• bon en maths

D. Préférences (20 points)

There are things we like to do and other things we do not like to do. Select five of the following things and say how you feel about each one.

Mes préférences

► J'aime (Je n'aime pas) dépenser mon argent.

1. _____
_____

2. _____
_____

3. _____
_____

4. _____
_____

5. _____
_____

► spend my money

• wait for the bus

• answer the teacher

• pass the exam

• lose my bag

• visit my grandparents

• earn money

• choose new clothes

• wear old clothes

• take my little brother to a party

Nom _____

Classe _____ Date _____

E. Cadeau d'anniversaire (20 points)

For your birthday, your uncle in Montreal gave you money to buy clothes. Write him a short letter thanking him and telling him how you will use the money.

Thank him for the money.

Tell him . . .

- what clothes you need
- to what type of store you are going to go
- what you are going to buy
- how much money you are going to spend.

Sign your letter.

Mon cher oncle,

_____

_____

_____

_____

Amitiés,

_____

F. Conseils (20 points)

Give advice to the following friends, suggesting what they should or should not do. Use the suggestions provided or use your imagination to give other advice.

1. Robert wants to get an "A." (Tell him to pay attention in class.)

2. Sophie wants to lose weight. (Tell her not to buy a pizza.)

3. Stéphanie wants to go swimming. (Tell her to go to the pool.)

4. Georges needs money. (Tell him to sell his CDs.)

5. Olivier needs to study for a test. (Tell him not to watch TV.)

Conseils

1. _____

2. _____

3. _____

4. _____

5. _____

Nom _____

Classe _____ Date _____ _____

Discovering
FRENCH
Nouveau!

BLEU

Unité 6
Resources

Unité 6

Multiple Choice Test Items

UNITÉ 6 Multiple Choice Test Items

Leçon 17

1. Cathy is going to buy two items she could wear on her head.
   Elle achète _____.
   a. un imper et une chaussette
   b. un collant et une cravate
   c. un chapeau et une casquette

2. Il fait froid. Où est _____?
   a. mon manteau
   b. ma chemise
   c. mon chemisier

3. Avec mon jean, j'aime porter un chemisier blanc et _____ noire.
   a. une veste
   b. une robe
   c. une jupe

4. Quand il va à une soirée élégante, Michel aime mettre un pantalon, une chemise,
   _____ et une veste.
   a. une casquette
   b. un collant
   c. une cravate

5. Elle va _____ un chemisier avec sa jupe.
   a. acheter
   b. imper
   c. porter

6. J'ai deux beaux _____.
   a. chapeau
   b. manteau
   c. manteaux

7. Je vais à la piscine, alors je vais mettre _____.
   a. des bottes
   b. une ceinture
   c. un maillot de bain

8. Il fait beau aujourd'hui. Tu vas mettre un short, un tee-shirt et _____.
   a. des bottes
   b. un survêtement
   c. des lunettes de soleil

9. Les sandales, les tennis et les baskets sont des _____.
   a. lunettes
   b. bottes
   c. chaussures

Nom _____

Classe _____ Date _____ _____

Discovering
FRENCH
Nouveau!

B L E U

10. Je vais mettre un _____ avec mon tee-shirt. Il fait frais.
    a. collant
    b. sweat
    c. chapeau

11. Benjamin n'a pas de vêtements très à la mode. Son pantalon est _____.
    a. chouette
    b. génial
    c. démodé

12. —_____ du manteau?
    —Il coûte 150 euros.
    a. Combien coûte
    b. Comment trouves-tu
    c. Quel est le prix

13. _____ du blouson noir?
    a. Qu'est-ce que tu penses
    b. Comment trouves-tu
    c. Tu penses

14. —Est-ce ce que le pull rose est trop cher?
    —Non, il est _____.
    a. bon marché
    b. à la mode
    c. quinze euros

15. —Tu cherches tes lunettes?
    —Oui, et je _____ mes lunettes!
    a. ne pense pas
    b. pense
    c. ne trouve pas

16. —Comment tu trouves la jupe? Moche?
    —Pas du tout! Elle est _____.
    a. joli
    b. élégant
    c. géniale

17. Ce pantalon est trop grand. Je vais mettre _____.
    a. une ceinture
    b. une casquette
    c. une chemise

18. 800, 900, _____.
    a. dix cent
    b. mille
    c. dix cents

Nom _____

Classe _____ Date _____ _____

Discovering
FRENCH
Nouveau!

BLEU

Unité 6
Resources

Multiple Choice Test Items

Keeping in mind the cost of these clothing items, indicate how much each of the following two people spends:

Sweater: 50 euros   Skirt: 65 euros
Hat: 35 euros   Pants: 52 euros
Wool overcoat: 250 euros   Dress: 82 euros
Raincoat: 85 euros   Tie: 27 euros

19. Charlotte va acheter une robe et un manteau.
    a. cent cinquante euros
    b. cent soixante-sept euros
    c. trois cent trente-deux euros

20. Simon va acheter un pantalon, un pull et un chapeau.
    a. cent quatre-vingt-sept
    b. cent trente-sept
    c. cent vingt-neuf

Leçon 18

1. —Qu'est-ce que vous achetez?
   —Michel _____ un beau blouson. Moi, j'achète un manteau.
   a. achètes
   b. achète
   c. achetons

2. —Vous achetez la veste bleue ou la veste noire?
   —Je _____ la veste bleue.
   a. préfère
   b. préférer
   c. préférez

3. Jean _____ sa cousine à notre fête.
   a. apporte
   b. amène
   c. amenons

4. J'_____ acheter une voiture au printemps.
   a. achète
   b. espère
   c. amène

5. Vous _____ voyager avec tante Annie.
   a. espères
   b. préférez
   c. espérer

6. —Est-ce qu'elles aiment les jupes?
   —Oui, mais elles _____ les jeans.
   a. préfère
   b. préfères
   c. préfèrent

Nom _____

Classe _____ Date _____ _____

7. —Qu'est-ce que tu _____ quand tu vas à une boum?
   —Des CD.
   a. amènes
   b. amenez
   c. apportes

8. _____ chemise est super!
   a. Ce
   b. Cet
   c. Cette

9. Mes parents vont acheter _____ appartement.
   a. sept
   b. cet
   c. cette

10. _____ sandales coûtent cher.
    a. Ce
    b. Cette
    c. Ces

11. —Tu préfères ces chaussettes-_____ ou ces chaussettes-là?
    a. ce
    b. ci
    c. le

12. Cet _____ est mon professeur.
    a. femme
    b. homme
    c. monsieur

13. Dans _____ magasin est-ce que tu achètes tes CD?
    a. quel
    b. quelle
    c. quels

14. —_____ chemise est-ce que tu préfères?
    —Celle-ci.
    a. La
    b. Cette
    c. Quelle

15. Avec _____ copains est-ce que tu vas aller à la boum?
    a. quel
    b. quelles
    c. quels

16. Quelles _____ est-ce que tu aimes porter?
    a. pantalon
    b. pulls
    c. chaussures

Nom _____

Classe _____ Date _____ _____

Discovering FRENCH *Nouveau!*

B L E U

Unité 6 Resources

Multiple Choice Test Items

17. —Où est-ce qu'elle _____ ses livres?
    —Dans son sac.
     a. apporte
     b. amène
     c. met

18. Vous _____ un manteau quand il fait froid.
     a. mets
     b. mettent
     c. mettez

19. —Est-ce que tu mets la télé?
    —Non, je _____ la radio.
     a. met
     b. mettes
     c. mets

20. Quelle robe est-ce qu'elle va _____ pour aller à cette soirée?
     a. met
     b. mettent
     c. mettre

Leçon 19

1. Nous mangeons trop, alors nous _____.
    a. maigrissons
    b. choisissons
    c. grossissons

2. Quand ils jouent au foot, ils _____ à maigrir.
    a. finissons
    b. réussissent
    c. choisit

3. L'été _____ en septembre.
    a. réussis
    b. maigris
    c. finit

4. Je _____ la robe bleue. La robe rouge est trop grande.
    a. choisis
    b. choisit
    c. choisir

Nom _____

Classe _____ Date _____ _____

"10" is the minimum grade required to pass the exam. Look at the grade report below and complete the following three sentences.

Martin: 9,5
Thomas: 12
Chantal: 11
Martine: 15
Sabine: 17
Didier: 8
Moi: 14

5. Martin et Didier _____ à l'examen.
   a. réussissent
   b. ne réussissent pas
   c. ne réussissons pas

6. Ma copine Sabine et moi _____.
   a. réussissent
   b. réussit
   c. réussissons

7. Chantal _____.
   a. réussit
   b. réussisse
   c. réussis

8. Mon imper est démodé. Je voudrais acheter un _____ imper.
   a. vieil
   b. belle
   c. nouvel

9. Je voudrais apporter mes _____ pulls à l'église.
   a. nouvelles
   b. beau
   c. vieux

10. —Cette affiche est très _____.
    —Oh non! Elle est moche.
    a. beau
    b. bel
    c. belle

11. Voici Mme Rivera. C'est notre _____ prof d'espagnol.
    a. nouveau
    b. nouvel
    c. nouvelle

12. Je voudrais trouver un _____ appartement.
    a. bel
    b. nouveau
    c. vieux

Nom _____

Classe _____ Date _____ _____

Discovering FRENCH *Nouveau!*

B L E U

Unité 6 Resources

Multiple Choice Test Items

13. Un vélo est _____ qu'une voiture.
    a. plus gros
    b. moins cher
    c. aussi petite

14. Andre Agassi est _____ que Plácido Domingo.
    a. plus sportif
    b. moins amusante
    c. aussi riches

15. Ma pizza est _____ que ton sandwich.
    a. plus bonne
    b. meilleure
    c. moins cher

16. Tu es plus grand _____.
    a. qu'il
    b. que lui
    c. que je

17. Les filles sont _____ que les garçons.
    a. plus intelligents
    b. aussi intéressantes
    c. moins gentille

18. La tante de ma mère est _____ que ma grand-mère.
    a. plus vieille
    b. plus vieux
    c. plus vieil

19. À ton avis, quels étudiants sont _____ que moi?
    a. plus intelligent
    b. plus timides
    c. plus belles

20. Michael Jordan est plus grand que _____.
    a. nous
    b. eux
    c. tu

Leçon 20

1. —Tu as cinq pièces d'un euro?
   —Non, mais j'ai _____ de cinq euros.
    a. l'argent
    b. un billet
    c. une bille

2. Bill Gates n'est pas _____.
    a. paie
    b. pauvre
    c. pièce

Nom _____

Classe _____ Date _____ _____

Discovering
FRENCH
Nouveau!

B L E U

3. —_____ billets de dix euros est-ce que tu as?
   —Trois. J'ai trente euros.
   a. Comment
   b. Combien
   c. Combien de

4. Si je _____ au loto, j'achète une voiture!
   a. paie
   b. dépense
   c. gagne

5. —Ce pantalon coûte cinquante-cinq euros et j'ai quarante-cinq euros.
   —Alors, tu _____ dix euros.
   a. envie de
   b. as besoin de
   c. paies

6. —Voici trois euros pour mon soda.
   —Non, non, Florent. J' _____ aujourd'hui!
   a. paies
   b. paie
   c. achetons

7. On _____ quand on va trop au restaurant.
   a. grossis
   b. grossit
   c. grossissons

8. Dans cet hôtel, _____ parle français, anglais et espagnol.
   a. il
   b. elle
   c. on

9. Vous _____ le bus?
   a. attendez
   b. entendons
   c. vendent

10. On _____ le mois de juillet pour aller à la plage.
    a. entend
    b. perd
    c. attend

11. Je _____ à mes mails.
    a. rends visite
    b. perds
    c. réponds

12. Elles _____ visite à leurs grands-parents le dimanche.
    a. rend
    b. rends
    c. rendent

Nom _____

Classe _____ Date _____ _____

Discovering
FRENCH *Nouveau!*

BLEU

Unité 6
Resources

Multiple Choice Test Items

13. Nous _____ notre maison.
    a. attends
    b. perdent
    c. vendons

14. Vous _____ souvent vos lunettes!
    a. perds
    b. perdons
    c. perdez

15. Nathalie, _____ à 11 h, s'il te plaît.
    a. rentre
    b. rentres
    c. rentrer

16. Morgane! Marie! _____ votre frère!
    a. Attendez
    b. Entendons
    c. Perds

17. Hugo, _____ pas ton argent!
    a. perdez
    b. ne perd
    c. ne perds

18. —Qu'est-ce qu'on va faire?
    —_____ à la piscine!
    a. Allons
    b. Vont
    c. Vais

19. —J'achète ce manteau?
    —Oh non, _____ ce manteau. Il n'est pas beau.
    a. achètes
    b. ne pas acheter
    c. n'achète pas

20. Les enfants? Pas de télé! _____ vos devoirs!
    a. Finis
    b. Fini
    c. Finissez

Nom _____

Classe _____ Date _____

Discovering
FRENCH
Nouveau!

BLEU

Unité 6
Resources

Comprehensive Test 2
Form A

UNITÉ 6 Comprehensive Test 2 (Units 4, 5, 6)   FORM A

Part I. Listening Comprehension (25 points)

1. Au grand magasin (8 points)

You are shopping for clothes in a department store in Paris. Listen to the prices of various items and select the appropriate number on your test paper. Then, blacken the corresponding letter—a, b, c, or d— on your answer sheet. You will hear each item twice.

Modèle: [La veste coûte 200 euros.]

   a. 300   b. 400   c. 200   d. 100

1. a. 60   b. 110   c. 130   d. 150

2. a. 80   b. 40   c. 50   d. 90

3. a. 350   b. 30   c. 300   d. 330

4. a. 15   b. 25   c. 20   d. 35

5. a. 580   b. 850   c. 680   d. 520

6. a. 105   b. 180   c. 150   d. 160

7. a. 25   b. 35   c. 45   d. 55

8. a. 89   b. 88   c. 90   d. 80

Nom _____

Classe _____ Date _____

Discovering
FRENCH
Nouveau

B L E U

2. La famille de Marc (7 points)

Look at Marc's family tree below. Listen to the statements about his family and decide if they are true (**vrai**) or false (**faux**). Then, blacken the appropriate letter—a or b—on your answer sheet. You will hear each item twice.

Modèle: [Jean-Paul est le père de Marc.]
      a. vrai   b. faux

  9. a. vrai   b. faux

10. a. vrai   b. faux

11. a. vrai   b. faux

12. a. vrai   b. faux

13. a. vrai   b. faux

14. a. vrai   b. faux

15. a. vrai   b. faux

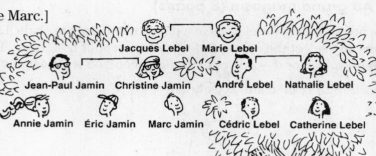

3. La réponse logique (10 points)

You will hear a series of ten questions. Listen carefully to each question and select the most logical response on your test paper. Then blacken the corresponding letter—a, b, or c—on your answer sheet. You will hear each question twice.

Modèle: [Qu'est-ce que tu achètes?]
      a. Cent euros.   b. À la pharmacie.   c. Des CD.

16. a. Oui, elle va faire une promenade.
    b. Non, elle est bleue.
    c. Non, mais j'ai une moto.

17. a. À dix heures.
    b. Un film américain.
    c. Je cherche une télé.

18. a. Sous la table.
    b. Marron et jaune.
    c. Il est bête.

19. a. Non, à gauche.
    b. Non, c'est loin d'ici.
    c. Non, c'est près.

20. a. Oui, il fait un sandwich.
    b. Non, la cuisine est en bas.
    c. Oui, elle mange dans la cuisine.

21. a. Oui, nous allons en classe.
    b. Non, continuez tout droit.
    c. Non, à pied.

22. a. Je vais jouer au volley.
    b. Oui, je viens de la plage.
    c. Non, la plage est très loin.

23. a. Je vais au match.
    b. Il n'est plus à la mode.
    c. Il fait froid.

24. a. D'accord, c'est une bonne idée.
    b. Peut-être, c'est difficile.
    c. Oui, il y a un cinéma.

25. a. Au prof d'anglais.
    b. À cette question.
    c. Parce que je veux répondre.

Nom _____

Classe _____ Date _____ _____

Discovering
FRENCH
Nouveau!

B L E U

Unité 6
Resources

Comprehensive Test 2
Form A

Part II. Language and Communication (40 points)

4. Les objets trouvés (5 points)

The people below are looking for their missing objects at the lost and found. Read the items and decide which word from the box correctly completes each sentence. Then, mark the corresponding letter—a, b, c, d, or e—on your answer sheet. (Note: Some words may be used more than once and others not at all.)

a. **leur**	b. **sa**	c. **leurs**	d. **ses**	e. **son**

26. Frédéric cherche _____ survêtement.
    a. ❑   b. ❑   c. ❑   d. ❑   e. ❑

27. Alice cherche _____ affiche.
    a. ❑   b. ❑   c. ❑   d. ❑   e. ❑

28. M. et Mme Lenoir cherchent _____ radiocassette.
    a. ❑   b. ❑   c. ❑   d. ❑   e. ❑

29. Stéphanie cherche _____ calculatrice.
    a. ❑   b. ❑   c. ❑   d. ❑   e. ❑

30. Marc et Isabelle cherchent _____ stylos.
    a. ❑   b. ❑   c. ❑   d. ❑   e. ❑

Nom _____

Classe _____ Date _____

5. Le bon choix (15 points)

One or more words have been omitted from the sentences below. Read the items carefully and decide which choice correctly completes each sentence. Then, mark the corresponding letter—a, b, c, or d—on your answer sheet.

31. Nous allons _____ du shopping cet après-midi.
   a. faisons   b. font   c. fait   d. faire

32. Tu connais Alice? _____ une fille très intelligente!
   a. Elle est   b. Ce sont   c. C'est   d. Il est

33. Qui _____ à la boum?
   a. viens   b. vient   c. viennent   d. venir

34. —C'est M. Mercier? —Non, ce n'est pas _____.
   a. lui   b. eux   c. il   d. moi

35. Hélène joue très bien _____ flûte.
   a. à la   b. la   c. une   d. de la

36. Dis, _____ bottes est-ce que tu vas choisir?
   a. quels   b. quelle   c. quel   d. quelles

37. J'ai un _____ appareil-photo.
   a. beau   b. mauvaise   c. vieux   d. nouvel

38. Mme Duval va _____ hôpital aujourd'hui.
   a. l'   b. à l'   c. à   d. au

39. Michel achète _____ veste-là.
   a. ce   b. cet   c. cette   d. c'est

40. Mes copains viennent _____ stade municipal.
   a. de   b. du   c. de la   d. la

41. Roger, _____ ton devoir!
   a. finis   b. finir   c. finissez   d. finit

42. Nathalie a 100 euros et Karine en a 150. Karine est _____ riche que Nathalie.
   a. meilleure   b. plus   c. aussi   d. moins

43. Mes voisins sont _____.
   a. japonais   b. mexicaines   c. canadien   d. espagnole

44. C'est la guitare _____ garçon là-bas.
   a. —   b. de   c. du   d. des

45. Est-ce que tu _____ ce vélo?
   a. choisit   b. attends   c. maigris   d. vends

Nom _____

Classe _____ Date _____

Discovering FRENCH *Nouveau!*

B L E U

Unité 6 Resources

Comprehensive Test 2

Form A

6. La chambre de Nicole (5 points)

Look at the picture of Nicole's room and read the sentences below. Decide which word from the box correctly completes each item. Then, mark the corresponding letter—a, b, c, d, or e—on your answer sheet. (Note: Some words may be used more than once and others not at all.)

| a. **dans** | b. **sur** | c. **derrière** | d. **sous** | e. **devant** |

46. Le sac est _____ la table.
    a. ❏   b. ❏   c. ❏   d. ❏   e. ❏

47. La chaise est _____ la guitare.
    a. ❏   b. ❏   c. ❏   d. ❏   e. ❏

48. La télé est _____ la table.
    a. ❏   b. ❏   c. ❏   d. ❏   e. ❏

49. Le sac est _____ la télé.
    a. ❏   b. ❏   c. ❏   d. ❏   e. ❏

50. Le cahier est _____ le sac.
    a. ❏   b. ❏   c. ❏   d. ❏   e. ❏

Nom _____

Classe _____ Date _____ _____

Discovering
FRENCH
Nouveau

B L E U

7. L'intrus (5 points)

Which word is the intruder? Read each item below to determine the word that does *not* correctly complete the sentence. Then, mark the corresponding letter—a, b, or c—on your answer sheet.

51. Annie _____ la radio.
    a. entend
    b. cherche
    c. dépense

52. Denis _____ les CD à son copain.
    a. apporte
    b. prête
    c. amène

53. M. Duval _____ visiter Paris cet été.
    a. veut
    b. met
    c. espère

54. Isabelle _____ du musée.
    a. vient
    b. va
    c. revient

55. Cet homme _____ au café.
    a. porte
    b. reste
    c. téléphone

8. Situations (5 points)

What would you say in the following situations? Read each item carefully and select the *best* expression. Then, mark the corresponding letter—a, b, or c—on your answer sheet.

56. *You want to know what Annie is going to do. You ask:*
    a. Qu'est-ce que tu dois faire?
    b. Qu'est-ce que tu vas faire?
    c. Qu'est-ce que tu fais?

57. *A woman on the street asks where the city library is. You answer:*
    a. Allez à la bibliothèque municipale.
    b. C'est la bibliothèque municipale.
    c. C'est près d'ici.

58. *You want to know if Pierre's portable player works. You ask:*
    a. Est-ce qu'il marche?
    b. Il travaille bien?
    c. Il va bien, n'est-ce pas?

59. *Your neighbor asks what is in your garage. You say:*
    a. Bien sûr, j'ai un vélo.
    b. Il n'y a pas de vélo.
    c. Il y a deux vélos.

60. *Patrick asks where your sister is. You answer:*
    a. Elle va faire une promenade.
    b. Je ne sais pas.
    c. C'est en ville.

Nom _____

Classe _____ Date _____

Discovering
FRENCH
Nouveau!

B L E U

Unité 6
Resources

Comprehensive Test 2
Form A

9. Des phrases embrouillées *(scrambled)* (5 points)

Your computer has scrambled the sentences below. Read each item and decide the logical order of the sentences. Then, mark the corresponding letter—a, b, c, d, or e—on your answer sheet.

61.    a. Moi aussi. Elle est à la mode.

62.    b. Qu'est-ce que tu penses de cette cravate?

63.    c. Une cravate.

64.    d. Elle est jolie mais je préfère la cravate bleue.

65.    e. Qu'est-ce que tu cherches, Christophe?

Nom _____

Classe _____ Date _____

Part III. Reading Comprehension (20 points)

10. À Villeneuve (5 points)

People are asking for directions to places in Villeneuve. Look carefully at the map and select the best answer to each question. Then, mark the corresponding letter—a, b, or c—on your answer sheet. (Note: The people talking are located at X on the map.)

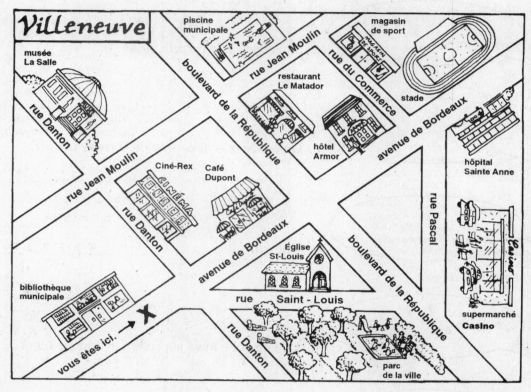

66. Pardon, madame. Où est l'église St-Louis?
   a. Continuez tout droit et tournez à droite.
   b. Tournez à gauche rue Danton.
   c. Continuez tout droit rue de Bordeaux.

67. Le musée La Salle est près d'ici?
   a. Non, il est près de l'hôpital Sainte Anne.
   b. Oui, tournez à gauche rue Danton.
   c. Non, il est très loin.

68. Il y a un hôpital avenue de Bordeaux?
   a. Non, tournez à gauche boulevard de la République.
   b. Oui, c'est tout droit.
   c. Oui, continuez à droite rue Pascal.

69. Où est la piscine municipale, s'il vous plaît?
   a. Elle est près du restaurant.
   b. C'est près d'ici rue du Commerce.
   c. À droite du stade.

70. Est-ce qu'il y a un ciné rue Danton?
   a. Non, boulevard de la République.
   b. Oui, tournez à gauche.
   c. Oui, tournez à droite rue Danton.

Nom _____

Classe _____ Date _____

Discovering FRENCH *Nouveau!*

B L E U

Unité 6
Resources

Comprehensive Test 2
Form A

11. On cherche des correspondants (5 points)

Five teenagers are looking for pen pals. Read their requests and the questions that follow. Select the ad which *best* answers each question. Then, mark the corresponding letter—a, b, c, d, or e—on your answer sheet.

Le club des Correspondants

a.
Garçon français,
16 ans, brun, yeux bleus, sympathique mais un peu timide, voudrait correspondre avec Américaine ou Anglaise parlant le français. Aime le sport, le ciné et la moto. Joindre photo. Réponse assurée.
   Olivier Lambesq
   25, place Gambetta
   24100 Bergerac

b.
Jeune Française,
15 ans, sportive (tennis, basket, ski) désire correspondre avec étudiants américains ou anglais du même âge pour échanger posters et CD de rock et de rap.
Écrire à:
   Dominique Loiseau
   32, rue du Dragon
   75006 Paris

c.
J'aime la danse,
le cinéma et la musique. J'ai 16 ans et je suis française. Je voudrais correspondre avec fille ou garçon de mon âge, de préférence porto-ricain ou mexicain, pour échanger CD de musique latine ou de guitare espagnole.
   Carole Gaune
   45, boulevard de la Mer
   76200 Dieppe, France

d.
Jeune Américain,
16 ans, voudrait correspondre avec jeunes Français du même âge parlant l'anglais. Aime le ciné, la musique classique et la moto. Joindre photo. Réponse assurée.
   Patrick Smith
   1329 Cole Street
   San Francisco, CA 94117

e.
Je m'appelle Julie,
et j'ai douze ans. Je voudrais correspondre avec un garçon canadien de 13 à 15 ans, parlant anglais, pour échanger CD. J'aime le jazz, le rock et le rap.
   Julie Cartier
   25, rue Colbert
   63000 Clermont-Ferrand.

Mots croisés

	1	2	3	4	5	6	7	8	9
I									
II									
III				■			■		
IV					■				
V						■	■		

---

71. Qui voudrait correspondre avec les Français de 16 ans?
   a. ☐   b. ☐   c. ☐   d. ☐   e. ☐

72. Qui pratique plusieurs sports?
   a. ☐   b. ☐   c. ☐   d. ☐   e. ☐

73. Qui a une moto?
   a. ☐   b. ☐   c. ☐   d. ☐   e. ☐

74. Qui aime écouter la musique espagnole?
   a. ☐   b. ☐   c. ☐   d. ☐   e. ☐

75. Qui cherche un correspondant canadien?
   a. ☐   b. ☐   c. ☐   d. ☐   e. ☐

Nom _____

Classe _____ Date _____

12. Cinq boutiques (5 points)

Look at the ads for five French specialty shops. Read the sentences which follow and decide if they are true (**vrai**) or false (**faux**) based on the information in the ads. Then, mark the corresponding letter—a or b—on your answer sheet.

76. La boutique Madelios vend des accessoires de vêtements.　　a. vrai　　b. faux

77. Mme Duval va chez VdeV pour acheter un survêtement.　　a. vrai　　b. faux

78. Chez Aster, le blazer est plus cher que la veste.　　a. vrai　　b. faux

79. Annie va chez Rallye pour acheter des baskets.　　a. vrai　　b. faux

80. Marc achète son équipement sportif au Jockey-Club.　　a. vrai　　b. faux

Nom _____

Classe _____ Date _____ _____

Discovering
FRENCH
Nouveau!

BLEU

Unité 6
Resources

Comprehensive Test 2
Form A

13. Stéphanie (5 points)

Carefully read the passage and questions which follow, selecting the best answer to each item. Then, mark the corresponding letter—a, b, c, or d—on your answer sheet.

> Aujourd'hui, c'est vendredi. Demain après-midi, il n'y a pas classe. Où est-ce que Stéphanie va aller? Est-ce qu'elle va aller en ville? Est-ce qu'elle va aller à la campagne (*countryside*)? Est-ce qu'elle va aller au cinéma? Est-ce qu'elle va aller chez ses copains? Stéphanie n'est pas sûre; elle hésite. Elle regarde le programme de télévision. Tiens! Il y a une comédie. Stéphanie adore les comédies! Demain après-midi, Stéphanie va rester chez elle. Elle va regarder la télé.

81. Demain, c'est _____.
   a. vendredi
   b. jeudi
   c. samedi
   d. dimanche

82. Demain après-midi, Stéphanie va _____.
   a. à l'école
   b. en ville
   c. au cinéma
   d. chez elle

83. Stéphanie va _____.
   a. regarder un programme amusant
   b. aller à la campagne
   c. regarder un film
   d. réparer la télé

84. Stéphanie ne va pas à l'école parce qu'elle _____.
   a. n'a pas envie d'étudier
   b. déteste ses profs
   c. n'aime pas la cafétéria
   d. n'a pas de classe

85. Stéphanie va regarder le programme _____.
   a. chez elle
   b. au cinéma
   c. chez ses copains
   d. à l'école

Nom _____

Classe _____ Date _____

Part IV. Cultural Awareness (15 points)

14. Méli-mélo culturel *(cultural jumble)* (15 points)

How much do you know about French-speaking people and their everyday life? Read each sentence below and decide whether the item is true (**vrai**) or false (**faux**). Then, mark the corresponding letter—a or b—on your answer sheet.

86. a. vrai   b. faux   French teens sometimes do small jobs for their neighbors to earn extra money.

87. a. vrai   b. faux   A Frenchman created the department store concept and opened his first store in Paris.

88. a. vrai   b. faux   Tourists go to Versailles to visit its famous **château**, built by Louis XIV.

89. a. vrai   b. faux   Haitians speak Créole and Spanish.

90. a. vrai   b. faux   In France, one must be at least 16 years old to drive a car.

91. a. vrai   b. faux   **Renault** is a large company specializing in computers.

92. a. vrai   b. faux   Most French young people have a positive attitude toward the United States.

93. a. vrai   b. faux   French teenagers take driving lessons as a part of their high school curriculum.

94. a. vrai   b. faux   **Ariane** rockets are built in Toulouse, France.

95. a. vrai   b. faux   For French young people, friendship rates first on the scale of personal values.

96. a. vrai   b. faux   **Compas** is a genre of music that is popular in Haiti.

97. a. vrai   b. faux   **Le Centre Pompidou** is a large sports complex on the outskirts of Paris.

98. a. vrai   b. faux   Tours is a town located southwest of Paris.

99. a. vrai   b. faux   Christian Dior and Pierre Cardin are famous French artists.

100. a. vrai   b. faux   Clothes in France are generally less expensive than those in the United States.

Nom _____

Classe _____ Date _____

Discovering FRENCH *Nouveau!*

BLEU

Unité 6 Resources
Comprehensive Test 2
Form B

UNITÉ 6 Comprehensive Test 2 (Units 4, 5, 6) FORM B

Part I. Listening Comprehension (25 points)

1. Au grand magasin (8 points)

You are shopping for clothes in a department store in Paris. Listen to the prices of various items and select the appropriate number on your test paper. Then, blacken the corresponding letter—a, b, c, or d—on your answer sheet. You will hear each item twice.

Modèle: [La veste coûte 200 euros.]

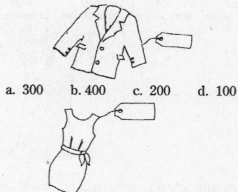

a. 300   b. 400   c. 200   d. 100

1. a. 225   b. 200   c. 235   d. 245   **5.** a. 340   b. 330   c. 310   d. 300

2. a. 80   b. 50   c. 60   d. 65   **6.** a. 100   b. 80   c. 200   d. 20

   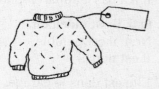

3. a. 80   b. 40   c. 400   d. 800   **7.** a. 130   b. 50   c. 100   d. 200

4. a. 35   b. 25   c. 45   d. 20   **8.** a. 400   b. 420   c. 800   d. 80

Nom _____

Classe _____ Date _____

2. La famille de Marc (7 points)

Look at Marc's family tree below. Listen to the statements about his family and decide if they are true (**vrai**) or false (**faux**). Then, blacken the appropriate letter—a or b—on your answer sheet. You will hear each item twice.

Modèle: [Jean-Paul est le père de Marc.]
      a. vrai   b. faux

  9. a. vrai   b. faux

10. a. vrai   b. faux

11. a. vrai   b. faux

12. a. vrai   b. faux

13. a. vrai   b. faux

14. a. vrai   b. faux

15. a. vrai   b. faux

3. La réponse logique (10 points)

You will hear a series of ten questions. Listen carefully to each question and select the most logical response on your test paper. Then, blacken the corresponding letter—a, b, or c—on your answer sheet. You will hear each question twice.

Modèle: [Qu'est-ce que tu achètes?]
      a. Cent euros.   b. À la pharmacie.   c. Des CD.

16. a. Mon copain.
    b. C'est mon quartier.
    c. Il n'a pas d'appareil-photo.

17. a. Oui, il est méchant.
    b. Non, il est pénible.
    c. Il est noir.

18. a. Elle est dans le garage.
    b. Elle marche très bien.
    c. Elle est jaune.

19. a. Non, ils sont à la maison.
    b. Non, ils regardent la télé.
    c. Oui, ils sont au salon.

20. a. En haut.
    b. En bus.
    c. En solde.

21. a. Elles sont propres.
    b. Tout droit.
    c. Oui, il y a les toilettes.

22. a. Oui, elle est blanche.
    b. Elle est moche.
    c. Elle est d'accord.

23. a. J'adore danser.
    b. Ma copine Annie.
    c. De nouveaux CD.

24. a. Parce qu'il est vieux.
    b. Je vais à la plage.
    c. Je vais manger.

25. a. Trois cents euros.
    b. J'ai besoin d'argent.
    c. Je n'ai pas de pièces d'un euro.

Nom _____

Classe _____ Date _____

Discovering FRENCH *Nouveau!*

BLEU

Unité 6 Resources

Comprehensive Test 2 Form B

Part II. Language and Communication (40 points)

4. Les objets trouvés (5 points)

The people below are looking for their missing objects at the lost and found. Read the items and decide which word correctly completes each sentence. Then, mark the corresponding letter—a, b, c, d, or e—on your answer sheet. (Note: Some words may be used more than once and others not at all.)

a. **leur**	b. **sa**	c. **leurs**	d. **ses**	e. **son**

26. Jérôme cherche _____ chemise.
   a. ❑   b. ❑   c. ❑   d. ❑   e. ❑

27. Le prof cherche _____ crayons.
   a. ❑   b. ❑   c. ❑   d. ❑   e. ❑

28. M. et Mme Boucher cherchent _____ livres.
   a. ❑   b. ❑   c. ❑   d. ❑   e. ❑

29. Sophie cherche _____ appareil-photo.
   a. ❑   b. ❑   c. ❑   d. ❑   e. ❑

30. François et Isabelle cherchent _____ chien.
   a. ❑   b. ❑   c. ❑   d. ❑   e. ❑

5. Le bon choix (15 points)

One or more words are missing from the sentences below. Read the items carefully and decide which choice correctly completes each sentence. Then, mark the corresponding letter—a, b, c, or d—on your answer sheet.

31. Je vais _____ ce polo.
    a. achète   b. acheter   c. acheté   d. achètes

32. —Où est Marc? — _____ en haut.
    a. Il est   b. C'est   c. Elle est   d. Ce sont

33. Qui _____ les CD?
    a. mettre   b. mets   c. met   d. mettent

34. —C'est Mme Duval? —Oui, bien sûr, c'est _____.
    a. lui   b. elle   c. sa   d. leur

35. Tu veux jouer _____ cartes avec moi?
    a. les   b. au   c. des   d. aux

36. _____ imper préfères-tu?
    a. Quelle   b. Quel   c. Quels   d. Quelles

37. Ma soeur a une _____ auto.
    a. vieille   b. nouvel   c. joli   d. belles

38. Ils étudient _____ bibliothèque.
    a. à   b. au   c. la   d. à la

39. Jérôme regarde _____ jean-ci.
    a. c'est   b. ce   c. cet   d. ces

40. Je n'ai pas _____ calculatrice.
    a. de   b. des   c. mon   d. de la

41. Les élèves, _____ attention maintenant!
    a. faire   b. font   c. fais   d. faites

42. Marc joue au tennis et Nathalie étudie. Marc est _____ sportif que Nathalie.
    a. peux   b. plus   c. peu   d. près

43. Ses copines sont _____.
    a. gentils   b. méchants   c. amusantes   d. timide

44. Voilà la voiture _____ Madame Vénard.
    a. de la   b. de   c. —   d. du

45. Est-ce que tu _____ à l'école?
    a. fais   b. finis   c. attends   d. réussis

Nom _____

Classe _____ Date _____

Discovering FRENCH *Nouveau!*

BLEU

Unité 6
Resources

Comprehensive Test 2
Form B

6. La chambre de Nicole (5 points)

Look at the picture of Nicole's room and read the sentences below. Decide which word correctly completes each item.

a. **dans**	b. **sur**	c. **derrière**	d. **sous**	e. **devant**

46. L'ordinateur est _____ le bureau.
   a. ❑   b. ❑   c. ❑   d. ❑   e. ❑

47. Le vélo est _____ la fenêtre.
   a. ❑   b. ❑   c. ❑   d. ❑   e. ❑

48. La guitare est _____ la chaise.
   a. ❑   b. ❑   c. ❑   d. ❑   e. ❑

49. La raquette est _____ le lit.
   a. ❑   b. ❑   c. ❑   d. ❑   e. ❑

50. La cassette est _____ la chaise.
   a. ❑   b. ❑   c. ❑   d. ❑   e. ❑

Nom _____

Classe _____ Date _____

Discovering FRENCH *Nouveau!*

B L E U

Unité 6 Resources
Comprehensive Test 2
Form B

7. L'intrus (5 points)

Which word is the intruder? Read each item below to determine the word that does *not* correctly complete the sentence. Then, mark the corresponding letter—a, b, or c—on your answer sheet.

51. Hélène _____ ses classes.
    a. aime
    b. étudie
    c. finit

52. Jean-Paul _____ sa mère.
    a. attend
    b. écoute
    c. téléphone

53. Stéphanie _____ les photos de Jacques.
    a. cherche
    b. dépense
    c. regarde

54. André va _____ le match.
    a. vendre
    b. gagner
    c. perdre

55. Luc _____ un nouveau pull.
    a. entend
    b. met
    c. porte

8. Situations (5 points)

What would you say in the following situations? Read each item carefully and select the *best* expression. Then, mark the corresponding letter—a, b, or c—on your answer sheet.

56. *You want to know if a swimming pool is nearby. You ask:*
    a. Pardon, comment est la piscine?
    b. Il y a une piscine près d'ici?
    c. Qu'est-ce qu'il y a à la piscine?

57. *Nathalie asks where you are coming from. You answer:*
    a. Je vais au centre commercial.
    b. Je viens de la bibliothèque.
    c. Je visite un café.

58. *A classmate asks if you have a pen. You answer:*
    a. Non, je n'ai pas de stylo.
    b. Oui, j'achète un stylo.
    c. Oui, son stylo est sur la table.

59. *You want to know where your teacher is going. You ask:*
    a. Où êtes-vous, monsieur?
    b. Comment allez-vous, monsieur?
    c. Où allez-vous, monsieur?

60. *Your mother asks how your sister is going to school. You answer:*
    a. Elle fait une promenade.
    b. Elle va à pied.
    c. Elle marche très bien.

Nom _____

Classe _____ Date _____

Discovering
FRENCH
Nouveau!

BLEU

Unité 6
Resources

Comprehensive Test 2
Form B

9. Des phrases embrouillées *(scrambled)* (5 points)

Your computer has scrambled the sentences below. Read each item and decide the logical order of the sentences. Then, mark the corresponding letter—a, b, c, d, or e—on your answer sheet.

61.    a. Nous allons écouter ses nouveaux CD.

62.    b. D'accord, je viens!

63.    c. Je vais chez mon cousin. Tu viens?

64.    d. Où vas-tu, Nathalie?

65.    e. Ça dépend. Qu'est-ce que vous allez faire?

Nom _____

Classe _____ Date _____

Part III. Reading Comprehension (20 points)

10. À Villeneuve (5 points)

People are asking for directions to places in Villeneuve. Look carefully at the map and select the best answer to each question. Then, mark the corresponding letter—a, b, or c—on your answer sheet. (Note: The people talking are located at X on the map.)

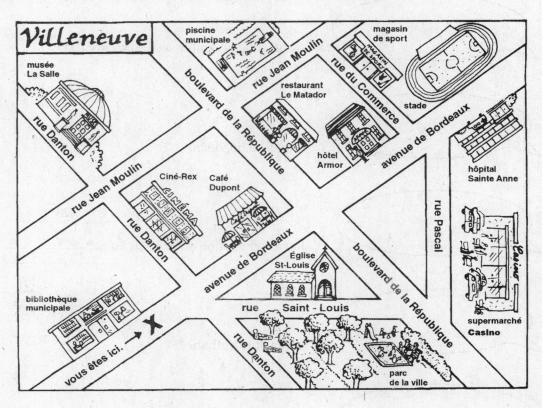

66. C'est près d'ici, le magasin de sport?
    a. Oui, très près.
    b. Non, c'est près du musée.
    c. Non, c'est assez loin.

67. Pardon, monsieur. Où est le parc de la ville?
    a. C'est tout droit.
    b. Tournez à droite rue Saint-Louis.
    c. Continuez tout droit et tournez à gauche.

68. Où est l'hôtel Armor, s'il vous plaît?
    a. Il n'y a pas d'hôtel.
    b. Tout droit, à gauche.
    c. Tournez à gauche boulevard de la République.

69. Il y a un supermarché dans le quartier?
    a. Oui, près du parc de la ville.
    b. Non, le supermarché est près de la piscine.
    c. Oui, rue Danton.

70. Où est-ce qu'il y a un magasin de sport?
    a. Tournez à gauche boulevard de la République.
    b. Tournez à droite rue Jean Moulin.
    c. Tournez à gauche rue du Commerce.

Nom _____

Classe _____ Date _____

Discovering
FRENCH
Nouveau!

BLEU

Unité 6
Resources
Comprehensive Test 2
Form B

11. On cherche des correspondants (5 points)

Five teenagers are looking for pen pals. Read their requests and the questions that follow. Select the ad which *best* answers each question. Then, mark the corresponding letter—a, b, c, d, or e—on your answer sheet.

Le club des Correspondants

a. Garçon français,
16 ans, brun, yeux bleus, sympathique mais un peu timide, voudrait correspondre avec Américaine ou Anglaise parlant le français. Aime le sport, le ciné et la moto. Joindre photo. Réponse assurée.
  Olivier Lambesq
  25, place Gambetta
  24100 Bergerac

b. Jeune Française,
15 ans, sportive (tennis, basket, ski) désire correspondre avec étudiants américains ou anglais du même âge pour échanger posters et CD de rock et de rap.
Écrire à:
  Dominique Loiseau
  32, rue du Dragon
  75006 Paris

c. J'aime la danse,
le cinéma et la musique. J'ai 16 ans et je suis française. Je voudrais correspondre avec fille ou garçon de mon âge, de préférence porto-ricain ou mexicain, pour échanger CD de musique latine ou de guitare espagnole.
  Carole Gaune
  45, boulevard de la Mer
  76200 Dieppe, France

d. Jeune Américain,
16 ans, voudrait correspondre avec jeunes Français du même âge parlant l'anglais. Aime le ciné, la musique classique et la moto. Joindre photo. Réponse assurée.
  Patrick Smith
  1329 Cole Street
  San Francisco, CA 94117

e. Je m'appelle Julie,
et j'ai douze ans. Je voudrais correspondre avec un garçon canadien de 13 à 15 ans, parlant anglais, pour échanger CD. J'aime le jazz, le rock et le rap.
  Julie Cartier
  25, rue Colbert
  63000 Clermont-Ferrand.

Mots croisés

	1	2	3	4	5	6	7	8	9
I									
II									
III				■		■		■	
IV					■				
V						■			

71. Qui cherche des Français qui parlent anglais?
  a. ☐   b. ☐   c. ☐   d. ☐   e. ☐

72. Qui est de nationalité américaine?
  a. ☐   b. ☐   c. ☐   d. ☐   e. ☐

73. Qui voudrait correspondre avec un(e) élève qui parle espagnol?
  a. ☐   b. ☐   c. ☐   d. ☐   e. ☐

74. Qui cherche une correspondante américaine qui parle français?
  a. ☐   b. ☐   c. ☐   d. ☐   e. ☐

75. Qui voudrait échanger des affiches?
  a. ☐   b. ☐   c. ☐   d. ☐   e. ☐

12. Cinq boutiques (5 points)

Look at the ads for five French specialty shops. Read the sentences which follow and decide if they are true (**vrai**) or false (**faux**), based on the information in the ads. Then, mark the corresponding letter—a or b—on your answer sheet.

76. Nathalie va au Jockey-Club pour acheter ses chaussures de danse.   a. vrai   b. faux

77. Aster annonce des prix spéciaux pour le printemps.   a. vrai   b. faux

78. Sylvie va chez VdeV pour regarder les bikinis.   a. vrai   b. faux

79. La boutique Aster se spécialise en vêtements masculins.   a. vrai   b. faux

80. On trouve les vêtements pour les petits chez Rallye.   a. vrai   b. faux

Nom _____

Classe _____ Date _____

Discovering
FRENCH
Nouveau!

B L E U

Unité 6
Resources

Comprehensive Test 2
Form B

13. Chez François (5 points)

Carefully read the passage and questions which follow, selecting the best answer to each item. Then, mark the corresponding letter—a, b, c, or d—on your answer sheet.

> Regardez ces photos. Ce sont les photos de François. Là il joue au foot. C'est son sport préféré. Là il est à la plage avec ses copains. Regardez ces deux filles. Cette fille-ci s'appelle Sophie. Mais non, ce n'est pas la copine de François. C'est sa cousine! Sa copine, c'est cette fille-là. Elle s'appelle Christine. Elle n'est pas française; elle est canadienne. Elle passe ses vacances chez son oncle qui est un ami du père de François.

81. Les jeunes regardent _____.
    a. l'appareil-photo de François
    b. l'album de photos de Sophie
    c. les photos de François
    d. les photos d'une copine de François

82. François est _____.
    a. assez beau
    b. sérieux
    c. sportif
    d. très jeune

83. François est à la plage avec _____.
    a. deux filles
    b. ses meilleures amies
    c. ses camarades
    d. ses cousins

84. Christine passe ses vacances chez _____.
    a. l'oncle de François
    b. son oncle
    c. François
    d. le père de François

85. Le père de François est _____.
    a. le père de Christine aussi
    b. canadien
    c. un ami de l'oncle de Christine
    d. l'oncle de Christine

Discovering
FRENCH
Nouveau

B L E U

Part IV. Cultural Awareness (15 points)

14. Méli-mélo culturel *(cultural jumble)* (15 points)

How much do you know about French-speaking people and their everyday life? Read each sentence below and decide whether the item is true (**vrai**) or false (**faux**). Then, mark the corresponding letter—a or b—on your answer sheet.

86. a. vrai   b. faux   **Une boutique de soldes** is a small store specializing in high fashion clothing.

87. a. vrai   b. faux   French teenagers usually earn their spending money through part-time jobs.

88. a. vrai   b. faux   The ground level of a building is called **le rez-de-chaussée**.

89. a. vrai   b. faux   **Les Champs-Élysées** is a popular Paris movie theater.

90. a. vrai   b. faux   In France, one must be at least 16 years old to ride a moped.

91. a. vrai   b. faux   **Griots** is a popular Haitian dish.

92. a. vrai   b. faux   **Toulouse** is the center of the French aviation industry.

93. a. vrai   b. faux   The term **mobylette** is often shortened to **moby**.

94. a. vrai   b. faux   **Un grand magasin** is a large shopping mall.

95. a. vrai   b. faux   In order to have an extensive wardrobe, French teenagers prefer to buy more clothes of lesser quality.

96. a. vrai   b. faux   Victor Hugo is a famous French artist.

97. a. vrai   b. faux   **Le marché aux puces** is an open-air fruit and vegetable market.

98. a. vrai   b. faux   For watching people at a French café, customers prefer to sit **à l'intérieur**.

99. a. vrai   b. faux   Many French department stores have branches in cities throughout the country.

100. a. vrai   b. faux   The **Parc de la Villette** in Paris is a science museum.

Nom _____

Classe _____ Date _____

Discovering
FRENCH *Nouveau!*

B L E U

Unité 6
Resources

Test Scoring Tools

UNITÉ 6   Listening Comprehension
Performance Test Answer Sheet

A. Conversations

1. a. ___	2. a. ___	3. a. ___	4. a. ___	5. a. ___
b. ___	b. ___	b. ___	b. ___	b. ___
c. ___	c. ___	c. ___	c. ___	c. ___
d. ___	d. ___	d. ___	d. ___	d. ___

B. Questions et réponses

6. a. ___	7. a. ___	8. a. ___	9. a. ___	10. a. ___
b. ___	b. ___	b. ___	b. ___	b. ___
c. ___	c. ___	c. ___	c. ___	c. ___
d. ___	d. ___	d. ___	d. ___	d. ___

UNITÉ 6   Reading Comprehension
Performance Test Answer Sheet

1. a. ___	2. a. ___	3. a. ___	4. a. ___	5. a. ___
b. ___	b. ___	b. ___	b. ___	b. ___
c. ___	c. ___	c. ___	c. ___	c. ___

6. a. ___	7. a. ___	8. a. ___	9. a. ___	10. a. ___
b. ___	b. ___	b. ___	b. ___	b. ___
c. ___	c. ___	c. ___	c. ___	c. ___

Nom _____

Classe _____ Date _____

Comprehensive Test 2 (Units 4, 5, 6)

Instructions

Please use a No. 2 pencil only. Make heavy black marks that fill the circle completely. Do not make any stray marks on this answer sheet. Make all erasures cleanly.

	A B C D E		A B C D E		A B C D E		A B C D E		A B C D E
1	① ② ③ ④ ⑤	11	① ② ③ ④ ⑤	21	① ② ③ ④ ⑤	31	① ② ③ ④ ⑤	41	① ② ③ ④ ⑤
2	① ② ③ ④ ⑤	12	① ② ③ ④ ⑤	22	① ② ③ ④ ⑤	32	① ② ③ ④ ⑤	42	① ② ③ ④ ⑤
3	① ② ③ ④ ⑤	13	① ② ③ ④ ⑤	23	① ② ③ ④ ⑤	33	① ② ③ ④ ⑤	43	① ② ③ ④ ⑤
4	① ② ③ ④ ⑤	14	① ② ③ ④ ⑤	24	① ② ③ ④ ⑤	34	① ② ③ ④ ⑤	44	① ② ③ ④ ⑤
5	① ② ③ ④ ⑤	15	① ② ③ ④ ⑤	25	① ② ③ ④ ⑤	35	① ② ③ ④ ⑤	45	① ② ③ ④ ⑤
6	① ② ③ ④ ⑤	16	① ② ③ ④ ⑤	26	① ② ③ ④ ⑤	36	① ② ③ ④ ⑤	46	① ② ③ ④ ⑤
7	① ② ③ ④ ⑤	17	① ② ③ ④ ⑤	27	① ② ③ ④ ⑤	37	① ② ③ ④ ⑤	47	① ② ③ ④ ⑤
8	① ② ③ ④ ⑤	18	① ② ③ ④ ⑤	28	① ② ③ ④ ⑤	38	① ② ③ ④ ⑤	48	① ② ③ ④ ⑤
9	① ② ③ ④ ⑤	19	① ② ③ ④ ⑤	29	① ② ③ ④ ⑤	39	① ② ③ ④ ⑤	49	① ② ③ ④ ⑤
10	① ② ③ ④ ⑤	20	① ② ③ ④ ⑤	30	① ② ③ ④ ⑤	40	① ② ③ ④ ⑤	50	① ② ③ ④ ⑤
51	① ② ③ ④ ⑤	61	① ② ③ ④ ⑤	71	① ② ③ ④ ⑤	81	① ② ③ ④ ⑤	91	① ② ③ ④ ⑤
52	① ② ③ ④ ⑤	62	① ② ③ ④ ⑤	72	① ② ③ ④ ⑤	82	① ② ③ ④ ⑤	92	① ② ③ ④ ⑤
53	① ② ③ ④ ⑤	63	① ② ③ ④ ⑤	73	① ② ③ ④ ⑤	83	① ② ③ ④ ⑤	93	① ② ③ ④ ⑤
54	① ② ③ ④ ⑤	64	① ② ③ ④ ⑤	74	① ② ③ ④ ⑤	84	① ② ③ ④ ⑤	94	① ② ③ ④ ⑤
55	① ② ③ ④ ⑤	65	① ② ③ ④ ⑤	75	① ② ③ ④ ⑤	85	① ② ③ ④ ⑤	95	① ② ③ ④ ⑤
56	① ② ③ ④ ⑤	66	① ② ③ ④ ⑤	76	① ② ③ ④ ⑤	86	① ② ③ ④ ⑤	96	① ② ③ ④ ⑤
57	① ② ③ ④ ⑤	67	① ② ③ ④ ⑤	77	① ② ③ ④ ⑤	87	① ② ③ ④ ⑤	97	① ② ③ ④ ⑤
58	① ② ③ ④ ⑤	68	① ② ③ ④ ⑤	78	① ② ③ ④ ⑤	88	① ② ③ ④ ⑤	98	① ② ③ ④ ⑤
59	① ② ③ ④ ⑤	69	① ② ③ ④ ⑤	79	① ② ③ ④ ⑤	89	① ② ③ ④ ⑤	99	① ② ③ ④ ⑤
60	① ② ③ ④ ⑤	70	① ② ③ ④ ⑤	80	① ② ③ ④ ⑤	90	① ② ③ ④ ⑤	100	① ② ③ ④ ⑤

Nom _____

Classe _____ Date _____

Discovering FRENCH *Nouveau!*

BLEU

Comprehensive Test 2 (Units 4, 5, 6)

FORM B

Instructions

Please use a No. 2 pencil only. Make heavy black marks that fill the circle completely. Do not make any stray marks on this answer sheet. Make all erasures cleanly.

Discovering French, Nouveau! Bleu

Unité 6 Resources
Test Scoring Tools

UNIT TEST 6 (Lessons 17, 18, 19, 20)

FORM A

Part I. Listening Comprehension

CD 15, Track 13

1. The Logical Answer (20 points)

You will hear a series of ten questions. Listen carefully to each question and select the most logical answer on your test sheet. Circle the corresponding letter: a, b, or c. You will hear each question twice. First listen to the model.

Modèle: Qu'est-ce que tu achètes?
   You should have circled the letter "c": **Des chaussures.**

Let's begin. Écoutez.

Un.   Dis, Stéphanie, où est-ce que tu achètes tes vêtements?
Deux.   Qu'est-ce que tu vas porter pour aller au restaurant?
Trois.   Pourquoi mets-tu un imperméable?
Quatre. Qu'est-ce que tu as envie de faire?
Cinq.   Comment trouves-tu cette casquette verte?
Six.   Est-ce que cette robe est chère?
Sept.   Qu'est-ce que tu vas apporter au pique-nique?
Huit.   Combien est-ce que tu gagnes?
Neuf.   À qui vas-tu rendre visite?
Dix.   Est-ce que tu as beaucoup d'argent?

UNIT TEST 6 (Lessons 17, 18, 19, 20)

FORM B

Part I. Listening Comprehension

CD 15, Track 14

1. The Logical Answer (20 points)

You will hear a series of ten questions. Listen carefully to each question and select the most logical answer on your test sheet. Circle the corresponding letter: a, b, or c. You will hear each question twice. First, listen to the model.

Modèle: Qu'est-ce que tu achètes?
   You should have circled the letter "c": **Des chaussures.**

Let's begin. Écoutez.

Un.   Vous désirez, mademoiselle?
Deux.   Pourquoi est-ce que tu mets ton pull?
Trois.   Qu'est-ce que tu vas porter pour le match de foot?
Quatre. Tu as envie de faire une promenade?
Cinq.   Qu'est-ce que tu penses de ces chaussures?
Six.   Est-ce que ce pantalon est bon marché?
Sept.   Qui est-ce que tu vas amener à la boum?
Huit.   Pourquoi est-ce que tu mets ton maillot de bain?
Neuf.   C'est un nouvel imperméable?
Dix.   Combien d'argent as-tu?

Discovering
FRENCH
Nouveau!

BLEU

Unité 6
Resources

Audioscripts

Listening Comprehension Performance Test

CD 15, Track 15

Partie A. Conversations

This part of the Listening Comprehension Test will let you see how well you understand spoken French. You will hear five short conversations. Look at your Listening Comprehension Test Sheet and read the corresponding questions. After you have heard each conversation the second time, select the correct answer and mark the corresponding letter (a, b, c, or d) on your answer sheet.

Let's begin.

1. *Listen to the following conversation between a sales clerk and Caroline.*

   HOMME: Vous désirez, mademoiselle?
   CAROLINE: Je cherche des lunettes de soleil.
   HOMME: Comment trouvez-vous ces lunettes-ci?
   CAROLINE: Elles sont jolies. Combien coûtent-elles?

2. *Listen to the following conversation between Béatrice and her brother Alain.*

   BÉATRICE: Qu'est-ce que tu vas mettre pour aller à l'école?
   ALAIN: Mon blouson et une casquette.
   BÉATRICE: Moi, je vais mettre un imper et des bottes.

3. *Listen to the following conversation between Jean-Paul and Philippe.*

   JEAN-PAUL: Quelle veste est-ce que tu vas acheter?
   PHILIPPE: Je vais acheter la veste jaune.
   JEAN-PAUL: Tu n'aimes pas la veste bleue?
   PHILIPPE: Non, elle est trop courte!

4. *Listen to the following conversation between Nathalie and Éric.*

   NATHALIE: Qu'est-ce que tu vas faire cet été?
   ÉRIC: J'espère aller à Paris. Et toi?
   NATHALIE: Moi, je vais travailler!
   ÉRIC: Ah bon? Pourquoi?
   NATHALIE: J'ai besoin de gagner de l'argent.

5. *Listen to the following conversation between Pauline and Nicolas.*

   PAULINE: Qu'est-ce que tu veux faire?
   NICOLAS: Je ne sais pas.
   PAULINE: Tu as envie d'aller au cinéma?
   NICOLAS: Euh . . . je n'ai pas d'argent.
   PAULINE: Bon . . . alors, faisons une promenade à vélo.
   NICOLAS: D'accord! C'est une bonne idée. Je vais mettre un jean.

CD 15, Track 16

Partie B. Questions et réponses

This part of the Listening Comprehension Test will let you see how well you can handle French questions. You will hear your French friend Michèle ask you five questions. Listen carefully. Then look at your Listening Comprehension Test Sheet and select the MOST LOGICAL answer to each question. Mark the corresponding letter (a, b, c, or d) on your answer sheet. You will hear each question twice.

Let's begin.

6. *You and Michèle are walking through the mall. She asks:*
   Qu'est-ce que tu fais avec ton argent?

7. *It is Saturday afternoon and Michèle has come by your house. She asks:*
   Tu vas mettre ton maillot de bain?

8. *You and Michèle are shopping. She asks:*
   Pourquoi choisis-tu ce tee-shirt?

9. *You and Michèle are in town walking along the street. She asks:*
   Qu'est-ce qu'on fait?

10. *It is the weekend and Michèle has phoned you. She asks:*
    Tu as envie de jouer au basket?

Comprehensive Test 2 (Units 4, 5, 6)

Part I. Listening Comprehension (25 points)

CD 15, Track 17

1. Au grand magasin (8 points)

You are shopping for clothes in a department store in Paris. Listen to the prices of various items and select the appropriate number on your test paper. Then, blacken the corresponding letter—a, b, c, or d—on your answer sheet. You will hear each item twice. First, listen to the model.

Modèle: —La veste coûte 200 euros.
You should have blackened the letter **"c": 200.**

Let's begin. Écoutez.

One.	—Oui, les chaussures coûtent 110 euros.
Two.	—Le polo est en solde pour 40 euros.
Three.	—Cette robe-ci coûte 350 euros.
Four.	—Combien coûtent ces lunettes de soleil?
	—Elles coûtent 25 euros.
Five.	—Le manteau coûte 520 euros.
	—Il est très chic!
Six.	—Ce sac est chouette. Combien est-ce qu'il coûte?
	—150 euros.
Seven.	—La ceinture noire coûte 35 euros.
Eight.	—J'adore ce blouson. Combien coûte-t-il?
	—Il coûte 89 euros, mademoiselle.

CD 15, Track 18

2. La famille de Marc (7 points)

Look at Marc's family tree below. Listen to the statements about his family and decide if they are true **(vrai)** or false **(faux)**. Then, blacken the appropriate letter—a or b—on your answer sheet. You will hear each item twice. First, listen to the model.

Modèle: Jean-Paul est le père de Marc.
You should have blackened the letter **"a": vrai.**

Let's begin. Écoutez.

Nine.	Marie est la tante de Marc.
Ten.	Catherine est la soeur de Marc.
Eleven.	Jean-Paul est l'oncle de Cédric.
Twelve.	Éric est le fils de Christine.
Thirteen.	Marie est la grand-mère d'André.
Fourteen.	Jacques est le mari de Marie.
Fifteen.	Nathalie est la cousine d'Annie.

CD 15, Track 19

3. La réponse logique (10 points)

You will hear a series of ten questions. Listen carefully to each question and select the most logical response on your test paper. Then, blacken the corresponding letter—a, b, or c—on your answer sheet. You will hear each question twice. First, listen to the model.

Modèle: Qu'est-ce que tu achètes?
You should have blackened the letter **"c": Des CD.**

Let's begin. Écoutez.

Sixteen.   Est-ce que vous avez une voiture?

Seventeen.   Qu'est-ce qu'il y a à la télé?

Eighteen.   De quelle couleur est ton chat?

Nineteen.   Les toilettes sont à droite?

Twenty.   Est-ce que Philippe est dans la cuisine?

Twenty-one.   Vous allez à l'école en voiture, n'est-ce pas?

Twenty-two.   Qu'est-ce que tu vas faire à la plage?

Twenty-three. Pourquoi mets-tu un pull?

Twenty-four. Tu as envie d'aller au cinéma?

Twenty-five. À quoi est-ce que tu réponds?

BLEU

FORM B

Comprehensive Test 2 (Units 4, 5, 6)

Part I. Listening Comprehension (25 points)

CD 15, Track 20

1. Au grand magasin (8 points)

You are shopping for clothes in a department store in Paris. Listen to the prices of various items and select the appropriate number on your test paper. Then, blacken the corresponding letter—a, b, c, or d—on your answer sheet. You will hear each item twice. First, listen to the model.

Modèle: —La veste coûte 200 euros.
        You should have blackened the letter **"c": 200.**

Let's begin. Écoutez.

One.	—Cette robe est jolie mais elle coûte 225 euros.
Two.	—Combien coûte la jupe bleue?
	—Elle coûte 60 euros.
Three.	—Nos chemises coûtent 40 euros.
Four.	—Combien coûte cette ceinture marron?
	—25 euros, monsieur.
Five.	—L'imper rouge coûte seulement 310 euros.
Six.	—Ces chaussures sont en solde pour 20 euros.
	—C'est vrai, elles sont en solde . . . mais elles sont démodées.
Seven.	—Le pull gris est chouette. Combien est-ce qu'il coûte?
	—100 euros, mademoiselle.
Eight.	—Je vais acheter cette veste pour 420 euros.

CD 15, Track 21

2. La famille de Marc (7 points)

Look at Marc's family tree below. Listen to the statements about his family and decide if they are true (**vrai**) or false (**faux**). Then, blacken the appropriate letter—a or b—on your answer sheet. You will hear each item twice. First, listen to the model.

Modèle: Jean-Paul est le père de Marc.
        You should have blackened the letter **"a": vrai.**

Let's begin. Écoutez.

Nine.	Jacques est le grand-père de Marc.
Ten.	Nathalie est la mère de Marc.
Eleven.	Christine est la mère de Marie.
Twelve.	Catherine est la fille de Christine.
Thirteen.	André est l'oncle d'Annie.
Fourteen.	Christine est la femme d'André.
Fifteen.	Éric est le cousin de Cédric.

Discovering
FRENCH
Nouveau!

BLEU

Unité 6
Resources

Audioscripts

CD 15, Track 22

3. La réponse logique (10 points)

You will hear a series of ten questions. Listen carefully to each question and select the most logical response on your test paper. Then, blacken the corresponding letter—a, b, or c—on your answer sheet. You will hear each question twice. First, listen to the model.

Modèle: Qu'est-ce que tu achètes?
You should have blackened the letter **"c"**: **Des CD.**

Let's begin. Écoutez.

Sixteen. Qui est sur la photo?

Seventeen. Est-ce que ton chien est sympa?

Eighteen. De quelle couleur est ta voiture?

Nineteen. Est-ce que tes parents sont chez eux?

Twenty. Comment est-ce que tu vas venir chez moi?

Twenty-one. Où sont les toilettes, s'il vous plaît?

Twenty-two. Qu'est-ce que tu penses de cette veste bleue?

Twenty-three. Qui est-ce que tu vas amener à la boum?

Twenty-four. Pourquoi est-ce que tu portes ton maillot de bain?

Twenty-five. Combien d'argent avez-vous?

UNITÉ 6 ANSWER KEY

Video Activities

Module 17 Le français pratique: L'achat des vêtements (Pages 23–28)

Activité 1. Dominique et Stéphanie
1. a	2. c
3. a	4. b
5. b	6. a
7. b	8. c

Activité 2. Dialogue: Aux Galeries Lafayette
1. b, c	2. a, c
3. b, c	4. b, d

Activité 3. Je cherche . . .
a. 1	b. 3
c. 5	d. 8
e. 10	f. 11
g. 14	h. 15
i. 2	j. 4
k. 6	l. 7
m. 9	n. 12
o. 13	p. 16

Activité 4. Vous désirez?
1. un tee-shirt
2. des chaussures
3. une chemise
4. un pantalon
5. des lunettes de soleil
6. des chaussettes

Activité 5. Combien coûte la veste?
1. d	2. a
3. b	4. c

Activité 6. Qu'est-ce que tu penses?
1. a	2. b
3. b	4. b

Activité 7. Où acheter les vêtements?
A. Sample answer: at discount places
B.
1. une boutique de mode
2. un grand magasin
3. une boutique de soldes
4. un marché aux puces
C. Sample answer: I would go to a **boutique de soldes** because it is less expensive than a **boutique de mode** but the clothes are of good quality.

Activité 8. Dans un magasin
Conversations will vary.

Module 18 Rien n'est parfait! (Pages 56–59)

Activité 1. Frédéric et Jean-Claude
1. c
2. b
3. a

Activité 2. Au Bon Marché
1. vrai	2. vrai
3. faux	4. faux
5. vrai	6. vrai
7. vrai	

Activité 3. Comment trouves-tu ce pull?
a. 1	b. 2
c. 5	d. 10
e. 7	f. 4
g. 3	h. 9
i. 8	j. 6

Activité 4. Quel objet?
1. Ce	2. Cette
3. Cette	4. Ce

Activité 5. Quelle veste désirez-vous?
1. cette	2. ce
3. ces	4. ce

Activité 6. Un grand magasin
A. 4, 2, 1, 5, 3
B. Sample answer: I would like to shop for clothes in France, so I would go to the clothing department at Le Bon Marché.

Activité 7. Un jeu: Bon Marché!
Games will vary.

Module 19 Un choix difficile (Pages 88–91)

Activité 1. Une occasion importante
1. vrai
2. vrai
3. faux

Activité 2. Un choix difficile
1. c	2. a
3. d	4. b
5. e	

Activité 3. Préférences
1. b	2. b
3. b	4. b
5. b	6. b
7. a	8. b

Activité 4. Comparaisons
1. plus
2. aussi
3. plus

Activité 5. Dans un centre commercial
A.
1. dans un magasin de vêtements
2. dans un magasin de vêtements
3. dans un magasin de vêtements
4. dans un magasin de sport
B. Sample answers: Similarities: large building, many different stores ; Differences: larger than any mall I've ever been in, has a post office.
C. Sample answer: I would go to the clothing stores to see what the latest fashions are.

Activité 6. Une présentation de collections
Designs and dialogues will vary.

Module 20 Alice a un job (Pages 124–129)

Activité 1. Où travaille Alice?
1. vrai	2. vrai
3. faux	4. faux

Activité 2. Alice et Jérôme
1. Jérôme	2. Alice
3. Jérôme	4. Jérôme
5. Jérôme	6. Alice

Activité 3. Qu'est-ce qu'on fait?
1. c	2. b
3. c	

Activité 4. Qu'est-ce qu'on vend ici?
1. c	2. a
3. b	4. d

Activité 5. D'accord!
1. d	2. f
3. a	4. g
5. c	6. e
7. b	

Activité 6. On joue au tennis?
1. jouons	2. faisons
3. allons	4. dînons (allons)
5. jouons	

Activité 7. Au magasin hi-fi
Students should have marked all items except e, g, and k.

Activité 8. J'ai un job!
Interviews will vary.

Lesson Quizzes

Quiz 17

Part I: Listening

A. Conversations (40 points)
1. a	2. c
3. a	4. a
5. b	6. c
7. a	8. b

Part II: Writing

B. Au grand magasin (30 points)
1. un chapeau
2. des chaussettes
3. un maillot de bain
4. une ceinture
5. un chemisier
6. une jupe
7. des collants
8. une casquette
9. un imper(méable)/un manteau
10. des lunettes de soleil

C. Les nombres (10 points)
1. 800	2. 3 000
3. 2 650	4. 1 500
5. 12 000	

D. Expression personnelle (20 points)
Note: Answers will vary.
- des tennis noirs
- des chaussettes blanches
- un tee-shirt rouge
- un jean bleu

Quiz 18

Part I: Listening

A. Questions et réponses (30 points)
1. c	2. c
3. a	4. b
5. a	6. b

Part II: Writing

B. Les verbes (20 points)
1. achetez
2. préfère
3. amènent
4. espère
5. mets

C. Questions et réponses (30 points)
1. Quel / cet
2. Quelles / ces
3. Quelle / cette

D. Expression personnelle (20 points)
Note: Answers will vary.
- Je préfère aller à un match de foot.
- J'espère visiter Paris.

Quiz 19

Part I: Listening

A. Questions et réponses (30 points)
1. c	2. b
3. b	4. a
5. b	6. c

Part II: Writing

B. Les verbes (25 points)
1. finissent
2. choisis
3. réussit
4. grossissez
5. maigrissons

C. Les vêtements (25 points)

1. nouveaux
2. vieilles
3. belles
4. vieil
5. belle

D. Expression personnelle (20 points)

- Je suis plus [moins, aussi] sportif (sportive) que mes copains.
- Je suis meilleur(e) [moins, aussi bon(ne)] en maths que ma copine.
- Je suis plus [moins, aussi] intelligent(e) que le prof.

Quiz 20

Part I: Listening

A. Questions et réponses (30 points)

1. a	2. c
3. b	4. c
5. a	6. b

Part II: Writing

B. Activités (25 points)

1. vend	2. entendez
3. répondent	4. attends
5. rends	

C. Conseils (25 points)

1. Réussis	2. N'attends pas
3. Ne mange pas	4. Ne va pas

D. Expression personnelle (20 points)

Note: Answers will vary.

- Le week-end, on va en ville.
- On va au cinéma.
- On n'étudie pas.

Communipak

Interviews

Interview 1 (sample answers)

Ma chemise est blanche. / Mon tee-shirt est blanc.
Mon pantalon est bleu. / Ma jupe est bleue.
Mes chaussures sont noires.
Mes chaussettes sont grises.

Interview 2 (sample answers)

Je préfère porter une chemise.
Je préfère mettre des tennis.
Je préfère porter un blouson.
J'ai deux casquettes.

Interview 3 (sample answers)

Il s'appelle Jason's.
Il est cher.
Oui, on vend des survêtements dans ce magasin.
Non, on ne vend pas de chaussures.

Interview 4 (sample answers)

Music World vend des CD.
Move it! vend des vêtements de sport.
Street Smart vend des chaussures bon marché.
On mange bien chez Jimmy's.

Tu as la parole

Tu as la parole 1 (sample answers)

J'achète des compacts.
J'achète des vêtements.
Je vais au cinéma.

Tu as la parole 2 (sample answers)

un nouveau pull.
je vais acheter une robe.
je vais acheter un manteau.

Tu as la parole 3 (sample answers)

un tee-shirt, un jean et des baskets.
Quand je vais à une boum, j'apporte des CD.
Quand je vais à une boum, j'amène ma cousine (mon copain).

Tu as la parole 4 (sample answers)

Je suis plus grand(e) que lui (qu'elle).
Je suis plus jeune que lui (qu'elle).
Je suis moins sportif (sportive) que lui (qu'elle).

Tu as la parole 5 (sample answers)

j'espère finir mes devoirs.
j'espère écouter mon nouveau CD.
j'espère aller souvent à la plage.
j'espère réussir à l'examen.
j'espère aller au café avec mes copines.
j'espère voyager en France.

Tu as la parole 6 (sample answers)

J'ai envie de visiter ma copine.
J'ai envie de faire une promenade.
Je n'ai pas envie de jouer au ping-pong.
Je n'ai pas envie de travailler.

Conversations Side A

Conversation 1

Est-ce que tu as un chapeau?
Est-ce que tu vas mettre un pull?
Est-ce que tu vas porter un imperméable ou un blouson?

Conversation 2 (sample answers)

Je vais porter mon survêtement.
Je vais porter mes tennis.
Non, je ne vais pas apporter mon portable.

Conversation 3

Combien d'argent as-tu?
Quels vêtements est-ce que tu vas acheter?
Dans quels magasins vas-tu aller?

Conversation 4

Je travaille dans Jones and Co.
Je vends des livres.
Je gagne sept dollars par heure.

Conversations Side B

Conversation 1 (sample answers)

Oui, j'ai un chapeau.
Oui, je vais mettre un pull.
Je vais porter un blouson.

Conversation 2

Est-ce que tu vas porter un jean ou un survêtement?
Est-ce que tu vas porter des bottes ou des baskets?
Est-ce que tu vas apporter ton portable?

Conversation 3 (sample answers)

J'ai soixante-quinze dollars.
Je vais acheter un pull et un jean.
Je vais chez Sammy's Discount Shop.

Conversation 4

Dans quel magasin travailles-tu?
Qu'est-ce que tu vends?
Combien gagnes-tu par heure?

Conversations Side A

Conversation 5

Est-ce qu'on étudie beaucoup?
Est-ce qu'on parle français en classe?
Est-ce qu'on a beaucoup d'examens?

Conversation 6 (sample answers)

On les vend chez Listen.
On les vend chez Outside.
On mange bien chez Anthony's Pier 4.

Conversation 7 (sample answers)

Est-ce que tu as envie d'aller au café?
Est-ce que tu as envie d'aller au cinéma?
Qu'est-ce que tu as envie de faire après?
As-tu besoin d'argent?

Conversation 8 (sample answers)

Je suis plus jeune que mon frère.
Je suis plus petit(e) que lui.
Je suis plus sportif (sportive) que lui.
Je suis moins gentil(le) que lui!

Conversations Side B

Conversation 5 (sample answers)

Oui, on étudie beaucoup.
Non, on ne parle pas toujours français en classe.
Oui, on a beaucoup d'examens.

Conversation 6

Où est-ce qu'on vend des CD et des cassettes?
Où est-ce qu'on vend des vêtements bon marché?
Dans quel restaurant est-ce qu'on mange bien?

Conversation 7 (sample answers)

Oui, je voudrais aller dans un café.
Non, je ne veux pas aller au cinéma.
Je voudrais faire une promenade après.
Oui, j'ai besoin d'argent.

Conversation 8

Est-ce que tu es plus jeune que ton frère?
Est-ce que tu es plus grand(e) que lui?
Est-ce que tu es plus ou moins sportif (sportive) que lui?
Est-ce que tu es aussi gentil(le) que lui?

Échanges

Échange 1

Answers will vary.

Échange 2

Answers will vary.

Échange 3 (sample answers)

Je vais à la campagne.
Je vais porter un survêtement et des bottes.
Je vais à un mariage.
Je vais porter une robe.
Je vais à une boum.
Je vais porter un jean et un polo, etc.

Tête à tête

Activité 1 Au grand magasin

Élève A

a.
Combien coûte l'appareil-photo?
Combien coûte la montre?
Combien coûte la veste?
Combien coûte la télé?
Combien coûte la chaîne stéréo?

b.
La bicyclette coûte deux cent vingt-cinq euros.
Le lit coûte quatre cent quarante-cinq euros.
L'imper coûte cent cinquante euros.
La robe coûte cent dix euros.
L'ordinateur coûte mille euros.

Élève B
a.
L'appareil-photo coûte cent vingt-cinq euros.
La montre coûte trois cents euros.
La veste coûte cent euros.
La télé coûte deux cent quatre-vingt-dix euros.
La chaîne stéréo coûte six cent cinquante
    euros.
b.
Combien coûte la bicyclette?
Combien coûte le lit?
Combien coûte l'imper?
Combien coûte la robe?
Combien coûte l'ordinateur?

Activité 2 Cadeaux d'anniversaire

Élève A (sample answers)
a.
Je vais acheter une affiche à Thomas.
Je vais acheter un tee-shirt à Carole.
Je vais acheter un CD a Damien.
Je vais acheter des lunettes de soleil à Cécile.
Je vais acheter un pull à Jean-François.
b.
une casquette
des chaussettes
un livre
une ceinture
une chemise

Élève B (sample answers)
a.
une affiche
un tee-shirt
un CD
des lunettes de soleil
un pull
b.
Je vais acheter une casquette à Alain.
Je vais acheter des chaussettes à Christine.
Je vais acheter un livre à Julien.
Je vais acheter une ceinture à Antoine.
Je vais acheter une chemise à Sophie.

Activité 3 Comparaisons

Élève A
a.
(–)
Est-ce que Marc est plus ou moins élégant que
    Julien? (+)
Est-ce que M. Duval est plus ou moins jeune
    que M. Lassalle? (–)
Est-ce que les bottes sont plus ou moins
    chères que les chaussures? (=)
Est-ce que la jupe est plus ou moins longue
    que la robe? (–)
b.
Thomas est moins riche que Richard.
Christine est aussi sportive qu'Alice.
Charlemagne est moins gentil que Bijou.
Les lunettes de soleil sont moins chères que
    la ceinture.
Les baskets sont plus grandes que les
    sandales.

Élève B
a.
Sophie est moins grande que Claire.
Marc est plus élégant que Julien.
M. Duval est moins jeune que M. Lassalle.
Les bottes sont aussi chères que les
    chaussures.
La jupe est moins longue que la robe.
b.
(–)

Est-ce que Christine est plus ou moins
    sportive qu'Alice? (=)
Est-ce que Charlemagne est plus ou moins
    gentil que Bijou? (–)

Est-ce que les lunettes de soleil sont plus ou
    moins chères que la ceinture? (–)
Est-ce que les baskets sont plus ou moins
    grandes que les sandales (+)

Unit Test Lessons 17, 18, 19, 20

Form A

Part I: Listening Comprehension

1. The Logical Answer (20 points)
1. c	2. a
3. a	4. c
5. a	6. c
7. b	8. a
9. b	10. a

Part II. Language

2. The Right Number (6 points)
1. 501	2. 114
3. 1 200	4. 975
5. 820	6. 3 000

3. The Right Item (12 points)
Choose six items from:
un chapeau
un pantalon
une veste / un blouson
des lunettes de soleil
des bottes
des chaussettes
une casquette
une cravate
un manteau
une ceinture
un maillot de bain

4. The Right Verb (14 points)
1. finit	2. choisissons
3. attend	4. entendez
5. répond	6. mets
7. achète	

5. The Right Comparison (10 points)
1. moins . . . que	2. plus . . . que
3. aussi . . . que	4. plus . . . qu'
5. meilleur	

6. The Right Choice (10 points)
1. c	2. b
3. c	4. b
5. c	6. c
7. c	8. b
9. c	10. b

7. The Logical Choice (8 points)
1. a	2. b
3. a	4. a
5. c	6. b
7. a	8. c

Part III. Written Expression

8. Composition (20 points)
Answers will vary.

Form B

Part I. Listening Comprehension

1. The Logical Answer (20 points)
1. c	2. b
3. b	4. a
5. a	6. c
7. b	8. c
9. a	10. c

Part II. Language

2. The Right Number (6 points)
1. 710	2. 3 000
3. 166	4. 1 800
5. 524	6. 480

3. The Right Item (12 points)
Choose six items from:
un chapeau
un pantalon
une veste / un blouson
des lunettes de soleil
des bottes
des chaussettes
une casquette
une cravate
un manteau
une ceinture
un maillot de bain

4. The Right Verb (14 points)
1. finissent	2. choisis
3. attendons	4. entendez
5. réponds	6. met
7. achètes	

5. The Right Comparison (10 points)
1. moins . . . que	2. plus . . . qu'
3. moins . . . que	4. aussi . . . que
5. meilleur . . . que	

6. The Right Choice (10 points)
1. b	2. c
3. c	4. c
5. b	6. c
7. b	8. c
9. c	10. a

7. The Logical Choice (8 points)
1. b	2. c
3. b	4. a
5. c	6. a
7. b	8. a

Part III. Written Expression

8. Composition (20 points)
Answers will vary.

Form A/B (Alternate)

Part III. Cultural Awareness

8. Culture (20 points)
1. c	2. b
3. c	4. b
5. a	6. c
7. b	8. a
9. a	10. b

Listening Comprehension Peformance Test

A. Conversations
1. a	2. d
3. c	4. b
5. c	

B. Questions et réponses
6. c	7. a
8. c	9. d
10. d	

Reading Comprehension Performance Test

1. a	2. c
3. b	4. a
5. c	6. b
7. b	8. c
9. b	10. a

Writing Performance Test

Suggested Answers
Please note that the answers provided are
only suggested answers. Answers will vary.

A. Voyage à Nice (10 points)

un maillot de bain
des lunettes de soleil
une casquette
des sandales
des chemises

B. Vêtements d'hiver (10 points)

1. un manteau
2. un imperméable
3. des bottes
4. des pulls
5. une nouvelle veste

C. Comparaisons (20 points)

Florence Je suis aussi grand(e) qu'elle.
Patrick Je suis plus sportif (sportive) que
lui.
Tom Je suis moins timide que lui.
Silvia Je suis meilleur(e) en français qu'elle.
(Je suis moins bon[ne] en français qu'elle.)
Vanessa Je suis aussi bon(ne) en maths
qu'elle. (Je suis meilleur[e] en maths qu'elle.)

D. Préférences (20 points)

1. Je n'aime pas attendre le bus.
   J'aime répondre au professeur.
2. J'aime réussir à l'examen.
   Je n'aime pas perdre mon sac.
3. J'aime rendre visite à mes grands-parents.
   J'aime gagner de l'argent.
4. J'aime choisir de(s) nouveaux vêtements.
   J'aime porter de(s) vieux vêtements.
5. Je n'aime pas amener mon petit frère à
   une boum.

E. Cadeau d'anniversaire (20 points)

Merci pour l'argent.
J'ai besoin de nouveaux vêtements pour l'été.
Je vais aller dans un grand magasin.
Je vais acheter un short et un blouson.
Je vais dépenser 50 dollars.
Elaine

F. Conseils (20 points)

1. Fais attention en classe.
2. N'achète pas de pizza.
3. Va à la piscine.
4. Vends tes CD.
5. Ne regarde pas la télé.

Multiple Choice Test Items

Leçon 17

1. c. un chapeau et une casquette
2. a. mon manteau
3. a. une veste
4. c. une cravate
5. c. porter
6. c. manteaux
7. c. un maillot de bain
8. c. des lunettes de soleil
9. c. chaussures
10. b. sweat
11. c. démodé
12. c. Quel est le prix
13. a. Qu'est-ce que tu penses
14. a. bon marché
15. c. ne trouve pas
16. c. géniale
17. a. une ceinture
18. b. mille
19. c. trois cent trente-deux euros
20. b. cent trente-sept

Leçon 18

1. b. achète
2. a. préfère
3. b. amène
4. b. espère
5. b. préférez
6. c. préfèrent
7. c. apportes
8. c. Cette
9. b. cet
10. c. Ces
11. b. ci
12. b. homme
13. a. quel
14. c. Quelle
15. c. quels
16. c. chaussures
17. c. met
18. c. mettez
19. c. mets
20. c. mettre

Leçon 19

1. c. grossissons
2. b. réussissent
3. c. finit
4. a. choisis
5. b. ne réussissent pas
6. c. réussissons
7. a. réussit
8. c. nouvel
9. c. vieux
10. c. belle
11. c. nouvelle
12. a. bel
13. b. moins cher
14. a. plus sportif
15. b. meilleure
16. b. que lui
17. b. aussi intéressantes
18. a. plus vieille
19. b. plus timides
20. a. nous

Leçon 20

1. b. un billet
2. b. pauvre
3. c. Combien de
4. c. gagne
5. b. as besoin de
6. b. paie
7. b. grossit
8. c. on
9. a. attendez
10. c. attend
11. c. réponds
12. c. rendent
13. c. vendons
14. c. perdez
15. a. rentre
16. a. Attendez
17. c. ne perds
18. a. Allons
19. c. n'achète pas
20. c. Finissez

Comprehensive Test 2

(Units 4, 5, 6)

Form A

Part I. Listening Comprehension (25 points)

1. Au grand magasin (8 points)

1. b	2. b
3. a	4. b
5. d	6. c
7. b	8. a

2. La famille de Marc (7 points)

9. b	10. b
11. a	12. a
13. b	14. a
15. b	

3. La réponse logique (10 points)

16. c	17. b
18. b	19. a
20. a	21. c
22. a	23. c
24. a	25. b

Part II. Language and Communication
(40 points)

4. Les objets trouvés (5 points)

26. e	27. e
28. a	29. b
30. c	

5. Le bon choix (15 points)

31. d	32. c
33. b	34. a
35. d	36. d
37. d	38. b
39. c	40. b
41. a	42. b
43. a	44. c
45. d	

6. La chambre de Nicole (5 points)

46. b	47. e
48. b	49. e
50. a	

7. L'intrus (5 points)

51. c	52. c
53. b	54. b
55. a	

8. Situations (5 points)

56. b	57. c
58. a	59. c
60. b	

9. Des phrases embrouillées (5 points)

61. e	62. c
63. b	64. d
65. a	

Part III. Reading Comprehension (20 points)

10. À Villeneuve (5 points)

66. a	67. b
68. b	69. a
70. b	

11. On cherche des correspondants (5 points)

71. d	72. b
73. a or d	74. c
75. e	

12. Cinq boutiques (5 points)

76. a	77. a
78. b	79. a
80. b	

13. Stéphanie (5 points)

81. c	82. d
83. a	84. d
85. a	

Part IV. Cultural Awareness (15 points)

14. Méli-mélo culturel (15 points)

86. a	87. a
88. a	89. b
90. b	91. b
92. a	93. b
94. a	95. a
96. a	97. b
98. a	99. b
100. b	

Unité 6
Resources

Answer Key

Discovering
FRENCH
Nouveau

BLEU

Comprehensive Test 2
(Units 4, 5, 6)

Form B

Part I. Listening Comprehension

1. Au grand magasin (8 points)
1. a	2. c
3. b	4. b
5. c	6. d
7. c	8. b

2. La famille de Marc (7 points)
9. a	10. b
11. b	12. b
13. a	14. b
15. a	

3. La réponse logique (10 points)
16. a	17. b
18. c	19. c
20. b	21. b
22. b	23. b
24. b	25. a

Part II. Language and Communication

4. Les objets trouvés (5 points)
26. b	27. d
28. c	29. e
30. a	

5. Le bon choix (15 points)
31. b	32. a
33. c	34. b
35. d	36. b
37. a	38. d
39. b	40. a
41. d	42. b
43. c	44. b
45. d	

6. La chambre de Nicole (5 points)
46. b	47. e
48. c	49. d
50. b	

7. L'intrus (5 points)
51. b	52. c
53. b	54. a
55. a	

8. Situations (5 points)
56. b	57. b
58. a	59. c
60. b	

9. Des phrases embrouillées (5 points)
61. d	62. c
63. e	64. a
65. b	

Part III. Reading Comprehension

10. À Villeneuve (5 points)
66. c	67. b
68. b	69. a
70. c	

11. On cherche des correspondants (5 points)
71. d	72. d
73. c	74. a
75. b	

12. Cinq boutiques (5 points)
76. b	77. b
78. a	79. a
80. b	

13. Chez François (5 points)
81. c	82. c
83. c	84. b
85. c	

Part IV. Cultural Awareness

14. Méli-mélo culturel (15 points)
86. b	87. b
88. a	89. b
90. a	91. a
92. a	93. b
94. b	95. b
96. b	97. b
98. b	99. a
100. a